THE
EQUALITY
EFFECT

Improving life for everyone

Danny Dorling is a Professor of Human Geography at the University of Oxford. He has also worked in Sheffield, Newcastle, Bristol, Leeds and New Zealand/Aotearoa. He grew up in Oxford and went to university in Newcastle upon Tyne. He has published over 40 books including many atlases and: *Population Ten Billion* (2013); *All That is Solid* and *Inequality and the 1%* (2014); *Injustice: Why social inequalities still persist* (2015); and *A Better Politics: How government can make us happier* (2016).

The Equality Effect was written with the help of a great many people. It grew out of a much shorter book: *The No-nonsense Guide to Equality* which was published by New Internationalist five years ago. This fully updated and greatly extended version is kindly illustrated by the cartoons of Ella Furness. Ian Nixon carefully redrew all the figures. Andrew Kokotka designed the cover. Anna Barford, Noel Castree, Theresa Hayter, Aniko Horvath, Bob Hughes, Sebastian Kraemer, Carl Lee, Brian Martin, Avner Offer, Chris Philo, Simon Reid-Henry and Sally Tomlinson all either made comments on various drafts and/or on the concept of this book; I am grateful to all of them. David Gordon, Tina Gotthardt, Ben Hennig, Tom Mills, Kate Pickett, Nigel Waters and Richard Wilkinson helped with advice and comments. Alison and David Dorling both helped to iron out the English, the argument and the structure, and David valiantly fact-checked and grammar-checked it all again and again, suggesting many more new additions. Dan Raymond-Barker is marketing the book and agreed its full-length format given how much more we now know and can include than we knew just five years ago about equality. Finally, this book would not exist without its editor, Chris Brazier, who helped me plan the book from the outset, improved the text and co-ordinated its production. Even something as small as a book cannot be created without a great many people contributing to the joint endeavour. Human beings have always worked best in groups. Groups work best through the equality effect.

To those who desire more

THE
EQUALITY
EFFECT

Improving life for everyone

DANNY DORLING

Illustrations by
Ella Furness

Foreword by
Owen Jones

The Equality Effect
Improving life for everyone

First published in 2017 by
New Internationalist Publications Ltd
The Old Music Hall
106-108 Cowley Road
Oxford OX4 1JE, UK
newint.org

Reprinted 2017

Edited by Chris Brazier
Designed by Ian Nixon
Front cover by Andrew Kokotka,
montage from malerapaso/ismagilov/iStock
Illustrations by Ella Furness

Printed by TJ International Ltd, Cornwall, UK, who hold
environmental accreditation ISO 14001

British Library Cataloguing-in-Publication Data
A catalogue record for this book is available from the British Library.
Library of Congress Cataloging-in-Publication Data
A catalog record for this book is available from Library of Congress.

ISBN 978-1-78026-390-8
(ISBN ebook 978-1-78026-391-5)

Contents

Gasoline (petrol) consumption
Wasting young lives
Ecological footprints
Air travel
Crimes committed
Education and environment
Cycling and walking

Why contraception was revolutionary
The right to equal treatment
Why women's rights change everything
Fertility and income inequality
Health and equality
Housing: building equality
Rent regulations in more equal European countries
It does not have to happen all at once

Why the weekend gives us a taste for equality
Cuba, Costa Rica and Kerala
Norway, Sweden, Denmark and Finland
Crime, gender equality and intervention
Japan, Germany, despair and hope
Oases in apparent deserts of inequality
Americans are becoming less happy

How the rich are hiding their wealth
The one per cent have the most to lose
Not all is well in Spain
Basic income and living wages
The political labels of old
How to ensure that taxes are paid
Redistribution and reparation
What we dream of
Harmony

Foreword by Owen Jones

For too long – outside the circles of the political left – 'equality' has often been seen as an abstraction, a wishy-washy concept. To some, equality is something out-of-touch do-gooders spend their lives talking about. But the case for greater equality – as this book wonderfully shows – is hard-headed. Greater equality is good for all of us. Societies with greater equality tend to do better on a whole range of metrics: from their educational performance to their well-being, from levels of crime to financial stability. Higher levels of inequality breed mistrust, segregation and division. They are bad for aspiration: whether for your children to have a better life than you had or for your own chances of finding a secure job in communities where the old industries have been stripped away.

The distribution of wealth matters. Britain's ruling Conservative government once promised that 'we're all in this together'. Even if that were true, this Labour Party poster from the 1930s sums up why equality of sacrifice does not mean quite the same for everyone.

But the West's ruling ideology justifies and rationalizes inequality. Those at the top deserve to be there, so this ideology suggests, because they are more intelligent, more

capable, harder working, and so on. Those at the bottom are lazy and feckless and thick. The truth is this: wealthy business owners depend on the state to provide infrastructure like road and rail; to fund research and development which can be appropriated for innovative products; to provide an education system to train up their workforce; to sustain law and order to protect their property;

to subsidize low wages with in-work benefits; and so on. Without the largesse of the state, innovation – which is appropriated to make profit – is impossible.

And then there is the fact that some are born with odds stacked against them from day one. The birth weight of a child from a poorer background is lower than a child from more affluent circumstances. Some are born with more 'cultural capital': parents with a broader vocabulary, in houses full of books, who are better placed to help with homework. Repeated studies show that children with more affluent parents have much broader vocabularies from an early age than those born into poorer families. Living in an overcrowded house damages educational prospects, health and wellbeing. A poor diet, or hunger, equally damages your potential at school. The stresses of poverty can inflict significant damage.

Years before the financial crash, living standards in the US and the UK stagnated, even as corporations posted healthy profits. What did that mean? It meant workers took on more personal debt to sustain their living standards, damaging the economy. The government had to spend more money on in-work benefits, all at a cost to the taxpayer – money that would have been better spent on services and jobs and houses. It was damaging to the worker, to the taxpayer, and to society as a whole.

Equality matters: the wealth that is collectively produced by the hard graft of workers, supported by the contribution of the state, should be far more equitably distributed. This is not just the right thing to do: it's for the good of society as a whole. Here is a book which details – with irrefutable evidence – both the damage caused by inequality, and the benefits we all derive from living in more equal societies. We should all learn from it – and, above all else, act on it.

1
The Equality Effect

Greater economic equality benefits all people in all societies, whether you are rich, poor or in-between. The truth of this has only become evident recently, and is contentious because it contradicts the views of many in the elite. Countries that have chosen to be more equal have enjoyed greater economic prosperity while also managing to develop in ways that are more environmentally sustainable. In contrast, countries that have taken the road of growing inequality, such as the UK and the US, have seen increasing complaints from their populations about the costs or scarcity of healthcare, housing and many other basic necessities. Poorer countries that are more unequal also see more suffering. The evidence is now overwhelming that we need to set in motion the equality effect.

The tide has already begun to turn. It is early days, but we can now see where we are heading and those of us who argue for greater equality are beginning to make the running again. Those who would foster inequality are now on the back foot. In the UK and the US, inequality advocates made the running from 1978 all the way through to the financial crash in 2007-8. With hindsight, egalitarians were often on the back foot during those three decades. Whereas, in great contrast, from the 1920s right through to the early 1970s, economic equality was increasing most of the time in the US, UK and most other affluent states in the world and the views of those who argued for equality were much more popular. Today we are again at a crossroads. Other forms of equality – gay rights, women's rights, civil rights, disability rights – continued to be fought for in the 1960s, then won in later decades, and then more widely introduced after the 1990s, but often without the economic emancipation that could have enhanced their impact. Wage inequality between women and men remains high because overall wage inequality is high. People who resent being low-paid take out their anger on people they see as potentially inferior to them: women, immigrants, people with disabilities, people with different sexualities, in fact any group of people with a trait that can be used to differentiate them from a supposed majority.

Today even rightwing politicians sometimes talk of wanting to increase economic equality. They often express their concern for those 'left behind' economically, but it is hard to see any evidence that they are interested in much more than the votes of such people. However, the fact that they have changed how they talk demonstrates a more widespread change in our common understanding. Their immediate predecessors talked of 'rewarding talent', 'a rising tide lifting all boats', 'allowing the tall poppies to bloom' to the supposed (but not actual) benefit of all. Now even the perpetrators of growing inequality claim they are against it, but they do not admit to their own complicity in creating, maintaining and even increasing it.

The tide may be turning again towards greater economic equality, but the case for it needs to be made clearer – otherwise rightwingers will again subvert the argument. They will claim they are against inequality while quietly promoting a rebranded version of it.

The case for greater equality is *not* just the reverse of the case against income and wealth inequality. Gaining greater equality has a set of particular positive effects on a society that we can call 'the equality effect'. Greater economic equality makes us all *less* stupid, *more* tolerant, *less* fearful and *more* satisfied with life. It may bring even greater benefits than that. We are not sure because we have tolerated immense inequality for so long that we can't be certain of all that is possible when we eventually do treat each other with economic respect. Until recently the idea that greater equality of economic outcome could have a positive effect was viewed as a dangerous idea.

'It is so easy for people to have sympathy with suffering. It is so difficult for them to have sympathy with thought. Indeed, so little do ordinary people understand what thought really is, that they seem to imagine that, when they have said that a theory is dangerous, they have pronounced its condemnation, whereas it is only such theories that have any true intellectual value. An idea that is not dangerous is unworthy of being called an idea at all.'

Oscar Wilde, 1891[1]

When you read the words 'ordinary people' in the quotation above, did it make you a little uncomfortable? The person who wrote those words, Oscar Wilde, was a champion of greater equality but he lived in times that were so unequal that using 'ordinary' as an insult then raised few hackles. He was writing in 1891 and was calling the elite 'ordinary' in an attempt to encourage some of them to think differently.

The world changed so much in the century that followed that we are now ever so careful before we publicly pronounce a group as being 'ordinary' although, of course, we are all, in most ways and most of the time, just ordinary, common, people. It was rising economic equality, achieved long after Oscar Wilde died, that led to our now being so careful over our choice of words to describe others. You would be shocked if you were transported back in time to 1891 to hear how people talked about the poor, women, people living in other countries, even children. Children were then often beaten and in the upper classes were told they had to be 'seen, but not heard'. So much improved when we became more economically equal; but it is only in hindsight that we can now recognize that this improvement was the equality effect in action.

The equality effect can appear magical. In more equal countries, human beings are generally happier and healthier: there is less crime, more creativity, more productivity, more concern over what is actually being produced, and – overall – higher real educational attainment. The evidence for the benefits of living more economically equitable lives is now so overwhelming that it has begun to change politics and societies all over the world.

For the three decades prior to 2008, some countries, including the US and the UK, chose a path that led to greater inequality, often on the assumption that there was no viable alternative. Yet, even under intensifying globalization, the people of many other nation-states have continued to take a different road and have chosen ever greater equality. Today, it is often through the examples of how life differs between more and less economically equitable countries that we are able to measure the equality effect.

The time will come when this positive equality effect will be as readily accepted as the benefits of women voting or of former colonies gaining independence, which were seen as outlandish ideas only a century ago – and that time may come very soon. The benefits come as we gain greater equality than previous generations enjoyed and can look back on the past to register the effect. We no longer have to rely on just 'a dangerous idea' because we now have evidence of what happens when some countries choose to become more economically equitable and others don't. But we also have short memories. We forget that not long ago people argued vehemently against women being allowed to vote or whole countries having their freedom. And so we often fail to ask what we are doing today that will be regarded with horror in the future.

The basic thrust of this book is that human beings are found to be happier and healthier the more economically equal they are. Greater equality is not sufficient for widespread happiness, but it is necessary. This is borne out by looking at statistics from all over the world today – as well as by surveying long stretches of human history with the benefit of hindsight.[2]

Greater economic equality does not mean all people doing very similar work, or living in very similar types of families, or similar homes. It does not mean all schools being the same or all people being paid exactly the same. It means moving towards all people being fairly respected and rewarded for the work they do, the contributions they make and the needs they have. Money is relative. If some people are over-rewarded, others are effectively fined.

Equality means being afforded the same rights, dignity and freedoms as other people. These include the right to access resources, the dignity of being seen as able, and the freedom to choose what to make of your life on an equal footing with others. Believing that we all deserve such parity is very far from suggesting that we would all do much the same if we actually had more equal opportunities.[3]

People differ greatly from one another in what they most enjoy doing and are best at. We both come with and develop different propensities to be good at different things. We are often best at doing what we most enjoy doing – or end up most enjoying what we are best at. And we almost all enjoy being praised for doing a good and useful job, being praised for being a good neighbor or parent, or being otherwise helpful, kind and unselfish. Under greater economic equality, people are freer to choose to do what they are best at. Efficiency increases.

Look at the picture above. It shows a happy band of people going up a slope. They are all helping each other. Yes, one is at the front and one is at the back (but definitely not left behind), also some are short and some are tall, some fat, some thin, some disabled – we all have disabilities. We have learnt from the Paralympics that no-one should be denied the opportunity to give it a shot. If you have ever climbed hills, you will know what happens. You see the top and, when you get there, the view is much better but you also see another top. You might need a rest, but you don't give up because you want to see the view from even higher up. And climbing as a group is far more enjoyable and far safer than trying to climb on your own. Together we can seek greater equality, but we also achieve it just in the trying.

Although leftwing and green politicians tend to advocate greater equality more vocally, and rightwing and fascist ones might become members of their particular political parties in order to oppose it, equality is actually not the preserve of any political label. Great inequality has been sustained or increased under systems labeled as socialist and communist. Some free-market systems have seen equalities grow and the playing field become more level. Anarchistic systems can be either highly equitable or inequitable. Many such social systems existed in the past before the rule of law and the concept of property became widespread, and they were not all greatly equitable or inequitable.

The politics of economic equality and inequality is not the preserve of any one single group. It is easily conceivable that economic inequalities between men and women could reduce to zero and yet widespread inequalities remain between rich and poor. In some ways that has already occurred in some countries between people who are gay, straight or in-between, but that does not make those countries necessarily happy places if within each group economic inequalities are still widespread. Although Oscar Wilde would still be amazed at what has been achieved, he would undoubtedly argue that we must now search for the next shore of greater equality to land on, rather than simply celebrate what has been achieved so far.

The uninspiring nonsense of inequality advocates

Advocates of inequality are predictable and often annoyingly repetitive in their arguments. They tend to churn out uninspiring nonsense about the especially deserving rich and the undeserving majority, how doing others down (minimizing labor costs) will somehow help all in the end, and why any wealth created needs to be unequally distributed. For inequality advocates, the only alternative to great inequality that they can imagine is the equal sharing of misery. They suggest, with no evidence at all, that under greater equality everyone is less happy. When the evidence is actually examined the five countries in the world in which people are actually happiest are Switzerland, Iceland, Norway,

Finland and Denmark, which all also 'have strong social security systems'.[4]

Often advocates of inequality are ignorant of contemporary alternatives and also fail to recognize that their equivalents in the past are now forgotten whereas past champions of equality are remembered and celebrated, including Emmeline Pankhurst, Martin Luther King and Oscar Wilde. Can you remember the names of any who opposed them who are today revered?

Advocates of inequality can draw on largely US-based 'corporate misinformation networks' funded by tobacco, coal, oil, chemical and biotech companies, with their satellite policy foundations that try to pretend to be independent of their paymasters. The purpose of these groups is to 'portray the interests of billionaires as the interests of the common people'.[5] But the data these organizations collect is biased, one-sided, superficial and based on numbers which can be used to tell any kind of story you wish depending on how you select among them. Often they resort to telling stories about fictional individuals or groups, as when they pit 'benefit scroungers' against 'hard-working families'. And they always select the stories that – miraculously – work to sustain their money, their power and their interests.

Inequality advocates like to tell stories rather than interpret and evaluate evidence. They also accuse egalitarians of being advocates of uniformity when, in fact, the opposite is the case. When economic inequalities are great, the children of the poor are channeled towards menial, unproductive work but the rich and powerful must also play particular roles and are less free to be who they might really like to be. They steer their children into segregated schools and universities, which eventually herd them towards high-paid jobs such as finance, law or the family business, and which determine their future friendship groups, future spouses and partners. When high economic inequality is tolerated, the freedom to choose who you want to be, and to do what suits you best, is curtailed for the rich as well as the poor.

In times and places of greater equality we are (and have been) freer to choose our individual roles and how we each can best contribute. Under great inequality, the vast majority of people are condemned to lives of uniform and monotonous relative poverty, while many of the rich have remarkably similar lifestyles and are uniformly drab in their acquisition of status symbols. Can you imagine what future generations will make of the desire in Britain, and other countries that permit this, to pay for personalized license plates on vehicles? In future, people might well ask why a few chose to mark themselves out as arrogant, narcissistic and willing to waste money by buying such license plates. But at times of great economic inequality the affluent have always adorned themselves with silly symbols, from codpieces to cravats, which are always later perceived as symbols of stupidity and arrogance.

Later in this book examples are given from many different countries, but I am writing it in Britain and will take that country as my first and most usual example. In the UK today, total household wealth is £11,000 billion (worth around $13,400 billion as I write, though it would have been nearer $16,500 billion before the Brexit referendum in June 2016; readers from other countries will perhaps forgive me if, in these uncertain times, I do not attempt to translate all the sterling sums in what follows into US dollars). Almost half (45 per cent) of that wealth is held by the richest tenth of households. The poorer half of all households holds in total a fifth of that wealth (9 per cent) or 25 times less per household. Between 2012 and 2014 the wealth of the best-off tenth increased by three times more (21 per cent) than the wealth of the poorest half (which only rose by 7 per cent), but the wealth in the middle increased the least of all (by 4 per cent) making median average UK household wealth in 2014 £225,100. All of this makes the median about as unrepresentative as a median can get.

At the same time some seven per cent of UK households owned personalized license plates. In total, those license plates are estimated to be worth £2,000 million, equal to the total wealth of some 10,000 median households. Most of that £2,000 million will be the value of just the most distinctive minority of those personalized number plates. The money that the richest pay for personal license plates could raise the families of hundreds of thousands of children out of poverty. And, while you can't even see your own personal license plate while driving, others will read it as a sign of how little you care about their not having money.[6]

Under great inequality people might be encouraged to be more individualistic but they also lose individuality by status seeking, aping their betters, and worrying greatly about how they are perceived. There is far more variety when we are more equal, far more color in the world and we all have wider horizons. Just look at how dull and drab and sad the advocates of inequality are, at how they confuse greed with talent,[7] wealth with happiness and achievement with selfishness. Some people clearly think that having a license plate that says 'RICH 1' will impress others but then they are also surprisingly reticent about their own precise incomes being known. They just want you to think that they have more than you.

In 2016 one British Member of Parliament, Alan Duncan, was so incensed at the suggestion that he and his fellow politicians should reveal the income they acquired each year from outside sources that he said if this was revealed Parliament would become: 'stuffed full of low achievers, who hate enterprise, hate people who look after their own family and who know absolutely nothing about the outside world.'[8]

The 'outside world' looked in and mocked Alan at his suggestion that he was a high achiever who knew so much. He looked to all intents and purposes like a sneering little rich boy trapped in a self-congratulatory bubble. A few years earlier he could have said the same thing and not appeared so foolish. However, that

was before it was revealed that in 2007 he had claimed £598 from the taxpayer to have his ride-on lawn mower serviced, and in 2009 claimed £23,000 expenses overall. Alan used to work for Marc Rich, 'the disgraced commodities trader'.[9] Even in the highly unequal UK the tide is turning against those who would advocate that we remain as unequal and segregated as they have helped to make us. A new younger generation is longing for more freedom to mix with each other rather than to be separated by their accidents of birth.

As the tide turns against inequality, people become more critical of the outcomes it has produced. A few weeks after Alan spoke of the special talents of the rich, the *Financial Times* ran the headline 'New head of UK schools watchdog has no teaching experience'.[10] This newspaper for financiers was reporting on the uproar that accompanied the highly paid appointment of Amanda Spielman as the new chief inspector of schools. She had no experience of teaching but had instead 'worked in corporate finance for more than 15 years, including stints at Nomura International, Mercer Management Consulting and Kleinwort Benson'. In more equitable countries such rash and easily parodied decisions are less often made, not least because a wider set of views are respected. In more equal countries having made a great deal of money is not seen as evidence that you are an especially able person.

Inequality worldwide

Inequalities in income and wealth are by no means inevitable and countries vary markedly in the degree of inequality that they consider socially acceptable. In Switzerland, for example, the richest one per cent takes proportionately half the income that the equivalent group in the UK commandeers, while the poorest tenth of households in Switzerland enjoy three times as much (in real terms) as their equivalents in the UK survive on.

In Norway inequalities are even lower than in Switzerland, the poor are respected more and the tenth of families on high incomes are 'only' seen as being worth 6 times more per person than the poorest tenth. In Denmark the ratio is even lower at 5:1. In Germany, meanwhile the ratio is nearer 6.5, in France 7.5, in New Zealand/Aotearoa it is 8, in Canada and Australia nearer 9, in the

UK 10, in Israel 15 and in the US nearly 19 times as much. These simple numbers describe the society in each country as well as almost any other summary statistic currently available, although later on in this book the statistics of what the best-off one per cent take is used as an even simpler and even more effective summary.

The statistics just quoted are derived from recent reports of the Organization for Economic Co-operation and Development (OECD),[11] which is a club that only the richest states on earth are eligible to join. These statistics emphasize just how much variation there is, even between affluent countries. Worldwide, the variation is even greater. Rich countries tend to be among the most economically equitable in the world. This is hardly surprising. With a lot of money to go round in an affluent state, only the greediest and most ill-informed could believe that poverty is justifiable in their immediate neighborhood, or even across the other side of their city.

There are wide variations in the freedom to choose what to make of your life between different places in the world, and these are often very different from what is commonly suggested. In countries as unequal as the US and the UK, people are not 'united', despite that word appearing in the name of both. The very richest can easily afford second or third homes, which they leave empty most of the time, exacerbating the housing problems of the poor. The rich can frequently use hotels and often have their beds made by others who have to undertake such work because other options are not available to them. More equitable solutions are always possible. Stay in a Youth Hostel in the UK and you make and unmake your own bed. It really isn't very hard to make a bed, but it is hard and miserable work to make many dozens of beds a day. For people in more equitable countries, staying in a hotel is a treat rather than something commonplace.

Across Western Europe, welfare states – which would be better termed social states, as opposed to antisocial ones – were constructed in the aftermath of the Second World War.[12] This is partly why the poorest tenth of Germans now live on 60 per cent more than the poorest tenth of people in the US. A decade ago that difference was 50 per cent. Germany has not become more equal in the intervening years but it has become better off overall in relation to the US. In fact, Germany has become a little more unequal but economic inequality grew faster in the US over the same period, and median incomes hardly grew at all. So if you could not choose where in a society you might be placed, but were given the option of living in the US or Germany you would on average be advised to choose the latter.

Living standards for everyone rise more quickly in more equitable nations. People work harder when they are doing something worthwhile, rather than making the beds of those too lazy or too stuck-up to make their own. After adjusting for the cost of living, in Sweden the poorest tenth live on almost twice as much as the poorest tenth of Americans. Even in the UK they have a sixth more, but in more unequal Israel the poorest tenth have to subsist on 10 per cent less even than the poor in the US.[13] In Israel and the US, the poorest tenth are mostly seen as belonging to a different religion or race, which apparently makes such inequalities more palatable to the rich and to those who see themselves as part of a 'natural' majority. In the UK, the poor are a different class, definitely 'not like us'. Economic inequality creates disdain for others and creates labels where people define themselves as not being part of other groups.

It was partly the US government's European Recovery Program, the Marshall Plan, which helped construct the current social states of the rich world, including Germany. That plan was enacted at a time when the US was becoming rapidly more economically equal itself. Similarly, the US undertook social engineering in post-War Japan, which is the main reason why income inequalities are still so low in that country today (see Table 1 below). That is why most people in Japan do not see themselves as belonging to different social classes or ethnic groups any more. Just a few generations earlier in Japan, your future was dictated by the class you were born into: peasant, artisan, merchant, samurai, daimyo, shogun or royalty. Today, only a token royalty remains, and below that is a mass middle class and then a small group who are destitute and who struggle, including day-laborers and the homeless. Increasing economic equality due to any cause, including the outcome of war and natural disasters, changes the normal social relationships in a country because it changes people's acceptance of their place in society.

Although the US has been responsible for acts that have helped secure greater equalities elsewhere in the affluent world, in recent decades various US governments have pursued a different course domestically, intervening less to redress inequalities. As a result, people's life chances in North America (as reflected through income inequalities) are now almost as unequal as those in much of Africa. North America might be much richer than Africa south of the Sahara, but later in this chapter Table 1 and Table 2 show the latest UNDP measure of inequality. They show the ratio of the income of the richest fifth to that of the poorest fifth of the population, and highlight how most recently that measure of economic inequality has become higher in the US than in Uganda, Nigeria, Côte d'Ivoire and Malawi, and is now equal to Mozambique. This was not the case a few years ago, and is mainly due to high and possibly still rising inequality in the US, alongside a possible recent fall in economic inequality in much of Africa. As economic inequality rose in the US, people became understandably angrier, but most did not direct that anger at those who championed the inequality because they had been taught that 'wealth creators' were their friends and that it was 'immigrants' who were their enemies. Ironically, immediately after Donald Trump was elected president in November 2016 the Canadian immigration website crashed as so many Americans inquired about emigrating to slightly more equitable Canada.

The quintile inequality ratio – how much more the best-off fifth of households have than the worst-off fifth – is 5.8:1 in Canada as compared to 9.8:1 in the US. Canada is much less unequal than the US, but the sheer size of its southern neighbor dominates the overall record for the North American continent, which also includes Mexico and the Bahamas. However, in Canada the rise in inequality has very recently, for the time being, ceased – at least for the quintile measure reported below. The statistics of inequality are complex, but the overall picture is clear. There is no set path whereby inequality should be expected to always be increasing. It has been falling in many places in the world recently, and it fell greatly in the UK and US during most of the past century. Inequalities today seen as reasonable in the UK and US would be considered atrocities if they were suddenly imposed on more equitable places.

People adapt to both growing equality and growing inequality – they quickly become used to what they think they have to live with and that changes their identities, feelings and attitudes towards others. Living with more equality makes you resistant to treating others as inferiors or superiors and so creates increased respect all round. It is hard to explain just how strong this effect is to someone who has not lived in a place or time of greater equality. Growing up under a regime of high inequality can make many feel that they themselves are worth less (even that they are worthless) while others come to believe that they are naturally super-gifted or deserve to be where they are because of their own endeavors, discounting their own good fortune.

Often external forces alter nation-states and impose greater inequality or equality upon them. For much of the 20th century, the US supported dictatorships in Latin America and the Caribbean. This contributed to South America becoming the most unequal continent by the millennium. Its countries are now, however, free from military dictatorship and in many cases have recently undergone social revolutions, which may themselves have been produced by the very high levels of inequality. The latest data in Table 1 confirms that inequality in Argentina and Chile, for example, is now falling, albeit from monstrously high levels.

The table shows the ratio of mean incomes of the best-off 20 per cent of households to the worst-off 20 per cent. All countries in the United Nations Development Programme's 'highest affluence group' are included. The source of this data is the Human Development Reports for 2015 (Table 3) and 2005 (Table 14).

The table is ordered from the most equal to the most unequal of affluent countries in the world as measured most recently and shows the most recent changes in the statistic used to order each country. A decrease in inequality, a negative number in the final column that shows change, indicates a recent growth in equality. However, even when income inequality is falling, wealth inequalities can continue to increase because better-off people have more assets and can save more of their incomes. Wealth

Table 1: Household income inequality in the most affluent countries of the world, 2004-13

Rank	County	Quintile Ratio 2005–2013	Ratio from 2004 or earlier	Change 2004–2005/2013
1	Slovenia	3.6	3.9	-0.3
2	Sweden	3.7	4.0	-0.3
3	Czech Republic	3.9	3.5	0.4
4	Denmark	4.0	4.3	-0.3
5	Norway	4.0	3.9	0.1
6	Finland	4.0	3.8	0.2
7	Slovakia	4.1	4.0	0.1
8	Netherlands	4.5	5.5	-1.0
9	Hungary	4.6	4.7	-0.1
10	Austria	4.5	4.9	-0.4
11	Germany	4.7	4.3	0.4
12	Belgium	5.0	4.5	0.5
13	France	5.1	5.6	-0.5
14	Poland	5.2	5.8	-0.6
15	Switzerland	5.2	5.8	-0.6
16	Ireland	5.3	6.1	-0.8
17	Croatia	5.3	4.8	0.5
18	Japan	5.4	3.4	2.0
19	Estonia	5.6	7.2	-1.6
20	Lithuania	5.7	5.1	0.6
21	Canada	5.8	5.8	0.0
22	Australia	5.8	7.0	-1.2
23	Greece	6.4	6.2	0.2
24	Italy	6.9	6.5	0.4
25	Latvia	6.9	5.3	1.6
26	Spain	7.6	5.4	2.2
27	United Kingdom	7.6	7.2	0.4
28	United States	9.8	8.4	1.4
29	Israel	10.3	6.4	3.9
30	Argentina	10.6	18.1	-7.5
31	Chile	12.6	18.7	-6.1

inequalities are also more easily hidden and harder to measure. The elite try to hide their wealth more than any other group, including income derived from holding that wealth.

Inequality and class

People sometimes just consider mean average income and think that the best place to live anywhere in the world must be the US because it is there that some of the highest mean average incomes in the world are found. However, despite much rhetoric about the 'American Dream', membership of the richest group in US society is largely determined by how rich a person's parents were back when they were born, and not by their own efforts.

The US today has one of the lowest rates of social mobility among all nations in the rich world. And a child born poor in the US is more likely to die poor than in any other affluent country. The graph below (Figure 1.1) demonstrates that there is a strong correlation between social mobility and income inequality, with the US losing out on both counts. Social mobility is measured here by comparing the parents' income with their child's income in adulthood. Inequality is measured by the same quintile ratio as shown in the table above. The positions of countries in the graph only change slowly over time and were first made generally known through publication of the groundbreaking book *The Spirit Level* in 2009, though this chart is based on updated figures.

When income inequality is high, the dot representing the country is placed further to the right, and when it is low it is placed towards the left. Where social mobility is high, such that a parent's occupation and income has less bearing on a child's occupation and income, the dot is drawn high. The fact that many of the dots appear very near to the straight diagonal line demonstrates just how related social mobility and income inequality are. Each influences the other. Denmark and Australia fit least well, but they still fit the overall pattern. In both countries income inequality should be a little lower given their rates of social mobility. Perhaps one reason that the Danes are the happiest people in the world today is that they enjoy even greater social mobility than their high levels of current income equality would suggest. Of course, social mobility is far less of

Figure 1.1: Social mobility is higher in more equal countries

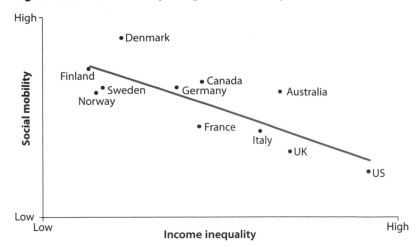

Original source: Intergenerational income mobility data from Blanden J (2009) Centre for Economic Performance, LSE. Paper No. CEEDP0111.
Via www.equalitytrust.org.uk

Note: This figure has been redrawn from one appearing on the Equality Trust website which was first drawn by Kate Pickett and Richard Wilkinson in 2009 and which has now been redrawn using the most recent data, showing an even closer relationship between the two variables than seen before.[14]

an issue in a country where the well-off are not that different from the worse-off.

Table 1 above showed that economic inequality is relatively high and rising in Italy, higher still in the UK and rising just as much as in Italy, while it is even higher in the US and has been rising faster still. Given that, it should be no surprise that social mobility is lowest in these particular affluent countries and also in that order of inequality. Researchers who study inequality become obsessed with the statistics, but in general very different measures all tend to tell the same story. Thus for many years it has been true that in the Scandinavian countries low income inequality, greater happiness and high social mobility are the norm. Later, in Chapter 6 of this book, small recent changes in inequality statistics in the Scandinavian countries are discussed, but here it is important to note that they are small.

Social mobility is about how much your choices and chances are constrained by your family background. The most common measure of it is to look at a person's chances of doing better (or worse) economically than their parents – technically referred to as intergenerational income mobility. Social mobility is high in more economically equitable countries because in those countries children have access to more similar resources. They will tend to go to similar schools, receive similar educational opportunities, and also be able to access a wide range of career options – few of which will lead to either very highly paid or very lowly paid jobs. More economically equitable countries are also less socially segregated and geographical residential districts are more mixed so that young adults are far freer to meet other young adults from different parts of society. The poor are less poor and therefore less excluded. Parents worry less about whom their children mix with and what career path they take because a person's income bracket is of much lower importance. The rich are less rich and the poor are less poor. All are therefore much freer to follow their heart's desire.

In great contrast to more economically equal societies, social mobility is very low in all the world's most unequal rich countries. There, the income of your parents really matters in determining your likely income in future. The reasons are not hard to understand. Affluent parents are very likely to give their children a leg-up, to pay for them to attend selective better-funded schools or to live in areas where the teachers are less stressed because they have to teach fewer children experiencing extreme poverty. These economically unequal societies are far more socially segregated. Within them, young adults are far less likely to meet and interact with those who are much worse-off or better-off than they are. Even if they do meet, such mixing often breaks social taboos that have arisen because of the economic inequality.

In the UK or the US, if a poor young person marries a richer person, there is an assumption that they are after their partner's money. Prenuptial agreements become common in such circumstances – contracts to ensure that the money stays in the richer family should the couple divorce in future. But, much more importantly, the stakes (even at very young ages) become so high in more economically unequal countries. If you are affluent, then allowing your children to follow their heart and do the kind of work they would like to try to do, or to marry the person they love, could lead them and your future grandchildren into living a life of poverty, because poverty is so much more common in more economically unequal societies. Social mobility is so very low in the most unequal of societies mostly because the affluent try so very hard to ensure their offspring are all affluent. The alternative is seen as failure, and that failure does almost always happen for some of the grandchildren or great-grandchildren of the very affluent, so it is an understandable fear. In England the upper-middle-class talk of their children being a 'disappointment' if they do not grow up to be as well off as they are.

It is worth noting that rates of social mobility can be relatively high in countries such as Germany, Canada and Australia, which are not the most equitable, but also not the most economically unequal. Countries can have educational or employment systems that are more equitable than their society at large, and so a younger generation need not be bound by what divided their parents so much. This is one of the reasons why rates of inequality change over time. A new generation can emerge that is less bound by its social background and so all the country dots in Figure 1.1 above do not lie on the straight line. Those countries that lie above that line are slowly becoming a little more socially mobile and hence will probably become more economically equal in the long run. Those lying below the line may well be heading in the opposite direction.

Equality and poverty

So far all the evidence presented in this chapter has concerned affluent countries, and only a very small subset of all the evidence that exists has been presented. The reason for concentrating so much on these countries initially is because it is in these countries that the implications of economic inequality are most clear to see. The social advantage of becoming better off in more unequal countries rapidly reduces when inequalities rise due to factors such as concerns about your social status. You begin to worry more about the future of your children. You may feel you have to spend more money on a home in an area that will give them access to a school that will help them secure a good job, or you may decide you cannot rely on state/public schooling. You may start to worry about whether you have enough money, even if you have a lot, because those above you will tend to have so much more. These worries are far less common in more economically equal countries – because both deep poverty and great wealth are less common.

In poorer countries, for most people there are more important and more immediate concerns than long-term planning for the next generation's future. These concerns often involve where the next meal will come from. They may also involve anxiety about whether you will be employed: each morning you may wait by the side of the road to see if a builder or farmer will pick you to work that day. Should you live at the whim of an unregulated landlord, as hundreds of millions do, you may have to work hard to ensure that you will be able to keep the shelter you have next month. You will also have to worry about trying to save some money in case you become ill. You may not have ready access to clean water. In such countries inequality matters a great deal

The sociology of water

because the most abject poverty will be far more widespread in those poorer countries where the elite tolerates great inequality. Infant mortality rates are higher in poor countries that are more unequal and so people have more children to ensure that enough of them survive to adulthood and can care for their parents in old age.

When a poor country is more unequal, it is less likely to have established even rudimentary social care and medical systems and universal free access to primary education. This is because the better-off in unequal poor countries think that they personally have little to gain from such overall social improvements; but even the better-off benefit when the extreme practices of greed common in the most unequal of countries are curtailed.

The personal benefits of gaining some wealth, even just a little, if you live in a country where poverty is common are obvious. And yet, as Table 2 below shows, economic inequalities are currently falling in most of the very poorest countries on earth. In recent years the poor have caught up a little with those in the best-off fifth of each society, but it is quite possible, even probable, that there will be a small group in each country who are making a very large amount of money and whose earnings are not well recorded. The same happens in rich countries, where annual records such as the *Sunday Times* Rich List in the UK and the *Forbes* index of billionaires in the US reveal the results of their growing take. Such records of the wealth of the very richest are also available for poorer countries but are very unreliable.

Data are hard to come by for the world's poorest countries – on everyone, not just the rich. The household surveys the UNDP relies upon will be less reliable in poorer countries and were even less reliable just a few years earlier. Nevertheless, a step does appear to have been taken towards greater equality recently. We will not dwell on the numbers in the table immediately below because they are all we have and we cannot compare them to other sources. But if anyone tells you that inequality is rising everywhere, please ask them why they think that is true, and show them this table of numbers.

Although data for individual countries may be unreliable, data for all countries combined are far more reliable as errors tend to

Table 2: Household income inequality in the world's least affluent countries, 2004-13

Rank	County	Quintile Ratio 2005–2013	Ratio from 2004 or earlier	Change 2004–2005/2013
1	Pakistan	4.1	4.8	-0.7
2	Niger	4.5	20.7	-16.2
3	Burundi	4.8	9.5	-4.7
4	Nepal	5.0	5.9	-0.9
5	Mali	5.2	12.2	-7.0
6	Ethiopia	5.3	4.3	1.0
7	Guinea	5.5	7.3	-1.8
8	Sierra Leone	5.6	57.6	-52.0
9	Yemen	5.6	5.6	0.0
10	Guinea-Bissau	5.9	10.3	-4.4
11	Tanzania	6.2	6.7	-0.5
12	Burkina Faso	7.0	13.6	-6.6
13	Madagascar	7.4	11.0	-3.6
14	Cameroon	7.5	9.1	-1.6
15	Senegal	7.8	7.5	0.3
16	Mauritania	7.8	7.4	0.4
17	Uganda	8.8	8.4	0.4
18	Nigeria	9.1	12.8	-3.7
19	Côte d'Ivoire	9.4	9.2	0.2
20	Malawi	9.7	11.6	-1.9
21	Mozambique	9.8	7.2	2.6
22	Kenya	11.0	9.1	-1.9
23	Rwanda	11.0	4.0	7.0
24	Gambia	11.0	13.8	-2.8
25	Swaziland	14.0	23.8	-9.8
26	Central African Rep.	18.0	32.7	-14.7
27	Lesotho	20.4	44.2	-23.8

Ratio of mean incomes of the best-off 20% of households to the worse-off 20%. All countries in the United Nations Development Programme's lowest affluence group. Source: World Development Reports: UNDP 2015, Table 3; UNDP 2005, Table 14. Note that there are many caveats given in the sources to these tables as to why the figures may not be that comparable over time for poorer countries in the world.

cancel themselves out when statistics are combined, unless there is some systematic error pushing all biases in one direction. In 2016 the former lead economist of the World Bank's research department, Branko Milanovic published a groundbreaking study of global inequality. In it he demonstrated that inequalities do not always increase, they also often fall – especially so today. He showed that between 1988 and 2008 the incomes of people in the second-poorest and middle quintiles of the global income distribution rose by between 20 per cent and 75 per cent in real terms.[15] Housing costs for these groups had not yet grown as rapidly and so they were genuinely better off. These were the greatest rises enjoyed by any global quintile group worldwide. They are mainly a result of the recent rise in living standards in China and it can certainly be argued that if China is excluded from the analysis then global inequalities have increased.[16]

Milanovic found that, judged by income inequality, the world as a whole had become more equal over the previous 30 years. However, the very richest one per cent also saw huge gains in their income – much larger than those of anyone else in the best-off two global quintiles. The poorest quintile, meanwhile, saw smaller gains – and there were even falls in income for many of the very

Figure 1.2: Global income growth from 1988 to 2008 by income percentile

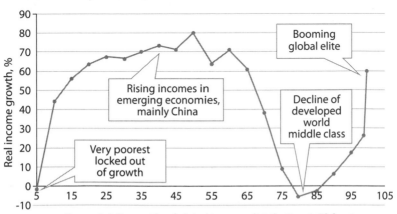

Poorest ← Percentile of global income distribution → **Richest**

Source: B Milanovič, *Global Income Inequality by Numbers*, Nov 2012, redrawn nin.tl/Atlanticgraph

poorest in Africa. So, although income equality increased overall, that headline summary hides a variety of trends for different groups of people all living at the same time on this increasingly interconnected planet.

Milanovic recently showed that the global distribution of incomes is changing shape. He showed that the UK and the US are unusual in their recent acceptance of growing inequality; that, both globally and locally, inequality tends to rise and fall over time in waves; and that Thomas Piketty is not quite correct to see the post-War period as unusual. The graph that first highlighted Milanovic's findings was published in *The Atlantic* magazine in 2014 and is shown in Figure 1.2.

How some countries recently set out to become more unequal

Before considering the benefits of the equality effect we have to consider the spread of economic inequality that allows us now to measure that effect. At the beginning of the 20th century, most affluent countries were very similarly unequal and then became very similarly equal by the middle decades of that century, so it was very difficult to ascertain what specific effects could be associated with very different degrees of inequality and equality. However, since the 1970s the affluent countries of the world have diverged. Because of that divergence we are now able to quantify what the effects of varying levels of economic equality appear to be.

Figure 1.3 will look like an unholy mess at first sight but don't worry – each line of it will be more clearly shown in charts that appear later in this book and will be separately explained. But this summary graph shows what percentage of a country's total personal income has been taken by the richest one per cent of the population each year from 1900 to 2015 – in 12 countries for which good data has been available for the past few years.

It was 44 years ago, in 1973, that inequalities in the US reached an all-time low – at this point, the richest one per cent of people earned only 7.7 times the average US wage – a remarkably high level of economic equality. Table 3 below makes Figure 1.3 easier to read and is included because the data contained in the graph

Figure 1.3: The take of the best-off 1% in 12 countries, 1900-2015

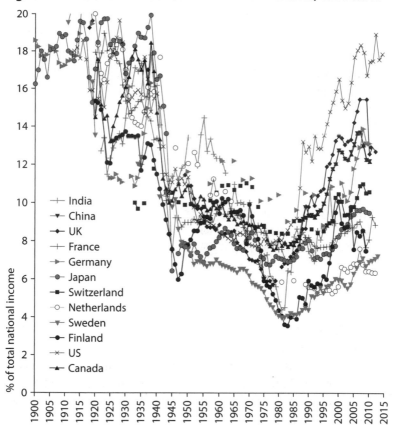

Years of consecutive data connected by a line. Where no data is shown it is missing for that year.

Source: World Wealth and Income database – accessed March 2017: http://wid.world/

are so important, but so hard to read. The table shows for how long we have had access to these data about extreme inequality in each country, what the start and end proportions were and also when the maximum and minimum inequality was achieved within each country. In most cases this data has only very recently come to light and been analyzed.

These figures really do matter because they show not just how much inequality has varied across time but also that it varies greatly between affluent countries at any one point in time. When people tell you that high inequality is inevitable because the whole

Table 3: Percentage income share of the best off 1% in 12 countries: earliest, lowest, highest, latest records

Country	Earliest record		Lowest recorded value		Highest recorded value		Latest record	
United States	1913	17.96	1973	7.74	1928	19.60	2014	17.85
United Kingdom	1918	19.28	1978	5.72	1919	19.59	2012	12.70
Canada	1920	14.40	1978	7.60	1938	18.41	2010	12.22
Germany	1900	18.63	1995	8.84	1917	22.42	2010	13.13
India	1922	12.72	1981	4.39	1938	17.82	1999	8.95
Switzerland	1933	9.98	1983	8.39	1939	11.78	2010	10.63
France	1920	17.95	1983	6.99	1923	18.91	2012	8.94
Japan	1900	16.25	1945	6.43	1938	19.92	2010	9.51
Netherlands	1914	20.96	1993	5.24	1916	27.88	2012	6.33
Finland	1920	15.27	1983	3.49	1920	15.27	2009	7.46
Sweden	1903	26.99	1981	3.97	1916	28.04	2010	7.24
China	1982	7.87	1983	7.70	2007	13.72	2010	12.22

Source: World Wealth and Income Database, accessed in March 2017.

world has become more unequal, you need a graph and table like this to tell them that they are wrong.

It is true that almost everywhere was more equal within recent living memory than it is today. If you live in the US, it will be hard to imagine a world in which the (big) boss earns just 7.7 times more than the average worker – yet this was the case in the US itself as recently as 1973. People in the Netherlands, Finland and Sweden, by contrast, would be appalled if inequalities in their countries rose up to those levels. They are already horrified that they have risen up from their own minimums of, respectively, five, three-and-a-half and four times the average worker's wage. However, the most recent data for the US, UK and Canada show the average pay of the top one per cent being respectively 18, 13 and 12 times average earnings. The situation was far worse in the distant past. In Sweden and the Netherlands in 1916 the top one per cent of the population took 28 per cent of all national income! Perhaps it was partly this legacy of appallingly gross inequality that led these countries to become the international leaders on equality that they are now.

Britain was even more equitable than the US in the 1970s and peak equality lasted a little longer in the UK. I grew up in that era of much greater equality in the UK. I was 10 years old in 1978 when the rich were least rich, when the best-off one per cent earned only 5.7 times the average income. By 2007, that figure had risen to 15.4 times. Almost every year since I was aged 10 I have watched the very rich get even richer and, below them, the affluent take more and more of what was left, leaving less and less for most people, especially for the poorest, whose numbers have grown. The somewhat heartless statistics in the graph and table above tell a story both of the apparently relentless growth of inequality in some rich countries, and of other countries choosing to keep levels of income inequality comparatively low.

Since 2007 the picture in the UK has become murky. The income share of the richest one per cent appeared on the face of it to have fallen abruptly to 12.7 per cent by 2012, from a high of 15.4 per cent just five year earlier. More recent statistics are not available. However, this is the income that the rich declare for taxable purposes and there are concerns that the very highest paid in the UK have been finding new ways to disguise their income. We will touch on this later, but it is first worth considering what happens to the politics and culture of a society that allows income inequality to grow and grow.

The MPs' expenses scandal in the UK revealed that fiddling expenses to hide illicit income was rife even amongst politicians. However, in many ways they are just behaving like many other very highly paid people in Britain. In April 2016, Peter Skinner was convicted of a fraud undertaken when he was a Labour Member of the European Parliament. He was a former Economics and Business lecturer, had been a member of the European Economic Monetary Affairs Committee for 15 years, a board member of the European Financial Services Forum, and claimed £500,000 over three years 'to pay for luxuries including hotels and clothes, as well as payments for his ex-wife'.[17]

The extent of fraud and the amounts of money being hidden tend to be much higher in times and places of great inequality. Everywhere has its scandals, but they vary in how common they are and making precise estimates of the actual income of the very rich is difficult because of fraud and hidden wealth. Amongst politicians scandals are more common on the political right. Peter Skinner was unusual. But for another similar example, look up the life and times of Patrick Brazeau, a Conservative Canadian Senator who was due to stand trial on charges of fraud in 2016 (his trial was delayed until June 2017 following his suicide attempt).[18] Then consider whether Patrick and Peter might have led very different lives had they not entered early adulthood in countries that were becoming so much more unequal and had they not been so conditioned by the environment around them which was largely not of their making.

Canadians experienced much the same trend as in the UK and US when it comes to looking at the take of the top one per cent. In 1974, when Patrick Brazeau was born, the richest one per cent of Canadians 'only' took 8.8 per cent of all income in Canada and that had fallen to 7.9 per cent by the time he was aged 10. But their take rose to 9.6 per cent by his 20th birthday, and to an enormous 12.7 per cent by his 30th.

When the best-off one per cent in your country are hoovering up so much then others feel entitled to boost their own incomes illicitly, or at least they appear to worry less about their own behavior. By the time Patrick was sworn in as a Canadian Senator at the age of 34 it looked as if economic inequalities in Canada might possibly be beginning to fall – but he had grown up in a country where the rich had taken more and more for most of the years that he had been alive. That doesn't just leave much less for the rest; it also especially corrupts those near the top. By 2014 Patrick was under investigation in the Senate for his previous potential financial irregularities, and was managing a strip club in Ottawa.[19]

It is easy to begin to believe that almost all politicians are corrupt and some are simply better at hiding this than others. In the UK one politician was lauded for only having claimed a black-and-white television license fee in his expenses. However, no-one questioned why he felt the need to do even that, given his very high official income. Very little publicity was given to the fact that the Member of Parliament to claim the least expenses was a relatively unknown MP when the expenses scandal broke in 2010: a man called Jeremy Corbyn.[20] Jeremy became leader of the Labour Party in 2015 and saw its membership rise to become the largest political party in Europe in less than a year. His message was simple and unusual – you have to be principled; you have to do the right thing. Bernie Sanders said much the same in the US and narrowly missed becoming the Democratic Party candidate for president in 2016. But before that, at the very end of 2015, Justin Trudeau was elected prime minister of Canada, and said his 'first legislative priority is to lower taxes for middle-income Canadians and raise taxes for the top one per cent of income earners'.[21]

If you have lived through the last four decades in the US, Canada or the UK, then simply by observing what has happened around you it looked (until very recently) as if the best-off would always take more and more. You might have concluded that, if you didn't join them, or at least begin to behave like them, your life and the lives of your children would suffer. The few politicians not on 'the take' are still seen as oddballs. In contrast to them, people who behaved as Donald Trump has behaved during most of his life appeared to do well, although it is claimed he would have done better had he made no business decisions at all during his 'working' life and simply invested the money in normal stocks and shares.[22] When Trump won the US presidency in late 2016 he opened up his life and views to more scrutiny than any other human on the planet has ever received.

But look again at the graph and table above and you'll see that the same trend of ever-rising inequality did not apply to the same extent in Germany, and hardly at all in the Netherlands, Sweden or France over this same period. There is greed and corruption everywhere – but it is better controlled in some countries than others. In more equitable countries, people are impressed by politicians like Jeremy Corbyn (who do not make extravagant expenses claims) and are dismissive of people like Donald Trump (who make claims of many kinds for their supposed brilliance).

Rich and poor in China and India

Let's turn away from rich-world problems for a moment and look, in Figure 1.4, at the two largest countries in the 12-country graph above: China and India.

Both China and India have followed the general trends seen in much richer countries. The inequality trend of the last century best documented in the richest countries of the world is also a global trend. Inequality fell, and then rose, and today we may be at something of a tipping point in both China and India as well as in many richer countries. The 1980s market reforms in China rapidly increased economic inequality. Inequalities were falling in India before 1981. We can be very sure that the same occurred in China before that date as the economic reforms in China allowing inequalities to rise came in very shortly after then. Because China also became much richer over this period, for a time, growing economic inequalities were not seen as a great problem there, but they are seen as such now. In contrast, in India, which had much slower economic growth than China, growing economic inequalities have caused greater friction. According to the latest world happiness report people are less happy in India than in China, but they are not especially happy in either of these very large countries.

Greater equality matters because under it more people are treated as being fully human, as deserving. Worldwide, you have to ask how global inequalities might look today had a reformer in the Chinese Communist Party been more concerned about inequalities rising in that country in the 1980s and 1990s. Was the rise in inequalities in China inevitable, as it moved towards mass-producing the world's merchandise? And now that growing inequality within China is so much more of a concern to the Chinese elite, might we see it fall?

One of the reasons inequality matters in China is that the statistics for that country have been revised. The new data in Figure 1.4 suggest, somewhat surprisingly, that inequalities within China in 1982 – before the Deng Xiaoping market reforms – were actually larger than in India. It is good that new statistics have been released – and worrying just how unreliable the old ones were. It is also interesting to see the recently reported fall in both China and India in the take of the best-off one per cent. Again, we have to be concerned about the reliability even of these updated statistics, but if the falls are partly caused by the very rich trying harder to hide their incomes then that is also an indication that

Figure 1.4: The take of the best-off 1% in India and China, 1922-2012

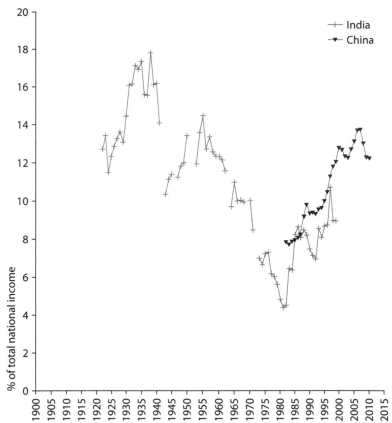

Years of consecutive data connected by a line. Where no data is shown it is missing for that year.

Source: World Wealth and Income database – accessed March 2017: http://wid.world/

inequality is being seen as more important now than it was a few years ago.

It is also now possible that many states, including China, are running out of options for increasing national incomes further and so those in power have chosen to take a bigger share from the rich in what they see to be a temporary necessity. In China, because there is infighting between different political and financial factions of the elite, the apparent recently renewed concern with 'inequality' may just offer a comfortable narrative to justify attacks that are otherwise not motivated by such concerns. This may not matter in the short term, as long as it reduces inequality, but in the long term a serious concern to reverse rising inequality would require greater political commitment.

Of course, within the vast countries of China and India there are huge variations. How many of the poorest billion people in the world would no longer be poor had more of India taken the path chosen by the citizens of Kerala state (explored in more depth in Chapter 6), which has prioritized health, education and social well-being over decades, with strikingly positive results? Had the industrialist Jehangir Ratanji Dadabhoy Tata not supported the 1975-77 state of emergency in India, would that emergency have resulted in a turn-around of policy towards opening up to transnational capital, and would the trend toward growing inequality for a billion people there have still become established? And would his steel company now own and be threatening to close the forges near where I used to live, in England's former steel capital of Sheffield? There are times when just a single alternative action can make all the difference.

Had 1960s revolutionaries in parts of Latin America been denounced just a fraction less by those who taught the men who went on to run the military regimes of the 1970s, would the world be different now? Latin America has recently seen a decline in inequality but economic inequality there became incredibly high following the rule of the dictators. And what might have occurred across Africa, the continent to suffer the greatest falls in income in the 1980s as worldwide inequalities then grew, had campaigners in Britain just been a little more radical than they were in the 1930s and altered British and other colonialist attitudes earlier?

In the years that followed revolution in China, despite famine and hardship, far fewer children died from poverty than in India, not least because fewer were born. Chinese fertility rates came down in a single generation from six live children being born per mother to just over two – and this was before the introduction of the notorious one-child-per-family policy.

From the early 1980s onwards, inequalities in India soared. We now know that they rose just as quickly in China but that rise was initially not included in the official statistics. Nevertheless, the increase in inequality has not yet brought unfairness in either country back to the levels experienced before 1949 – unlike in the US and the UK, where inequality levels now surpass those earlier post-War highs. And, unlike the first countries to become industrialized, China and India have the errors of the West to learn from – both old errors and very recent ones.

The data for India is now very out of date, but in both countries the latest data suggest that a return to the past very high levels of inequality is unlikely. Today, children growing up in urban China enjoy levels of good health similar to those in the US, partly because there are so few children and because such a large amount of China's growing wealth has been spent on their welfare. Both communist countries and those with democratic socialist governments tend to spend more on healthcare, partly because that is the right thing to do and partly because it can be used to legitimize the other things they do.[23] In India, despite similar levels of inequality to China, this is not the case, and an average child growing up in India today is growing up with health risks the Chinese escaped a generation ago. It is very possible for two countries to have similar levels of inequality but very different outcomes for children. But for both China and India, home to a third of the population of the planet, it is greater equality in future that would serve them best.

The international landscape

At the start of the last century, almost everywhere in the world, the richest one per cent received between 10 and 30 per cent of all the personal income. Who those richest people were changed in China from feudal lords to communist officials (and their friends), and in India from the Raj to local entrepreneurs (and the most corrupt politicians), but there is always a top one per cent. By 1980, almost nowhere did this elite receive as much as 10 per cent. By the end of the first decade of this century, inequalities had risen again, but we also had a wider variety of outcomes between countries in terms of equality and inequality than has ever previously been recorded. Worldwide, we collectively appear to be making new choices and winning at least some of the battles.

The British historian Tony Judt said before his death in 2010:

> 'Never before has there been more scope for choice. Never before have the range of inequalities exhibited by these dozen states been as wide as in 2010. Those who wish to see greater equalities won again need to know both how they were lost some 30 to 40 years ago and how in other countries they have been protected. Where inequalities are highest, it is all the harder to recover or improve the situation because: "Inequality is corrosive. It rots societies from within".'[24]

The complex Figure 1.3 above is dissected in the rest of this book by extracting and discussing pairs of countries such as China and India, and later chapters also add statistics about the top one per cent in many other countries for which no data were available only five years ago. However, at this point a note of caution is required concerning what appeared to be very recent drops in inequality – especially concerning the apparent dramatic fall in the take of the top one per cent in the UK in recent years.

The UK introduced a 50-per-cent top rate of income tax for a very short period, in April 2010, a month before a Labour government lost power. This had several effects, including incentivizing many in the richest one per cent to pay their tax early, at the lower old rate of 40 per cent.[25] But it also coincided with a rapid jump in the number of people in the UK registering new companies with no employees, the numbers of which rose by nine per cent in the year to 2011, but by only two per cent and one per cent in the subsequent two years.[26] That increase is *unlikely* to have been due to a sudden transient increase in entrepreneurial zeal, but was most likely due to the advice of very affluent individuals' accountants on how to reduce their tax liabilities. It is not impossible that other very recent turns in inequality such as those shown in India and China are partly due to the super-rich becoming better at hiding their income and wealth. But even that could be a sign that we have reached a turning point – they are now more afraid of the tax authorities. Right now it is very hard to tell and wildly different statistics were being bandied around in 2016 and early 2017. Never, though, had economic inequality been of such interest to so many people worldwide as it has been recently.

In the US, the average pay gap between bosses and workers fell between 2014 and 2015, the most recent years for which we have data. In 2014, the average pay of the CEO of one of the 500 top-ranked companies in the US was 373 times that of the average worker. By 2015 that ratio had fallen to 335 times, partly because many trade unions had been successful in very recent pay disputes, increasing the average annual pay of workers by $900 a year to $36,900. More importantly, the average pay of the bosses appeared to fall from $13.5 million a year to $12.4 million. However, even if we are at a global tipping point, there is still an awfully long way to go and we have to be very careful when assessing the pay of CEOs because it is not at all transparent.

Alternative estimates of the US CEO to average worker pay ratio published in *The Atlantic* in late 2016 put it at an almost unbelievably high 949:1 in 2014 and so it may be almost as high as that today, if falling.[27] In 1980 the same US pay ratio was 42 times, rising to 107 times in 1990. From 2017 onwards

The scales of injustice

the US Securities and Exchange Commission will 'require public companies to disclose the ratio of the pay of their CEOs to the median compensation of their employees'.[28] Again, all this additional scrutiny suggests we may be at a turning point, even if we cannot be that precise about just how bad inequality currently is in a country like the US or the UK, where the very rich try so hard to hide their income.

Here is another way of viewing the trends shown in the complex Figure 1.3 graph from earlier in this chapter. The 12 countries included are typical of worldwide trends. For 60 years, inequalities fell rapidly almost everywhere. The income share of the top one per cent in society is just one measure of inequality, but it is a good measure in that using it ensures that you focus on the rich, their take and their behavior. Even a cursory study of inequality reveals that the greed of the rich is the real problem, not some laziness amongst the poor. In practice, the 'one-per-cent-take' statistic correlates closely with other measures of inequality, but it may be one of the best statistics to focus on because the very richest have such a disproportionate effect. People compare their own situations with those just above them and with the richest more than with those just below. Scholars who study inequality are coming to believe it is vital to concentrate on the rich as the major problem, rather than to continue the historical tradition of focusing so much on the poor.[29]

The incremental, imperceptible changes that add up to progress

The graph above, Figure 1.3, of overall global inequalities, can appear very depressing if not dissected and examined in detail, but, as it is taken apart in the rest of this book, I will try to show you how your eye has been drawn to the bad news and how you are not seeing the potentially good news so clearly. The same can happen when you listen to the news on radio or television, which tends to concentrate on disaster and failure. As the US essayist Rebecca Solnit put it in a much-quoted recent summary:

> 'We lose hope when we lose perspective – when we lose sight
> of the 'accretion of incremental, imperceptible changes' which

constitute progress and which render our era dramatically different from the past, a contrast obscured by the undramatic nature of gradual transformation punctuated by occasional tumult.'

The countries where inequalities are rapidly rising again have been shaded most darkly in Figure 1.3, but notice that, in most of the countries included, the best-off one per cent of people still earn less than a tenth of all income and thus less than 11 times the overall average income of the rest, despite the recent rises in inequality. Furthermore, in very recent years the apparent falls in inequality across so many countries cannot all be due to the kind of tax-avoidance behavior that typifies the richest in the UK. Some will be, but offshore tax havens are now being exposed more and more and we are finding out far more about the wealth hidden within them.

It is important to remember that the majority of the rich countries of the world still enjoy levels of equality similar to those experienced by Canada, the US and the UK when they were at or near their most equal. Exceptionally, within unequal affluent countries, and much more widely elsewhere, you hear of individuals who honestly treat other people as equals to amazing effect. But it is far easier to treat others as equals in times and places of greater widespread equality. Then you do not have to behave like a saint in order not to fiddle your expenses. It is easier to behave well when you are all more equal. And we have known this for many centuries. It led to one of the most famous declarations of all time about the right to be treated as an equal and to be healthy, free and happy as a result:

'We hold these truths to be self-evident, that all men are created equal, that they are endowed by their Creator with certain unalienable Rights, that among these are Life, Liberty and the pursuit of Happiness.'

US Declaration of Independence, 1776

The men who drafted and signed the world's most famous document advocating greater equality included many who owned slaves and a large majority who would not have considered women as men's equals. Nevertheless, they signed a declaration that is still held in awe today.

Today, on its website, the officials of the US House of Representatives celebrate key gains in greater equality, writing:

> 'The House's first African-American member was elected in 1870. The first Hispanic member took office in 1877, the first woman member in 1917, the first Asian-American member in 1957, and the first African-American woman member in 1969. In 2007, Representative Nancy Pelosi of California was elected as the first woman Speaker of the House.'[30]

Nowhere are losses of equality listed as achievements. In future the 2008 election of Barack Obama will be added to that list. Had Hillary Clinton won the presidency in 2016, her name would have been added. Donald Trump's electoral victory is very unlikely to be immortalized in the same way. Progress is never linear; but those who are not progressive are forgotten more quickly unless they become the very worst of tyrants.

Greater equality is often won only after great insult has been recognized. Future egalitarians may look back on us today and ask why we did not consider children's rights more fully than we do today. They may wonder why we did not value more highly the rights of those at the end of life, of prisoners of war, of criminals, of people considered deranged or simple, of animals, of diversity in nature, of future generations and their rights to a habitable planet, and of others whom we are unable yet to recognize as a disregarded group. If we act now, then future generations may look back at us today and say we were living in the years when the trend changed and we helped to change it. Many things become much clearer with hindsight, but, given what we know about the benefits of greater equality today, it is already clear what we should be striving for now.

Equality is a process, a direction that you take, and only in very limited technical senses an end that you achieve. There is a big gap between women getting the vote – the technical equality – and equal political participation. That is why in this book I so often precede 'equality' with the word 'greater'. Other groups are constantly being recognized as equally human, which is usually the first step towards greater equality being won. People do not

Figure 1.5: The take of the best-off 1% in 14 countries, 1900-2015

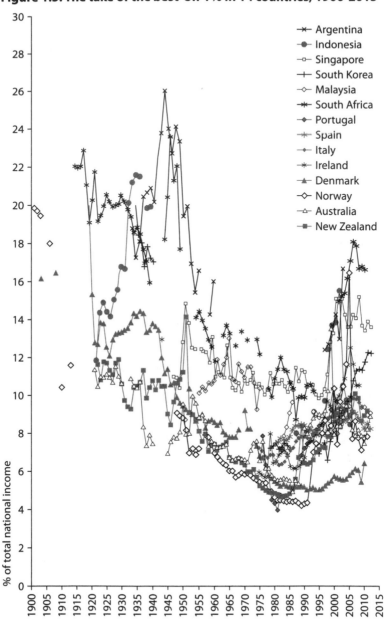

Years of consecutive data connected by a line. Where no data is shown it is missing for that year.

Source: World Wealth and Income database – accessed March 2017: http://wid.world/

easily bomb, torture or starve others they recognize as being human, as being like them, as being part of the same family – the human family. We need to stop people, especially the rich, being so bigheaded and pigheaded. We need to remember that 'there, but for the grace of God, go I'. We have to strive for greater equality endlessly, not to create a world of pure equality, but just to get our basic rights accepted as normal, including the right not to have to live in poverty. As we become more equal the list of rights we win grows longer.

One sign of great progress being made is that good inequality data for a further 14 countries has been released, more than doubling the number that can now be studied if we are concerned with the take of the richest one per cent. That data is shown in Figure 1.5 above and Table 4 below again summarizes what the graph shows. At various points in the rest of this book pairs of these countries will also be examined to look at their particular trends more closely.

Table 4: Percentage income share of the best off 1% in 14 countries: earliest, lowest, highest, latest records

Country	Earliest record		Lowest recorded value		Highest recorded value		Latest record	
Argentina	1932	18.77	1997	12.39	1943	25.96	2004	16.75
Australia	1922	11.63	1982	4.61	1951	14.13	2011	9.17
Denmark	1903	16.21	1994	5.00	1917	27.61	2010	6.41
Indonesia	1921	11.82	1982	7.17	1933	21.55	2004	8.46
Ireland	1938	16.93	1977	5.64	1938	16.93	2009	10.50
Italy	1974	7.46	1983	6.34	2007	9.86	2009	9.38
South Korea	1933	21.13	1998	6.58	1933	21.13	2012	12.23
Malaysia	1951	8.76	1983	7.87	1965	12.99	2012	9.11
NZ/Aotearoa	1921	11.34	1986	4.88	1999	13.44	2012	8.85
Norway	1900	20.18	1989	4.13	1900	20.18	2011	7.80
Portugal	1976	7.89	1981	3.97	2005	9.77	2005	9.77
Singapore	1947	10.94	1995	9.84	2008	15.15	2012	13.57
South Africa	1914	22.03	1987	8.78	1946	23.61	2011	16.68
Spain	1981	7.50	1981	7.50	2006	9.14	2012	8.20

Source: World Wealth and Income Database, accessed in March 2017.

Geography is the key to uncovering why growing inequality is never inevitable – because it never happens everywhere at once. Look at the most recent years in the graph above and try to discern that a change might be happening. There is a turn towards growing equality again, a turn last seen in most of these countries only after the Second World War had ended – although it began earlier in Denmark, Italy, New Zealand/Aotearoa and Australia, just after the First World War, which was the conflict that most involved them.

1 'Oscar Wilde (1891) 'The Critic as Artist', in *Intentions*, James R Osgood & McIlvaine, 1891, pp.93-211, online-literature.com/wilde/1305/
2 S Oishi & S Kesebir, 'Income inequality explains why economic growth does not always translate to an increase in happiness, *Psychological Science*, 26, 10, pp 1-9, Sep 2015, nin.tl/growthisnothappiness
3 Avner Offer, *The Challenge of Affluence*, Oxford University Press, 2006.
4 BBC news, 'Denmark the "happiest country" and Burundi "the least happy"', 16 Mar 2016, nin.tl/happinessratings
5 George Monbiot, 'Frightened by Donald Trump? You don't know the half of it', *The Guardian*, 30 Nov 2016, nin.tl/Trumpfright
6 ONS, *Main results from the Wealth and Assets Survey: July 2012 to June 2014*, 18 Dec 2015, nin.tl/wealthassets
7 Simon Heffer, 'MPs' expenses: Parliament is no place for the talented', *The Telegraph*, 5 Feb 2010, nin.tl/talentandParl
8 M Wilkinson, 'Senior Tories warn David Cameron he has started a tax returns "witch-hunt"', *The Telegraph*, 12 Apr 2016, quoting Alan Duncan, former minister, nin.tl/taxwitch
9 H Watt, 'Alan Duncan claimed thousands for gardening: MPs' expenses', *The Telegraph*, 10 May 2009, nin.tl/gardenexes
10 G Viña, 'New head of UK schools watchdog "has no teaching experience"', *The Financial Times*, 10 Jun 2016, nin.tl/noteaching
11 OECD, *In It Together: Why Less Inequality Benefits All*, Paris, 2015.
12 New Zealand had introduced a social state and great equality before the Second World War. For more information start with: nin.tl/p26F3w
13 N Stotesbury & D Dorling, 'Understanding Income Inequality and its Implications: Why Better Statistics are Needed', *Statistics Views*, 21 Oct 2015, nin.tl/betterstats
14 See The Equality Trust, *The Spirit Level Slides*, 2017, nin.tl/SpiritLevelslides
15 B Milanović, *Global Inequality*, Harvard University Press, 2016.
16 M Roberts, 'Globalisation and Milanović's elephant', *The next recession blog*, 14 Sep 2016, nin.tl/nextrecession
17 'Expenses fraud ex-MEP Peter Skinner jailed for four years after falsely claiming more than £100,000', *The Telegraph*, 29 Apr 2016, nin.tl/Skinnerjailed
18 J Elliot, Brazeau trial delayed until June 2017, *CTV News*, 4 Mar 2016, nin.tl/Brazeau
19 J Willing, '"A job is a job", Sen. Brazeau says of strip club gig', *Ottawa Sun*, 20 Feb 2014, nin.tl/stripclubgig

20 M Hussein, 'Islington North MP Jeremy Corbyn is the country's lowest expenses claimer', *Islington Gazette*, 8 Dec 2010, nin.tl/Corbynlowestexes

21 C Harris, 'Justin Trudeau signals new style on 1st day as Canada's 23rd prime minister', *CBC News*, 4 Nov 2015, nin.tl/Trudeaufirstday

22 C Groden, 'Donald Trump would be richer if he'd have invested in index funds', *Fortune Magazine*, 20 Aug 2015, nin.tl/Trumpricher

23 S Jones, 'Castro's legacy and the envy of many nations: social care in Cuba', *The Guardian*, 27 Nov 2016, nin.tl/Cubasocialcare

24 Tony Judt, *Ill fares the land*, Allen Lane, London, 2010.

25 Burkhauser et al, 'What has been happening to UK income inequality since the mid-1990s?', *ISER Working Paper*, p 13, Feb 2016, nin.tl/UKincomes

26 See BIS, *Enterprise Directorate, Enterprise and Economic Development Analysis Team Analysis 2015*: nin.tl/Govuploads (look for 'legal status time series')

27 W Lazonick & M Hopkins, 'Corporate executives are making way more money than anybody reports, *The Atlantic*, 15 Sep 2016, nin.tl/waymorepay

28 R Kerber, 'CEO-worker pay gap stays wide despite wage hikes: unions', *Reuters*, 17 May 2016, nin.tl/CEOworkergap

29 On why it is now worth concentrating on the rich see: Susan George, *Whose crisis, whose future?* Polity, 2010.

30 On the House of Representatives website, see: house.gov/content/learn/history

2

When we were more equal

The history of human equality may surprise you. Hunter-gatherers valued equality and co-operation above all other human traits. The happiest and most sustainable societies left hardly any trace, because they were sustainable. In contrast, pyramids and castles are only built by enslaving the poor. Great cultural advances tend to come through revolutions against inequality. The last such revolution lowered inequalities worldwide from 1918 through to 1978. But in recent years, a few English-speaking rich countries have been demonstrating to the world what goes wrong when inequality is allowed to rise.

Those who favor inequality have for some time known the danger of teaching and understanding Geography. This was not simply the academic study of exploration, conquest and colonies; it was also the discipline that allowed you to compare different places – to see what was possible elsewhere and so could be changed closer to home. An 1879 testimony to a Select Committee of the British Parliament was in no doubt about the threat:

> 'Geography, sir, is ruinous in its effects on the lower classes. Reading, writing, and arithmetic are comparatively safe, but geography invariably leads to revolution.'[1]

History allows us to see how equality waxes and wanes over time, while Geography widens our horizons so we can see what is actually possible elsewhere. But the study of equality is about more than Geography and History. It involves Politics, Sociology,

Economics, Mathematics and Science, including Comparative Psychology and Biology.

Trying to understand inequality has recently become very popular. For example, the Worldwide Web contains numerous videos of what have come to be called Frans de Waal's monkeys. Frans and his colleague Sarah Brosnan first reported that Capuchin monkeys in cages react with extreme anger to being treated unequally. Their findings were disseminated most widely in a letter to the journal *Nature* published in 2003.[2] The videos show how a monkey reacts when another monkey is unfairly given better treats for performing the same action. What you see is that the slighted monkey is not amused when another monkey is given grapes instead of cucumber. Over 10 million people have viewed just one video of a Capuchin monkey annoyed that another monkey has been given grapes instead of cucumber![3] The idea of fairness, that we should be treated equally, goes back a very long way in our own history as well as that of other apes. An appreciation of equality is part of our very being.

When considering equality, it is hard to overstate the importance of humans being mammals. Mammals often live in groups and frequently there are hierarchies to be seen within those groups, from wolf packs to communities of chimpanzees. The key way in which humans differ from other mammals is that they create very elaborate mechanisms to control some people's tendency to try to dominate others and these mechanisms vary widely. Humans don't simply scream with anger, as Capuchin monkeys do.

Anthropologist Christopher Boehm described the development of egalitarianism among humans as resulting from the '...collective power of resentful subordinates [which] is the base of human egalitarian society.'[4] America's Founding Fathers were resentful subordinates. That is why the US Declaration of Independence said: 'We hold these truths to be self-evident, that all men are created equal...' The founding fathers were also all men. At some point in our evolution as a species, long before that 1776 declaration, women were subordinated. It is no coincidence that at around the same time as men in the United States were first so effectively demanding equality of treatment, this subordination was challenged most clearly – by Mary Wollstonecraft, most famously in her *A Vindication of the Rights of Woman* (1792). Inequalities between men and women, between the British and settlers in the United States, and between the rich and the poor in France, where revolution broke out in 1789, had all grown too great. Human beings have an intrinsic yearning for greater equality.

Hunting, fighting and feasting

It is now well established that hunter-gatherer societies relied on relationships of equality and group co-operation to survive. Individuals who acted in selfish ways could be ostracized and would not be likely to survive if they did not find another group to join.

Fear of being seen as selfish and of being rejected by others is innate in humans who are not psychologically damaged. Christopher Boehm went on to suggest that it was partly tool-making that resulted in humans evolving to favor the survival of those among them who were more inclined to be egalitarian. One of Boehm's key explanations as to why our ancestors became inclined to favor more egalitarian social structures (as compared to the average ape concerned with slights against themselves personally) concerns the advent of a particular group of tools: weapons.

Without weapons, the largest and fittest tend to dominate. With weapons, even the smallest can be a killer. Weapons also make it easier for a crowd of smaller humans to dominate a few larger humans, especially when spearheads are attached to long sticks or fired as arrows.

The good news – that we evolved in ways that allowed greater equality than other mammals, and developed ideas about treating other people fairly – is tainted by the bad news that weapons gave us the capacity to kill others if we became frightened enough. As social theorist and teacher Zygmunt Bauman put it: 'It is easy, in other words, to prod, push, seduce and entice non-evil people to commit evil things.'[5] However, Zygmunt lived to the age of 91, at a time when humans were learning in fits and starts for the first time how to be so many in number and yet to live peacefully.

In detailed analysis of our most recent weapons, it has been suggested that both conventional and nuclear bombs have been used and continue to be readied for deployment not because they serve a military purpose, but because so much money and effort have been invested in creating them. Sadly, we know that nuclear weapons and nuclear waste will be the longest-lasting legacy of the very few countries that developed them, with the US and what is now Russia prime among them. All this we have had to learn very quickly.

Zygmunt Bauman was writing the words above in the context of trying to explain how, towards the end of the Second World War, the German town of Würzburg was bombed simply because the Allies had run out of other targets and wanted to dispose of some bombs. Thousands of civilians, including many children, were killed. All the bombers were men, although often women had been recruited to work in the factories that made those bombs. That town was chosen purely because it was convenient, a riskless target without defenses and far from allied troops. However, the only reason to bomb it was to use up the bombs.

Figure 2.1: The rise and fall in nuclear weapons held worldwide, 1945-2015

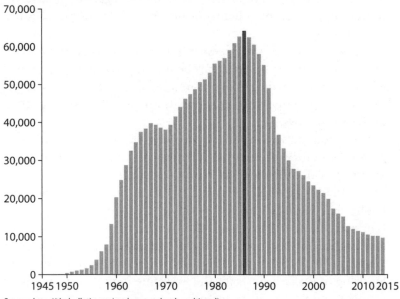

Source: http://thebulletin.org/nuclear-notebook-multimedia

Part of the reason we do not see war as more repellent is because we have in us, first, the ability to divide 'us' from 'them' and, second, the capacity to be so easily led. However, the creativity that ended up reinforcing those traits of seeing others as different could also help us to alter our behavior in future. We are not prisoners of our physical biology, but are far more often locked into newly evolved ways of thinking that are harmful to all. Often it is only when we have been creative that we have escaped these mental prisons. Despite thc global stockpile of nuclear weapons still standing at around 10,000 (it was over 60,000 at its peak in 1986), so far only two nuclear bombs have been dropped to kill.[6]

In many ways we have come a long way since we traveled in small bands foraging for food carrying only a few weapons. But just as we have recently learnt to reduce our nuclear arsenal, in the past we repeatedly had to learn the lesson that stockpiling many weapons leads to their being used. Today we can no longer afford to learn that lesson through making mistakes. So we have to ask what will be a safer world less likely to resort to war – one with more or less economic equality? The last time we reached an inequality peak in Europe was just before the First World War, and it is possible that the stupidity associated with great inequality not only made that war more likely but also led to its lasting so long. Just before the Second World War economic inequalities rose again abruptly in Germany and Japan, as we will see in more detail in Chapter 6. Growing inequality often leads to war or revolution.

The greater equality that evolved amongst hunter-gatherers, when found today in situations of increased mutual respect, leads to greater creativity than is often seen in more unequal societies. Later on in this chapter examples are given of how much more common inventing and publishing ideas now are in more equitable affluent societies. This is hardly surprising. If you deride a majority of people as being inferior they are unlikely to have the opportunity, let alone the enthusiasm, to be creative.

Creativity is a very old human instinct, but for most people the scope to be creative, as we now recognize creativity, only opened up in recent centuries in places and times of greater equality. However, we were very creative in other ways in the distant past, in effect inventing ourselves – modern humans. The more tools we made, the more creative we became. The variety became enormous in places such as the floor of the Great Rift Valley, especially between the two extinct volcanoes of Olorgesailie and Oldonyo Esakut. An opposable thumb was necessary for many of those inventions, but it is now widely argued that the greater equality then found between those volcanoes was essential for invention.

Greater equality was also a prerequisite for human settlement. To settle in an area, and especially to farm it, requires a degree of co-operation and co-ordination that cannot be sustained easily if the strong are constantly pouncing on the weak. Crops have to be planted. A small surplus needs to be stored and respected to get through the winter, to sow next year's harvest, and especially in case of drought.

However, once settled, a degree of surplus can be amassed that hunter-gatherers would never have been able to carry around with them. If not dissipated, a surplus creates a problem. It gives the people who hold the surplus power over others, and those others

Early commodity traders

may well, and rightly, resent that power. Many different kinds of mechanism were developed by imaginative people to prevent the destruction of many early human societies by a few individuals trying to hold on to large amounts of private property.

One way to deal with the accumulation of a surplus is to redistribute it regularly. Potlatch is the name given to those gatherings routinely held around the American Pacific northwest coast to feast, party and redistribute wealth. In fact *'The main purpose of the Potlatch is the redistribution and reciprocity of wealth'.*[7] In Canada, Potlatch redistribution was made illegal by act of parliament in 1884, the ban only being repealed in 1951. Similarly, in the US, Potlatch was banned *'largely at the urging of missionaries and government agents who considered it "a worse than useless custom" that was seen as wasteful, unproductive, and contrary to "civilized" values.'*[8]

Feasting was developed as a way of redistributing wealth. Celebrations were about coming together. The world's earliest surviving map is of folk dancing in a field – no doubt a more interesting thing to depict than the meal afterwards.[9] But not everywhere did we share.

The vast majority of early farming does appear to have taken place under quite equitable conditions. Apart from through archeological and folk records, this greater equality of the past is also revealed by many practices still surviving today. It is partly replacing our own agricultural labor with that of others that has made much greater inequalities possible: creating a peasantry, serfs, and then replacing people with more animal power and, ultimately, with machines (tractors).

When inequalities grow, fewer humans grow tall.[10] Human adult skeletons are found to be two to three inches shorter on average if dug up from the places and periods around when hunter-gathering had begun to be given up, and again a further couple of inches shorter if unearthed from where and when farming became widespread.[11] The reasons suggested for our diminishing heights include not enjoying such a wide variety of nutrients once we became sedentary. We could not (literally) walk away from the problems and places of the lean years. But some may also have received less than others when all were not largely collecting for themselves and their wider family.

More of us could live in a smaller area if we farmed; we could preserve knowledge in writing too when slightly larger settlements were established. If we did it sustainably and without creating great hierarchies – and hence differences in who got to eat what – then we would tend to live well but to leave little trace. We have an upside-down view of history where those who create most destruction and carnage, but leave a lot of rubbish and large buildings behind, are remembered (through archeology) with the greatest awe.

Equitable societies tend not to leave many follies behind. Across most of the continent of Africa, from the more equitable civilizations of the Americas, of Australasia and into Asia and Europe, where people lived well they left the least traces – generally just their bones and a few less perishable essential possessions. A sustainable society leaves as little trace of its existence as possible. The Indus Valley civilization of the second and third centuries BCE, for example, is famed for both its sustainability and for leaving no trace of palaces. Why would people in an equitable society waste their lives building enormous monuments? Monuments are built both to soak up surplus labor and to demonstrate superiority.[12] With superiority comes a rationale for conquest. And conquest sows the seeds of revolution, or war, and then often a return to greater equality.

Hierarchy, conquest, revolution

The word 'revolution' is at least seven millennia old. Revolutions have been occurring ever since there has been enough accumulation of power and wealth for it to be worth rebelling against. Without power, it is hard to hold on to wealth and, without wealth, unless you co-operate and share very well, you don't often have much power. It is partly because of a sudden accumulation of wealth that greater equality is so often lost. From Norman barons divvying out England's lands after 1066, to Russian oligarchs plundering the spoils of the former Soviet Union after 1989, greater equalities can quickly be eroded by military or economic conquest, as well as reinstated after them.

The phrase 'revolution' is often dated back to early Egypt. It may be older and may only be dated back to then because Egyptian writing is among the earliest that survives. There will have been countless earlier records that have been lost. In ancient Egypt the turn-around of society that resulted from the demoting of a particular Pharaoh was said to be like a *'revolution of the potter's wheel'*.

It is from Egypt that we also have the first recording of an appreciation that all are equally able to contribute and one that even suggests that those who appear to be worth the least and know the least might actually be the wisest. Over 5,000 years ago an Egyptian scribe wrote this saying on papyrus: *'Wise words are rarer than emeralds, yet they come from the mouths of poor slave girls who turn the millstones.'*[13]

Hierarchies arose first in places like Egypt because of its geography. It was there that the largest river nearest to the Great Rift Valley entered the sea, shortly after flooding, and hence irrigating and fertilizing the greatest area of surrounding land. African pharaohs are immortalized as the first named tyrants of the world and, instead of being remembered for their wise truths, their thousands of slaves are mainly remembered only as the anonymous and unwilling builders of vast monuments.

Our recorded history, especially ancient history, tends to be of non-egalitarian hierarchical societies because more egalitarian non-hierarchical societies had that tendency to blow short-lived surpluses in a Potlatch-type party without leaving many records carved laboriously in stone. More equality also brings more leisure time. When you party more and labor less, you leave far fewer stone monuments behind; often just the circle of a few standing stones.

You could not persuade a set of free-minded people to build a pyramid. You would have to enslave the laborers either physically, economically or emotionally to get them to work on huge monuments that serve no obvious utilitarian purpose or are unnecessarily grandiose. The same applies to stately homes and palaces, cathedrals, grand mosques and Olympic stadia – why do they have to always outdo the previous ones? Of course they are built 'to the greater glory of' someone, but whom? The answer is never 'those that have to do most of the work'. Some belief systems make us freer and more equal than others. When the

Quaker Cadburys made great profits from their chocolate business, they did not build some especially grand Quaker Meeting House, but Bournville model village to *'alleviate the evils of modern, more cramped living conditions'*.

Australian aboriginal religion is centered on story telling, not temple building. Modern-day Quakers never have priests and lay gravestones flat to represent the equality of all, especially in death. The most recent prevalent religion, called Science, does have hierarchies and creates hierarchies of living scientific saints, for example through the awarding of Nobel Prizes. However, in practices such as peer review, it contains aspects of equality. As with all new religions, it does not see itself as a religion but simply as telling the truth. Science also appropriated the ceremonial aspects of older religions, seen most clearly in university degree ceremonies. Modern-day science grew alongside the global growth of inequality that came with capitalism.

It has been suggested that many religions were partly established in response to growing inequalities and also in order to retaliate against the impact of those inequalities and the frequent enslavement of others that accompanied inequality (see box below). Once the idea of private property is legitimized – the ownership of more than a small number of personal items and a patch of land big enough to live on – then the idea of private property can quickly get out of hand. *Personal* property is limited to what you have about your person. *Private* property is limitless. If anything can be bought and sold, then you can own any amount of land, ideas, incalculable riches, and even other people – servants, staff and slaves.

The Jewish slaves who (along with many others) built pyramids had something to hold them together: the idea of an after-life to live for, something invaluable and special to them, promised by their one special god. There is a long-standing pattern to the attitudes of religious tradition to economic inequality. The Buddha was a rich aristocrat who gave it all up for something better than material wealth and again that promise of becoming special down the road. The early Christian traditions were all about piety and sharing, about creating heaven on earth. All these people were searching for a Utopia.

Christians told each other the story of a rich young man who asked Jesus how he could inherit eternal life. Jesus's reply was '...*I tell you the truth; it is hard for a rich man to enter the kingdom of heaven. Again I tell you, it is easier for a camel to go through the eye of a needle than for a rich man to enter the kingdom of God.'*[14] Apparently this revelation came as something of a shock to those first Christian disciples, not all of whom were poor. Jesus then is said to have responded: *'If you want to be perfect, go, sell your possessions and give to the poor, and you will have treasure in heaven. Then come, follow me.'* It was because the young man had become sad and was unwilling to do this that the eye of the needle was mentioned. The phrase possibly refers to a small gate in a city wall that a camel could fit through only if the saddle and the bags it carried were removed.

It has been claimed that *all* the great ancient religions began in times of unusually harsh inequality, ranging from that brought about following conquest, including oppression by a foreign power, to the problems of fair distribution following ecological collapse.[15] Subjugation, inequality and injustice breed dissent

Environmental degradation, religion and equality

Between the first and fourth centuries of the Common Era there was an extended sequence of environmental disasters. These resulted in pestilence and then plague spreading across the Roman Empire. The Roman deities were useful gods for a victorious ruler to believe in, and for a prosperous people to follow, but they were gods of fighting and war. Christianity concentrated on healing and promised a life after death; which was of some consolation amid all the excessive dying: *'As conversions to Christianity accelerated during the plagues, it moved from an outlawed religion of martyrs to the official religion of the empire by the end of the fourth century.'*[16]

In a similar pattern to when Christianity became widely adopted, the years when Islam came into being, when the Qur'an was first set down and when the prophet Muhammad lived, were also difficult years to live through. The difficulties were partly caused by excessive taxation, but that in turn may have been due to climatic and volcanic precursors, factors that we have only recently come to appreciate. Coping with environmental disasters has often meant having to overthrow long-standing tyranny, and such disasters have often been the trigger that was needed for change to crystallize – to get the established order out of a particular rut of thinking and behaving:

> 'The decades of fighting which led to the destruction of most of the Arabian kingdoms and chiefdoms seem to have also led to the elaboration of some definite "anti-royal" freedom-loving tribal ethos codified in the tribal historical traditions and poetry... The reflections of this ethos seem to be present even in al-Qur'an [which states... "The kings, when they enter a town, they corrupt it; they make the most glorious of its folk the most base, they do it this way."'[17]

During the sixth century, just at the time when the Qur'an was written, there was a global cooling of around 0.7-0.9°C. This was similar to that cooling which occurred during the little ice ages of the late 16th and 19th centuries. Such cooling harms harvests. There was also unusual worldwide tectonic and volcanic activity.

It is even claimed that: '*In the history of the Mediterranean region, we may compare it, perhaps, only with the tectonic catastrophe of the middle of the second millennium BCE, which was crowned with the greatest Santorini eruption in the Aegean Sea… that seems to have become fatal for the Minoan Civilization …*'[18] All these events are likely to have led to food shortages, caused widespread fear and made the tyranny of those kings who had entered the towns and corrupted them much harder to maintain than before.

Climatic change and environmental disasters have often had a strong influence on collective human thinking. In Europe, the reaction to the earthquake and tsunami that destroyed Lisbon in 1755 was to crystallize contemporary thinking towards becoming more scientific, believing that there was more to fate than the will of the (previous) gods. In the world today, enhanced global warming and the perceived threat to planetary ecosystems is again focusing minds in the same way that past events fostered the widespread adoption of new religions, of new ways of thinking. One interpretation of the present is to say that it bears the hallmarks of these past events, and that our commonly accepted beliefs are again being challenged by environmental degradation.

Climatic change has always influenced human society. The advent of ice ages coincided with harsher times in more northerly areas and was also the precursor to the invention of agriculture in the tropics and sub-tropics, and the transformation of fundamental beliefs. This can most easily be found in the creation and abandonment of huge monuments. The subject of such monuments, decaying into dust, was the motivation for Percy Bysshe Shelley's poem 'Ozymandias':

> 'Two vast and trunkless legs of stone stand in the desert…on the pedestal these words appear – / My name is Ozymandias, king of kings: / Look on my works, ye Mighty, and despair! / Nothing beside remains. Round the decay / Of that colossal wreck, boundless and bare / The lone and level sands stretch far away.'

and can create new groups who act in solidarity against those who enslave them. The history of Judaism, the religion that lies behind the most popular world religions of Islam and Christianity, is littered with stories of exodus. In Judea it took the execution of Jesus by the Roman colonizers for Christianity to be born.

Empire and religion

Just as much of our received wisdom concerning the Egyptians began with Victorian explorers marveling at the splendor of their palaces and the tombs of the few, so the Roman Empire was written up in the textbooks for schoolchildren during the latter days of the British empire as being a model of efficiency and order – as something to be emulated. In such schoolbooks the high levels of inequality it fostered, the supposed efficiency of all roads leading to Rome, of ultimate control by a single emperor, were presented as being for the common good. The US still follows this model with the upper house of Congress named after the Roman Senate and a touching, if unfortunate, belief that a single emperor-president can be infallible and should be held aloft as a great example – something that began to be widely questioned for its rationality in the early days of Donald Trump's presidency.

British textbooks implied the superiority of Roman-style empires so as to add justification to their new empire, although by then the suggestion was that all roads should lead to London, bringing tribute to the Empress Victoria. This imperialism was portrayed as being for the good of almost half of the world, that portion which Britain had colonized. More recently, the US has often tried to dress up its leaders' self-interested actions as being for the global good. In fact, Roman imperialism did not raise living standards for most of the subjects of that empire, neither did British imperialism two millennia later, just as US imperialism also fails to do so today in most of the countries of the world that are still dominated by US interests. Fewer and fewer people around the world today see US leaders as worrying much about the interests of most other people in the world.

Skeletons found from times and places of Roman colonization have indicated that people were shorter and in a worse state of health in times of high Roman influence. Far from Roman colonization being a civilizing influence, the bones of the skeletons show evidence of increased disease and starvation. There is even evidence of a curtailing of creativity in the diminishing quality of pottery found in those parts of Europe most effectively colonized by the Romans.

Innovation in general stalled in Europe and around the Mediterranean under the yoke of the Roman Empire. Inventions were largely imported from outside rather than created within. More egalitarian China produced a far greater variety of innovations than did subjugated Europe; from the wheelbarrow to printing and gunpowder, from new religious beliefs (the East Asian or Taoic religions) to innovations in both philosophy and ecology.

Across the North China Plain it is said that a hundred generations of farmers subsisted for centuries without either depleting the soil or needing organization by any all-powerful overlord. From India came the third great group of ancient religions, the Eastern or Dharmic religions. Also from India came huge numbers of original ideas spawned in long peaceful interludes, including new languages and new mathematics which then spread into the Islamic world, whose contribution to human history has been played down because it did not suit later European tyrants to admit that not all great ideas were first thought of in Greece, and hence from just within the current borders of Europe.

The traditional Western version of history still suggests that innovation and invention rarely occur outside Europe. These histories tend to start with the Greeks, because earlier European histories did too, and because Greece is the only European place about which very much prior to the current era can be written.

Almost all of the inventions of antiquity originate from times and places where people in general were given more time and space to think – and often these were places a long way from Europe. Steel, for instance, has been found in Turkey, dating from about 3,800 years ago and was forged in East Africa at least three-and-a-half millennia ago. Printing, as well as the obvious ceramics (china), came from China. Spices were cultivated in the East Indies and elsewhere in Asia, as – it is worth repeating – were many of the ideas that are often today still attributed to Greek philosophers.

The Christian variation on the religious theme of Judaism did result, among much else, in the establishment of monasteries where men were treated as more equal to each other than they were in the outside world, where learning could be continued, established knowledge protected and new ideas developed. Similarly, the Islamic variation on the Judaic theme resulted in an era of relative peace and quiet trade in goods and ideas in which Indian and Arabian mathematics could mix. For Europeans this thinking later replaced the Roman idiocy of representing 944 as CMXLIV (1,000 minus 100 plus 50 minus 10, plus 5 minus 1). The lack of a functioning number 0 in Roman mathematics limited European intellectual progress.

It was early inequality and tyranny in the Arabian Peninsula, several generations on from Roman tyranny in Judea, which led to the birth of Islam. The greater equalities under the new Muslim religion allowed mathematics to develop further and then spread westwards. This had been preceded by environmental degradation and by a series of outside shocks, similar in psychological impact to how the early Roman plagues helped usher in Christianity as a widespread alternative to Roman gods. In the case of Islam it was local groups that helped the new religion spread as they opposed kings trying to collect taxes in lean years.

History doesn't repeat but it rhymes. There is a constant rhyme in human history of tyrants emerging and people then banding together to oppose the new tyranny. New beliefs and theories are created, new constitutions and creeds constructed, and then often that which was created to oppose tyranny and inequality itself becomes corrupted and establishes a new tyranny. In medieval Europe, the Christian Pope became an all-powerful despot. All too often, institutions – originally established along egalitarian or emancipatory lines – later become purveyors of inequalities and injustice.

The tyranny within Saudi Arabia today, where a tiny royal family controls a huge country; the tyranny of the new Chinese empire that produces flat-screen mobile phones for the social-networkers of the world, using armies of industrial workers –

virtual slaves; the tyranny of the terror the US exerts on many smaller states (despite itself having arisen from complaints of such behavior by the British): these are just three of many examples of how the fight for greater equality has been usurped in the recent past.

We should not be surprised at the rise in inequality in many parts of the world today; nor should we be surprised if those rises are soon reversed or already being reversed; but we should learn and be wary that any gains made can easily be lost again in the future when we forget how hard it was to achieve them. Human memory is not good. That is why we tell and repeat stories so often, stories of gains won and lost. We tell stories in academic works and also in fiction, especially the most successful fiction. The famous first line from *Pride and Prejudice* by Jane Austen beginning *'It is a truth universally acknowledged, that...'* is all about an economic inequality. It continues: *'a single man in possession of a good fortune'*, who apparently *'must be in want of a wife'*.

The phrase *'all animals are equal but some are more equal than others'* was written by George Orwell in his book *Animal Farm* – a fable about equality and how easily it can be lost. It was a parody of the later results of the Russian Revolution. The Tsar of Russia had been a despot. He was overthrown in 1917, only for the revolutionaries that succeeded him in turn to give way to the potential despots among themselves. As a result, *'pushed to an extreme never tried anywhere else, the modern promise of bliss guaranteed by a rationally designed and rationally run, orderly society was revealed to be a death sentence on human freedom.'*[19]

Renaissance, mercantilism, enlightenment

Innovation, creativity and greater equality have a long history of being intermingled. Because all human beings have significant abilities, under any system based on equal treatment there is a much higher chance of new ideas not only being discovered, but also of those discoveries being recognized as innovative. The greater the degree of inequality and the more profound the hierarchy, the fewer people are credited with the possibility of having any useful ideas and those fewer good ideas that do emerge are often ignored. Under regimes of great inequality, underlings have to tell the emperor how good his fiddling is, even if it is awful and the city happens to be burning down as he plays.

Let us turn our attention again to Europe, near the center of what had been the Roman Empire, but roughly a millennium after it had effectively ceased to exist. The Renaissance that took place, in what was later to become Italy, was only made possible because of a greater acceptance of more equality. In 1452 a servant-girl gave birth to an illegitimate boy, Leonardo. He went on to become the best-known painter, sculptor and inventor the world has ever seen. Although his achievements are naturally ascribed to his talents, and he has been described as the most talented man to have ever lived, it is also true that he thrived because of when and, more importantly, where he was born. He was born just outside the town of Vinci in the Italian region of Tuscany, whose urban center was Florence.

By the middle of the 15th century, Florence had grown rich on unequal trade, buying cheap and selling dear, and on a little relaxation of the laws of usury to allow profit to be made from lending money. As yet these riches had not totally corrupted those who received them. Lorenzo de' Medici was the wealthiest of the bankers. However, he took what appeared to be gifted artists and scholars into his household where there '...was no seating order at table. Instead of the eldest and most respected sitting at the top of the table above the rest, it was the first to arrive who sat with Lorenzo de' Medici, even if he were no more than a young painter's apprentice. And even an ambassador, if he came last, took his place at the foot of the table.'[20]

Leonardo da (of) Vinci was just one of those young men who came to sit at Lorenzo's table (around the year 1480). It is ironic that the Renaissance sparked such creativity while also creating a new form of banking, epitomized by the Medicis, which made profit by lending to others at a time when it became again permissible to receive interest on those loans.

Most religions had described moneylending to receive interest as sinful prior to 1480.[21] Islam continues to do so today. However, the moneylending that began in earnest in Florence quickly spread through the mercantilism of the nearby Venetian republic and was imitated more widely. This was facilitated by a new source of wealth. Just a dozen years after Leonardo sat at Lorenzo's table, the ship *Santa Maria* ran aground on the coast of Hispaniola and the wealth of the Americas became available for plunder.

It was where and when religious rules against profiteering were most weakened that the vicious mercantilism of today began. One of the places made rich by banking, trade and the exploitation of the Americas – and later Africa and the East Indies – was the Dutch Republic, which is part of a larger constitutional monarchy today. But, very like Florence two centuries before, the Dutch Republic was a place that was at first more welcoming to new thinking than surrounding areas. Now remembered for the Golden Age of Dutch painting, this was also the time and place where it became possible for René Descartes (1596-1650) to establish a new early philosophy of science. He would also lament how money appeared to be taking on a life of its own and totally preoccupying people's minds in Amsterdam.

Religion, the environment, equality, riches and knowledge are all related in ways that can abruptly change. By the 17th century, the Catholic Church, which had once promoted and protected learning, had become far more controlling. Leonardo had been taken to trial for sodomy (and acquitted). The entire republic of Venice had been excommunicated. Galileo (1564-1642), the father of modern observational astronomy, came close to being declared a heretic, and in 1663 a later pope placed Descartes' books on the prohibited index, the *Index Librorum Prohibitorum*.

Christianity, which had become a very inegalitarian religion, was propping up despotic monarchs and corrupt clergy. It stifled all kinds of innovation and thought. It was within this amoral atmosphere, coupled with the added influence of new-found riches from the Americas, that modern-day capitalism was born. However, a few centuries on, another external shock, in this case the Great Lisbon earthquake and tsunami of 1755, would usher in more equality (see box overleaf).

It was Enlightenment thinking that culminated in that US Declaration of Independence in 1776. It was also the Enlightenment that resulted in the efficiencies of a production-line version of pin manufacture being celebrated in the works of the economist Adam Smith. So it was that both greater equality and the new human enslavement (and greater inequality) of

Independent shocks and new thinking in Europe

In Europe, it took the natural disaster of the 1755 earthquake and tsunami that destroyed six-sevenths of Lisbon and much else besides, to prompt questioning of the authority of a god (of any religion) that could sanction such misery. This resulted in increased freedom from religious dogma and the right to have any thoughts you like (not any amount of wealth). It came to be called the Enlightenment.

> 'The Enlightenment broke through "the sacred circle" whose dogma had circumscribed thinking. The Sacred Circle is a term used by Peter Gay to describe the interdependent relationship between the hereditary aristocracy, the leaders of the church and the text of the Bible. This interrelationship manifests itself as kings invoking the doctrine of the "Divine Right of Kings" to rule. Thus church sanctioned the rule of the king and the king defended the church in return.'[22]

So, over a thousand years after natural disasters helped bring Islam into existence, the Christian countries themselves had an epiphany. For the earthquake and tsunami to have had such a great impact on Lisbon, that city itself had to have grown very rich. This had occurred over the previous two centuries, as gold and silver plundered from the Americas was transported through Portugal and Spain into the

mass factory labor came out of ideas which could only have been spawned in a time when we were more equal.

The Enlightenment was also one of the first times when the ideas of a named woman were both taken seriously and recorded for posterity. Mary Wollstonecraft's *A Vindication of the Rights of Woman* is, in hindsight, perhaps the most significant thinking to have emerged from the Enlightenment. It was published in 1792, two years after she had written in support of the recent French Revolution, a revolt against both the monarchy and the established church. Mary Wollstonecraft was born just four years after the Lisbon earthquake and died giving birth at the age of 38. Although hardly recognized at the time, and mostly disapproved of on the few occasions her ideas were discussed by those who then held much power, she may have been the most innovative

rest of Europe and across to India and China; while slaves from Africa were transported back in return to the Americas.

The so-called 'discovery' of the Americas was akin to a natural disaster of epic proportions for the inhabitants of those American continents, who – if they survived the new diseases brought in from the old world and then the social upheaval of, in effect, aliens arriving from what might as well have been outer space (the conquistadors) – came to suffer great inequalities, destitution and enslavement. The 'discovery' also fundamentally altered world human geography. In human geography terms it recreated Pangaea, making the Americas an adjunct of Europe.

Suddenly Europe took center stage as the crossroads for trade – it became the place where the Silk Road hit the sea rather than a western peninsula of Asia. In effect, it became a continent despite not being an island. The wealth that amassed in Europe as a result of trans-Atlantic exploitation was one of the catalysts for later social change being so dramatic, but it took that 1755 environmental disaster to sway people away from the view that god approved of inequality and that he gave kings divine rights and men command over women. The subsequent French Revolution took place between 1789 and 1799 after particularly poor harvests added extra impetus. Environmental and social events are often far from unrelated.[23]

writer of the age, and a precursor to the greatest ongoing social revolution of all – the fight for women's equality.

Communism, colonialism, capitalism

Rebellion often results from finding contemporary inequalities unacceptable, remembering times of greater equality and from the catalyzing effects of natural or human-made disaster. Traditionally, it was the monarch who originally provided a focus for such rebellion. Once kings, queens and emperors are deposed, the next step is the establishment of republics and the hope of greater equality.

Western history marks out the creations of Greek, Venetian, Dutch, French and American republics – and, most recently, the creation of an economic union in Europe under no monarch –

as moments of great human achievement. These moments are partly remembered in celebration because, following rebellion, the freedom to be more equal can be easily lost again and new tyrannies can very quickly become established in the wake of old. However, shortly after celebration, revolution can often next result in terror, as occurred in France between the summers of 1793 and 1794. Often the terror is the work of counter-revolutionaries.

In all of human history, social *inequalities* rose most abruptly during the 19th century – and most clearly in those parts of the world that were industrializing. Before industrialization, fashions changed slowly and the consumption of material goods was low. There were limits to both growth and to the wealth that could be accumulated when people relied on wind, water and, indirectly, the sun as their primary sources of power. It was energy from the sun that grew the wood used to make charcoal, buildings and ships.

Before industrialization, most people were not necessarily poor. If they survived childhood disease they could live very reasonable lives, often working far fewer hours a day than their descendants laboring in factories or offices, but they had much less stuff. The richest amongst them especially had less compared to the rich of today. In recent years, in rich nations, it is often remarked that even some of the poorest among us can have access to goods and a degree of comfort not even enjoyed by kings in the recent past; the poor today in rich countries can have lots of stuff, but often still lack what humans frequently need most – they are not respected.

It was when the more natural and sustainable power sources were replaced by burning coal that so many more 'goods' could first be made. Steam was generated to drive machines that could more quickly transform one commodity into another: wool into jackets, iron into nails. But the machines could not run themselves. They needed people to tend them. There was suddenly, it appeared, no limit to what could be accumulated by a small group of people who enslaved another group to work for them, magnifying the effects of that labor by attaching human beings to looms and all manner of other machines. Wage slaves might appear to be politically free, but usually have little real economic choice over the work they can get, and hence little control over their own lives.

The first of the extra goods produced by these wage slaves might have appeared to be necessities. Cotton garments were manufactured in huge quantities. A great proportion of the world's people became clothed in garments manufactured in England. The wage slavery in England and Scotland was not the only thing that made this possible. It also occurred because actual slaves taken from Africa had been put to work in American cotton plantations and because the clothing industry across the whole Indian subcontinent was repeatedly and ruthlessly decimated. Cotton exports increased, spinning and manufacture in India decreased, inequalities were raised, both worldwide and within the newly industrializing countries and the newly impoverished colonies. Within Britain, as little of the surplus as possible was passed on to the mill workers. Within India only a few colonial collaborators fared well.

It was because of this new, steep rise in inequality that communism was born. Karl Marx was simply the person who was there at the right place and time and who most effectively addressed the rising inequality he saw around him. He had a ready audience, as far more people than he and his friend Friedrich Engels could see that inequalities were rapidly rising. Marx was the author of the most cogent analysis of the time, *Das Kapital*, and also co-author (along with Engels) of *The Communist Manifesto*.

It was the capacity of coal burning to power machines and make huge profit that made the times new – that provided the environmental 'shock'. The *'...initial fears centered on the possibility that the benefits of this new capacity would be confined to a tiny minority. Das Kapital embodied this fear and encapsulated the anger which moved millions in much of the 20th century.'*[24] Marx thought Russia almost the last place on earth likely to take up his suggestions, but it was Russians in exile planning a revolution who found his ideas to be the best then on offer.

Although he could not have known it, Karl Marx was writing at a time and in a place (Victorian Britain) of extremely, if not unprecedentedly, high inequality. By the 1850s in England, people's average heights were at an all-time low. They recovered only slowly. By 1918, average heights were only back to where they had been a century earlier in 1818.[25] The industrial revolution did not improve real living conditions for most people, even in England. This was made evident through what it did to their bodies – most of the British were stunted.

Life expectancy in the worst parts of Manchester and Glasgow fell to as low as 25 years of age for decade after decade in the early 19th century, and this was from within the powerhouses of the country at the center of the British Empire. Overall life expectancy was so low because so many infants died. Childhood diseases spread easily in dense, poverty-stricken slums. Most people who survived childhood would live much longer than 25 years, but they would also usually see several of their own children and then grandchildren die before reaching adulthood.

The global impoverishment that the spread of capitalism would bring – at first out of Amsterdam, then out of London and finally, financially, centered on New York – would result in the worldwide stunting of millions of children as imperialism brought recurrent famines to the India of the British Raj and opium war to China. The rise of capitalism is often heralded as a great economic success, but until 1917 it was only a success for those who owned great amounts of capital. Only after that year did economic inequalities begin to reduce across the world. Only from then onwards, right through to the 1970s, did the wealth generated in factories powered by burning coal begin to be spread.

Many Indians fought for and gained independence, followed by terror and mass exodus as Pakistan separated. Many Chinese fought for and gained a revolution – again one that was followed by terror. However, it was the 1917 revolution in Russia that had the greatest effect on inequality. That revolution came in the midst of the First World War and created both the need to pay for the costs of that war within Europe and a fear of revolution happening elsewhere. World war and the Russian Revolution fostered the dawn of a new growth in equality that came to have a dramatic effect on how people treated each other.

Figure 2.2 below shows the best current estimates for the income take of the richest one per cent in France and the UK over the period 1900 to 2015. The best-off one per cent took the most they may ever have taken in the UK in the year 1919: almost 20 per cent of all income. The time series for this particular statistic in the UK is very incomplete, but by 1937 the take of the British top one per cent had dropped to just below 17 per cent; by 1949 it was less than 12 per cent; by 1966 it was less than 8 per cent; and by 1976 less than 6 per cent of all income. A trend that began in the First World War when the rich had to be taxed highly to pay for the costs of war became self-reinforcing and economic equality rose and rose, decade after decade. The trend was accelerated by collective action. There were rent strikes in Glasgow, new political parties grew up, newspapers began to champion social causes

Figure 2.2: The take of the best-off 1% in France and the UK, 1918-2010

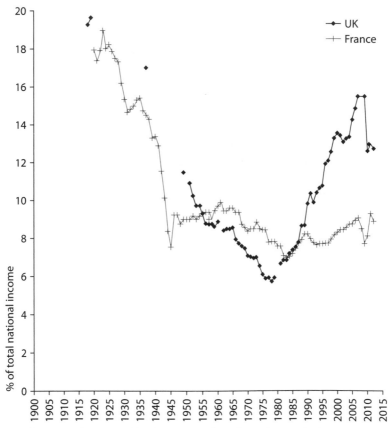

Years of consecutive data connected by a line. Where no data is shown it is missing for that year.

Source: World Wealth and Income database – accessed March 2017: http://wid.world/

more often, trade unions became more powerful, and politicians feared revolution.

The time series for France is more complete. In France economic inequality peaked in 1923 when the best-off one per cent took nearly 19 per cent of all income. That fell to below 17 per cent by 1929; to less than 12 per cent by 1942; less than 8 per cent by 1977; and reached a minimum of just less than 7 per cent in 1983. However, what is most interesting is how the French and UK inequality trends began to diverge in the 1980s. Inequalities remained relatively low in France but rose and rose in the UK until very recently when, in both countries, there was a sudden jolt to the long-term trend in 2008 with the advent of the global economic crash. That crash itself was brought on by rising inequality, by the very richest trying as hard as they could to make their investments go further by lending money to people at high interest rates to buy homes in the US and then Europe, at rates of interest for 'sub-prime' property that could not be repaid.

The 2008 global economic crash was an event that was remarkable because of its worldwide implications, but such events have occurred before. We may also have only just seen the first of what could be a series of financial crashes that could lead to a great change, as again has occurred before. What happened between 1917 and the late 1970s was a worldwide economic revolution. To understand it, it is important to realize why the Russian Revolution caused great fear among some of the most powerful people in the richest countries of the world. Suddenly it looked as if revolution was possible even in the most backward of places, which meant it could happen anywhere. For Britain, internal revolution was simultaneously occurring within what was to become the Republic of Ireland, which had been part of the United Kingdom for centuries but saw the Easter Rising of 1916 lead ultimately to Irish independence in 1922.

The graph above shows only the French and UK components of the much more complex graph described in detail in Chapter 1 (Figure 1.3). The French records are more complete. However, prior to 1950, other records suggest that the British had a similar experience to the French: one of rapidly growing equality from the mid 1920s to the mid 1970s.[26] The latest figure for the UK in the graph is for 2012. In the four years immediately before then, the best-off one per cent had seen their share of incomes rise even faster, while most British people's real incomes had fallen. And, as explained in Chapter 1, the apparent recent fall in the take of the top one per cent in the UK is more likely to be due to creative accounting than to a real fall – but we cannot yet be sure.

In the aftermath of the First World War, in addition to the British losing most of Ireland, there was: fear of revolution in England; a rise in progressive leftwing parties; a strengthening of trade unions; the first wave of feminism; the beginnings of various civil-rights movements. All of these led to slight decreases in the share of national income received each year by the very rich. But why did inequality continue to fall in places like Britain and France from 1920 onwards so continuously and so smoothly for so long? Why didn't the rich regroup more quickly?

One suggestion is that immediately after the First World War many poor countries were carved up and divided amongst the victors. This included those countries that had been colonies of the losers. The redistribution of the profits from colonial spoils enjoyed by the victors was another reason why it became possible to reduce inequalities within these rich countries in ways that were relatively painless for the very rich. Their share fell, but the cake grew in size as colonial markets were exploited.

Inequalities fell within rich countries like the UK and France between 1920 and 1970 partly because they were rising worldwide between countries: local traditional industries in poorer countries were decimated by the demand for free trade from rich countries. As the UK and France became much richer from imposing exploitative terms of trade upon poorer countries worldwide, they could respond to demands from the mass of their populations without hammering the wealthy too hard.

The greatest period of growing equality in both the UK and France (and in many other affluent nations, but not Germany) was between the two world wars, and it continued right through into the 1970s. This is seen in many monetary and physical measures. For instance, children's heights soared in most affluent countries where equalities increased. In Germany inequalities rose between the two world wars, which was one of the key reasons why there was a Second World War. Germans voted for the Nazi party in 1933 partly out of economic desperation and growing destitution: inequalities were rising and the overall economic cake was shrinking, as discussed further in Chapter 6.

After the Second World War a fear of fascism returning was one of the impetuses for ever-increasing economic equality. There was also an even greater fear of communism, which was heightened from the 1920s onwards after it became clear that the Russian revolution was not about to be reversed. The 1929 banking crash appeared to be Marx's predicted collapse of capitalism. Labor movements grew stronger. Even in the 1960s, many thought that communist countries were more efficient when they put astronauts into space before the Americans did. It wasn't until the 1980s that the communist countries came to be seen as economic basket cases – though China was already by then taking a different path. Politics mattered.

Paul Krugman, in his book *The Conscience of a Liberal* suggested that all the main changes in US inequality that occurred throughout the 20th century were driven by politics. Initially that politics resulted in much greater economic equality being achieved within the US than was being experienced in much of Europe. Ordinary people in the US had a high standard of living by the 1960s, especially when compared with most people living in Europe.

By the 1970s some of the tallest people on earth were born in the US. Inequalities within that country were at an all-time low, unprecedented numbers of young people were allowed to go to college and university, and civil rights were being won both by black groups and by women. Technological innovation permitted white American men to demonstrate that they could travel into space, including going to the moon and getting back alive. However, with hindsight, the refusal of Rosa Parks to give up her seat on an Alabama bus in 1955 had a greater long-term effect on what it meant to be American.

A kind of second American Revolution took place between 1928, when the richest one per cent of Americans took almost a fifth of all national income, and 1973, when that share had fallen to just 7.7 per cent, the lowest ever recorded (see Figure 2.3). Women, people from minority ethnic groups, youngsters, but above all poorer people in general, secured greater equality in the US than had existed since the time indigenous peoples dominated the land.

Social democracy versus corporate greed

In 1905 the US Supreme Court declared as unconstitutional a new law that had been introduced in New York State. This law limited bakers to working no more than 10 hours a day. The Court said this *'deprived the baker of the liberty of working as long as he wished'.*[27] The average working week then in the US was 60 hours.

In 1905, and for much of the 30 years that followed, the richest one per cent of US citizens managed to take home up to a fifth of all the national income each year – as much as 20 times the average worker's earnings – an estimate made by taking the arithmetic mean. The US top one per cent took much more than that if you took the median income, which is the point at which half the working population earns less and half more. The mean is not a very meaningful average when inequalities are great. Consider, for instance, what the mean wealth of women in England might have been when a tiny minority had married a man in possession of a good fortune but the rest had not.

A century ago, in England, two out of every five women in work were domestic servants.[28] They might well have been working more than 60 hours a week. Most of the remaining female employees worked in factories and mills, where at least their working hours were limited to 56 hours a week by the Factory Act of 1878. On the whole, the period was one of dog-eat-dog. Regulations were seen as evil and if a baker wished to work himself to an early death, but undercut his competitors by so doing – hence also hastening their deaths through overwork – then so be it.

'Less regulation' was the wish of many in power, but others successfully opposed the powerful. It was in response to such opposition that Britain had brought in that 1878 Factory Act and that New York State later introduced that 1905 law. And because those who opposed inequality became better organized, greater equalities were permitted and enforced, fought over for three decades and then reinforced for four decades more. That is the

**Figure 2.3: The take of the best-off 1%
in Canada and the US, 1913-2014**

Years of consecutive data connected by a line. Where no data is shown it is missing for that year.

Source: World Wealth and Income database – accessed March 2017: http://wid.world/

story of the first half of the chart above.

If just the Canadian and US lines are shown on the graph of the shares of income held by the best-off one per cent, then a very clear picture emerges. From the middle of the 1930s onwards they tracked each other downwards – rapidly – as the outcome of the 1929 stock-market crash and the mass unemployment that followed it eventually led to the rich being denied such an unfair share. They continued to be denied it until most adults alive in the 1930s were dead or were too old to be taken sufficiently seriously when they warned us of the folly of allowing inequalities to rise so high again.

Inequalities rose in the 1980s almost as fast as they had fallen in the 1930s. The increases were abrupt, beginning most clearly in 1982, but accelerating in 1986 and 1987, and rising significantly almost every year since. They rose as new North American theories of unfettering the markets for big business and banks began to hold sway – a little different from those ideas that would earlier have had a baker work well over 60 hours a week, or which saw it as acceptable for 40 per cent of employed women to be servants of the better off. Now the concern was with the ability of the very richest to make money, not with other people or equality.

The two North American lines were not in sync before 1938, but both enjoyed the same social progress and both suffered from the anti-social 'revolution' of the 1980s. However, the graph in Figure 2.3 shows that in Canada for a few years after 1989 there was a curtailing of the excesses of rapidly rising inequalities. That same brief dip was replicated in the United States when inequalities fell briefly in 1992, and again in 2001 and 2002 following the collapse of the 'dot.com bubble' and then again in both countries from 2010 onwards following the global market crash of 2008. It is too early to say, but it is not impossible that we are at another tipping point. However, the last tipping point took two decades to actually tip in the US and Canada, where inequalities did not actually start to fall rapidly until 1941.

It is worth reiterating that the two periods in which the trends changed were both times of political rebellion. It is not as if inequalities falling and then rising follow some kind of business cycle; rather, they follow political victories and failures. The years following the crash of 1929, all through to 1940, were when the trajectory of greater and growing equality for a generation was set. From the very bottom of society up there were strikes, union organization and early civil-rights agitation. From the top down came fear of revolution and rebellion, and a little well-meant paternalism. Within the Democratic Party in the US, a mood for change was successfully established, a new deal and social state offered, defended and extended throughout the 1950s and 1960s.

Just as the ownership and profit from colonies made increasing equality in Europe cheaper for European elites, greater equality in the US and Canada was partly made possible by North America's increasing dominance of international markets. As North American riches grew greatly, sharing the surplus became easier than would otherwise have been the case and than was the case in the 1930s depression. The greater sharing out in the US and Canada was often at the expense of people elsewhere in the world, people who were having free trade imposed upon them in a singularly un-free way. North American soldiers were fighting a great many hot wars and participating in a gigantic Cold War, mostly to pursue their leaders' selfish economic interests.

The second period in which the trends changed was from 1968 to 1979. In 1971 President Nixon, a Republican, ended the Bretton Woods international monetary system created in 1944 by John Maynard Keynes and Harry Dexter White, which had been based on fixed but adjustable exchange rates against a US dollar convertible into gold. The US would no longer guarantee a dollar was worth a fixed amount of gold after 1971. By this time most colonies had formally gained independence, the oil-producing countries had become more independent, industrialization was spreading, and the balance of world economic power was beginning to alter.

Human discovery of the uses to which coal and oil could be put is very closely intertwined with falls and rises in equality in later decades and earlier centuries. Inequalities began growing when coal-powered industrialization took shape and they grew again when the price of oil rose in the 1970s. Richard Nixon floated the dollar free partly so as to allow the US to buy more of its oil from abroad. Floating the dollar free also allowed Nixon to finance a particularly nasty quasi-colonial war, in Vietnam.

One plausible argument is that the move towards greater and greater equality ended in the 1970s because the US was no longer becoming richer and richer in comparison to the rest of the world, as it had before and especially in the two decades of its unprecedented economic growth after World War Two. That supremacy was possible only because Europe was war-ravaged. Continued economic growth at post-War US rates was unsustainable and, from 1980 onwards, it looked as if average living standards in North America could not continue to rise so quickly.

The 1980s North American revolution was organized by the most affluent, those who had become used to great rises in living standards year after year as the cake grew in size. They did not realize that these gains had not arisen solely (or even largely) because of the ingenuity of Americans, but mostly because of the effective exploitation of others. US far-right advocates, such as George Gilder, rose to prominence in the early years of Ronald Reagan's presidency from 1981. His *'four-word answer to poverty was "Get married, stay married" and that marriages break down "because the benefit levels destroy the father's key role and authority".'*[29]

In 1987, the American Enterprise Institute for Public Policy Research issued the following statement: *'"The way to move out of poverty is to finish high school, get married and stay married, and take (and keep) a job." This has been the neoliberal consensus on "poverty policy" ever since.'*[30] But that consensus is being challenged with the suggestion that it is inequality that is unethical, not divorce or unemployment. Very recently in the US, austerity measures were presented as being the only permissible policy discourse, even though many academics continued to explain that one cause of the US budget deficit is non-progressive taxation and to conclude that *'inequality is not only unethical but also it is economically disastrous'.*[31]

When Bernie Sanders stood against Hillary Clinton to try to secure the Democratic nomination to run for president, he stood against austerity and the arguments began to change more quickly in the US than they had for decades. But Donald Trump copied Bernie's language and tapped into the angst about inequality, despite Trump being an embodiment of wealth and privilege. The Democrats did not choose Bernie, and Trump won the 2016 election. Change is rarely simple, but extreme inequality always brings about change.

Very recently, public-sector cuts, especially when accompanied by regressive taxation (tax cuts for the rich), have been shown by economists to be statistically linked to worsening lives for the majority, which eventually result in increased rioting and violence. This relationship is so close that those who discovered it have even suggested that this is one mechanism that prevents

unjust governments from increasing inequalities even further. Thus *'one possible reason why austerity measures are often avoided –[is] fear of instability and unrest.'*[32]

For those of us *unfortunate* enough to live in inequitable countries, but *fortunate* enough to live in the rich world, we have to look back to before the 1980s to realize the great equalities that were lost and many of the ways in which life has changed. We have to work hard to remember what it was like to live in the US when Americans were more equal. When they were more equal, more found it easier to stay married to someone they loved, to find a job they liked and to stay longer at school than their parents. It was similar in Britain, but Britain is now almost as unequal as the US and, during 2011-15, its population underwent £81 billion ($130 billion) of public-sector cuts that were mostly to the detriment of those with less. Many of these planned cuts have yet to be fully implemented and more cuts are to come.

In Britain, the Conservative-led coalition government of 2010 said it would cut the debt, sought to curb possible inflation, drove down wages and tried to take control of the trade unions by curtailing their freedoms. When social inequalities had been as high before in Britain, the British elite in the end chose not to follow others in Europe when *'Benito Mussolini and Hitler had slashed the public debt, curbed inflation, driven down wages, and taken control of the trade unions in Italy and Germany, respectively.'*[33]

Back in December 2010 a UK government report misleadingly titled *'Tackling child poverty and improving life chances, consulting on a new approach'* argued that *'We are particularly concerned about evidence demonstrating that poverty is transmitted between generations'* and *'The evidence available indicates that simply increasing household income, though reducing income poverty, will not make a big difference to children's life chances.'*[34] People who quoted this report as evidence for their views were effectively denying that poverty was a major factor in the outcomes associated with poverty. They were suggesting that hardship dissuades people from being poor and hence helps tackle child poverty and improves life chances.

The concentration in the final pages of this chapter on anglophone affluent countries is necessary because it is the English-speaking rich countries that now serve as a warning to so much of the world. In the UK and the US there has been a revival of 1960s Cultural Deficit Theory – the discredited idea that underachievement among poor children was a result of deficiencies within the children, their families and communities.[35]

The cultural deficit models argued that, since poor parents failed to embrace the educational values of the dominant social classes, and continued to transmit to their children values which inhibited educational achievement, then the parents' culture was to blame if low educational attainment continued into succeeding generations.

Reviving discredited ideas allows extremist governments to recommend measures which then entirely ignore the structural reasons for educational underachievement, reasons such as the class divide, deepening poverty, inadequate school funding in poor areas, social class segregation in the education system and thousands of children being excluded from school. By 2016, when I began work on this book, UK state school budgets had been slashed through cutting funding per child at ages 16, 17 and 18 while the new 2015 Conservative government tried to pretend that the education budget was in some way ring-fenced.

Inequality was still worse, overall, in the US, although there were signs of the acceptance of gross inequality there teetering. This was partly because so many now had so little to lose. Then in the UK a slim majority voted to leave the European Union and in the US a minority voted in President Trump. Both events have been widely reported as being linked to the very high rates of economic inequality. And high economic inequality manifests

Figure 2.4: Change in wealth inequality by ethnicity in the US

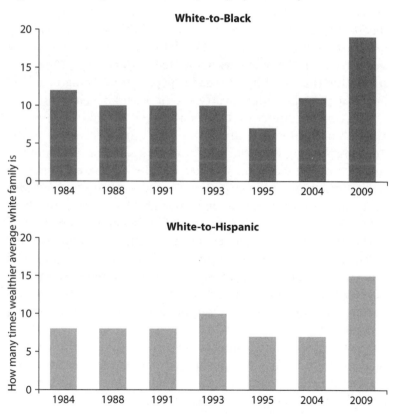

Notes: The Survey of Income and Program Participation was redesigned for the 1996 panel. The redesign may have affected the comparability of the data from 1998 and later years with the data from earlier panels.

Sources: For 2009: Pew Research Center tabulations of Survey of Income and Program Participation data from the 2008 panel; for 1984 2004: various US Census Bureau Reports including Current Population Reports.

itself in high inequality between men and women, by race and by class (between men and between women)[36] – and in myriad other levels of oppression all made manifest by some having much less than others, or as Vito Laterza put it:

'If we simplistically frame Trump's victory and the Brexit vote as a revolt of the dispossessed and the disenfranchised white working classes – based on a partial and biased reading of the actual data – there is a real risk that the solutions we come up with will contribute to reinforce various forms of white nationalisms and xenophobic alliances, rather than providing a clear and uncompromising alternative to them. The attention has to shift to the whole system, with its myriads of levels of discrimination and oppression."[37]

Within the US, wealth inequalities have recently risen rapidly as measured between households designated white and those labeled Black or Hispanic. This increase in inequality in wealth began before the economic crash of 2008, but was greatly exacerbated by it. The upper of the two charts above (in Figure 2.4) shows that, by 2009, the average black family had recourse to 19 times less wealth than the average white family.

When all the wealth of Black households in the US is averaged out, by 2009 there was just $5,677 to share out among every household. Just four years earlier that figure had been $12,124. The housing-market crash hurt Black families especially hard. However, Hispanics were similarly affected, with their average wealth falling from $18,359 per household in 2005 to just $6,325 by 2009. These are huge drops over very short time periods for millions of people already with relatively low levels of average wealth.

In contrast, the average US white family saw its mean household wealth fall from $134,992 in 2005 to $113,149 by 2009. Most white families are not that wealthy – the mean average is inflated by a very rich minority – but the median white family was still much richer than the median black or Hispanic family.[38] More recent figures do compare the median wealth of households in the US.

In 2011 the median white family had $111,146, the median Black household $7,113 and the median Latino household $8,348.[39]

The same paper that these figures are drawn from showed the median gain from having graduated at college was $60,000 for a white household, but less than $5,000 for Black and Latino households, despite it being so much harder for them to have achieved that graduation. Having low wealth in the country that perceives itself as the richest on earth is particularly demeaning.

In the UK, meanwhile, inequalities have also been rising fast, despite an apparent recent fall in the take of the top one per cent, which appears to be largely an attempt to hide more of its income from taxation. This rise in inequality widens the gaps between different social classes and, for those ethnic-minority groups over-represented in lower-income groups, it can mean not only poverty but also becoming more visibly differentiated from the more affluent majority.[40]

A 2011 summary of the evidence found that, when studying inequality and poverty as distributed by ethnicity and race in the UK, there was common experience of racism and discrimination.

> 'But as soon as nearly every issue is examined in more detail, such broad patterns start to break down. Discussing issues in relation to "minority ethnic groups" as a whole almost immediately becomes untenable due to the enormous variation between them. Even considering a smaller set of ethnic groups is very often also problematic... For other "groups", such as Chinese people, the variations of income as well as many other factors are so wide as to bring into question when it is useful to use this single group as a focus for analysis.'[41]

Today, by one measure, as much as 90 per cent of world wealth is held by just one per cent of the world's human inhabitants, and a disproportionate number of the global top one per cent live for at least part of the year in the UK and US. Inequalities between countries are falling slightly as they rise rapidly within some very affluent nations, so in those most unequal of rich countries all of us *feel insecure because our jobs, and so our incomes, social standing and dignity, are under threat...*' The result is, according to Zygmunt Bauman, that *'the explosive compound of growing social inequality and the rising volume of human suffering, relegated to the status of "collaterality" (marginality, externality, disposability, not a legitimate part of the political agenda) has all the markings of being potentially the most disastrous among the many problems humanity may be forced to confront, deal with and resolve in the current century.'*[42] Zygmunt died in January 2017, but left this warning from his reading of history about the importance of economic inequality.

1　R Cooke, 'We must assert the importance of geography in the curriculum', *The Independent*, 10 Jun 2002, nin.tl/CookeGeog
2　SF Brosnan & FBM de Waal, 'Monkeys reject unequal pay', *Nature* 425, 18 Sep 2003, pp 297-9, doi:10.1038/nature01963.
3　youtube.com/watch?v=meiU6TxysCg
4　C Boehm, *Hierarchy in the Forest: The Evolution of Egalitarian Behavior*, Harvard University Press, 1999.
5　Zygmunt Bauman, *Collateral Damage*, Polity, 2011.
6　thebulletin.org/nuclear-notebook-multimedia
7　nin.tl/o6Nqrw, referring to GM Sproat, quoted in D Cole and I Chaikin, *An Iron Hand upon the People* (Vancouver/Toronto 1990). Potlatch is common all around the Pacific but varies in how it is described. In New Zealand/ Aotearoa the term is Hāngi.
8　Ibid.
9　It is a map because it is thought to show the field boundaries around the dancers. Maps were drawn long before there was writing. A very concise history of cartography is given in D Dorling and D Fairbairn (1997) *Mapping, ways of representing the world*, Longman, London.
10　Recent research is beginning to show that the Roman invasion reduced the heights attained by those invaded. Advocates of inequality often claim it allows 'Tall Poppies' to grow without realizing that they can only look tall because it stunts the growth of so many around the few.
11　S Wells, *Pandora's Seed: The unforeseen cost of civilization*, Allen Lane, London, 2010. Women up to 9,000 BCE stood on average 5.6 inches above five feet in height. That fell to 1.2 inches above by 5,000 BCE and 0.7 inches by 3,000 BCE. For men, the drop was from 8.7 to 6.8 to 3.5 inches in those 6,000 years.
12　Only where religion was hierarchical were people made to build huge cathedrals, mosques and pyramids, rather than have more leisure. Numerous theories abound over men in particular needing to prove something, most recently by building tall phallic skyscrapers, earlier by having constructed great womb-like halls (the womb being the most powerful muscle in the human body). The psychology of inequality and equality is almost limitless, but it can be worth starting with issues of masculinity: S Kraemer, 'The Fragile Male', *BMJ* 321:1609-12, 2000.
13　EH Gombrich, *A Little History of the World*. New Haven, Yale University Press, 2008.
14　On the rich, needles and camels: nin.tl/nMcMMp
15　WF Ruddiman, *Plows, plagues, and petroleum*, Princeton University Press, 2005.
16　Ibid.

17 A Korotayev, V Klimenko, & D Proussakov, 'Origins of Islam: Political-Anthropological and Environmental Context', *Acta Orientalia Academiae Scientiarum Hung* 52(3-4): 243-276, 1999.

18 Ibid.

19 Bauman, op cit.

20 Gombrich, op cit.

21 The inner ring of the seventh circle of hell was reserved for those lending money according to one 14th-century interpretation of Christianity, Dante's *Divine Comedy*. See: nin.tl/r2qlus

22 This quote is from the egalitarian encyclopedia that is Wikipedia, a source much disliked by the new religion of science.

23 A summary of suggestions in Peter Gay, *The Enlightenment: An Interpretation*, WW Norton, 1996, and multi-authored Wikipedia: en.wikipedia.org/wiki/Age_of_Enlightenment. In 2002 and 2005 Susan Neiman and Jean-Pierre Dupuy also separately identified 1755 as the date after which we saw that we could overcome natural disasters if we organized ourselves better.

24 EA Wrigley, *Energy and the English Industrial Revolution*, Cambridge University Press, 2010.

25 R Floud, K Wachter et al, *Height, health and history: nutritional status in the UK, 1750-1980*, Cambridge University Press, 1990.

26 D Dorling, 'Fairness and the changing fortunes of people in Britain', *Journal of the Royal Statistical Society A*, 176, 1, 97-128, 2013.

27 HJ Chang, *23 things they didn't tell you about capitalism*, Allen Lane, London, 2010.

28 S Robson & M McGuinness, 'Gender inequality and women's poverty', in B Knight, *A minority view: What Beatrice Webb would say now*, Alliance Publishing Trust, London, 2011.

29 David Gordon, Professor of Social Justice, Bristol University, personal communication, 2011.

30 Ibid.

31 R Peet, 'Inequality, crisis and austerity in finance capitalism', *Cambridge Journal of Regions, Economy and Society* doi:10.1093/cjres/rsr025, 2011.

32 J Ponticelli & HJ Voth, *Austerity and Anarchy*, Centre for Economic Policy Research, London, 2011.

33 J Bakan, *The Corporation*, Constable, London, 2005.

34 Emphasis as in the original: nin.tl/v06inZ

35 Discredited by, among hundreds of others, D Gordon, in G Craig, T Burchardt and D Gordon, *Social Justice and Public Policy*, Policy Press, Bristol, 2008.

36 K Geier, 'Inequality Among Women Is Crucial to Understanding Hillary's Loss', *The Nation*, 11 Nov 2016, bit.ly/2kx5mVY

37 V Laterza, 'The dangers of the myth of Trump's white working class support', Vito Laterza's Blog, 10 Nov 2016, nin.tl/Trumpmyth

38 R Kochhar, R Fry, & P Taylor, 'Wealth Gaps Rise to Record Highs Between Whites, Blacks, Hispanics, Pew Center Research, 26 Jul 2011, nin.tl/oDIVYp

39 L Sullivan et al, *The Racial Wealth Gap: Why Policy Matters*, IASP/Demos, 2015, nin.tl/USracialwealthgap

40 See D Dorling, *Fair Play*, Policy Press, 2011.

41 H Barnard & C Turner, *Poverty and ethnicity: A review of evidence*, Joseph Rowntree Foundation, 2011, nin.tl/q24tqs

42 Bauman, op cit.

3

Why children need greater equality

In the world as a whole, the evidence is inescapable that we have been moving in a more equal direction. The strongest proof lies in child mortality rates in even the very poorest countries, rates that are lower now than they were among the rich in imperial Britain a century or so ago. A few countries have recently been bucking the trend and actively pursuing greater inequality, but in the long term it is clear that caring about our children means caring about equality and sustainability.

'The [US] Census Bureau recently announced a heartening five-per-cent gain in the median household income between 2014 and 2015, the largest one-year gain on record. Yet a look at the longer-term trends offers a sobering perspective. The jump in household income merely helps to make up for lost ground; the median earnings in 2015 were actually lower than back in 1999 – 16 years ago.'

Jeffrey Sachs, *The Boston Globe*, 2 October 2016[1]

It is no coincidence that Thomas More set Utopia on an island. He was a teenager when the Americas were discovered, a time when the adults around him first realized how much was unknown. He could not have known that this discovery would change everything, with 1492 sparking a series of events that would propel humanity to become a very different species. More things – more possibilities – were imagined, but no human was, or is, capable of imagining change on the scale that has occurred. The search for utopias is the constant attempt to stretch our imaginations from what is merely possible now to what is conceivable in future.

Four centuries after More coined the term Utopia, Oscar Wilde wrote that the only worthwhile maps of the world were ones that included Utopia. Utopia was no longer a sensible object of derision. So much was changing so quickly that what mattered was how the future could be shaped and how we, with our limited imaginations, could try to look into the fog of possibilities. The worldwide emancipation of women that was well under way by the late 1800s was clearly one of the greatest changes to the species. It was also clearly still just beginning at that point. Men had mostly dominated before and males did in many other mammal species, but the change is only clear in hindsight and few men saw it coming. We are changing as a species. We are inventing new concepts with increasing rapidity. 'Utopia', 'species' and 'teenager' are all words we invented as we began to see the world around us, and ourselves, differently.

From time immemorial humans had watched many of their children die before them. Such suffering was thought unavoidable up to a century ago, when over a tenth of the children of even the richest people in the world, the English servant-keeping classes, died in childhood. Today child mortality rates in urban China are falling so fast that within a year or two of 2017 they could be as low as in the United States. Already less than one per cent of babies born in urban China die before their first birthday. In Iceland only two in every thousand infants die in that first year and the rate is still falling. Worldwide rates are falling so fast that we know that they cannot fall any faster than they are now, because they cannot fall below zero. Never have we known such progress, but very few people saw this as possible even just a few decades ago.

People who believe that a much better future is possible for all – utopians – are rare, but becoming more common. For example, so many British people bought white poppies to wear on Remembrance Sunday 2016 (thereby remembering victims of war while expressing commitment to peace) that stocks ran out – and sales had been rising in each of the previous three years.[2] More people than ever before do not believe that war is justifiable. And utopians have frequently been proved right in the long run: the impossible has often become possible. Our species is transforming into something new. We now understand that it was not the gods who suddenly decided that almost all children should live to see adulthood, but rather that we made this possible ourselves through our social and political priorities. Our agonizing about the current state of things is the main drive to achieving progress. We rightly complain about all the greed, selfishness and stupidity in the world. Occasionally we need to recognize what this complaining achieves and to recognize the progress that is won.

We have to stop saying that dystopia is inevitable, that war and suffering are unavoidable, and move on to thinking about how things could be better. What sort of world might be possible and what would make that happen? So let us think first about that world in which almost all our children will make it to adulthood. We have never had as few children per family worldwide as we are having now. Surely they can have a better life and a fairer deal than we have had? And surely they will be able to act more sustainably so that generations to come can also see their lives improve.

Equality and child mortality

Babies are great levelers because they are all more or less similar – and also initially the same as they were 10,000 years ago. Greater equality has some very clear benefits to infants. In affluent societies with more equitable income distributions, fewer babies are born undernourished. They also suffer less from diseases caused by the alcohol or drugs taken by their mothers while they were in the womb. This is because use of alcohol and drugs is less prevalent amongst adults in more equitable societies.[3]

In poorer societies, infants are more likely to die within their first year of life than in richer ones, but in more equitable poor societies those risks are also reduced. In 2009, worldwide, 42 babies died for every 1,000 born. However, in Cuba infant mortality rates were 10 times less at 4 per 1,000, even less than in the hugely wealthier United States (7 per 1000). In very unequal and poor India, the rate in 2009 was 50 deaths per 1,000 born and in more equitable (in some ways) and a little less poor China it was 17 per 1,000. For every grieving parent in China each day there were three in India.[4] Where would you rather have a child if you were an average citizen – China or India?

Just six years later, in 2015, the global infant mortality rate had fallen to 32 deaths for every 1,000 live births, 10 fewer than in 2009. These six years were a remarkable period of world demographic history. There has been no period in human history where infant mortality rates have fallen this fast worldwide. From 1990 to 2009 the rates fell from 63 per 1,000 to 42 per 1,000, or by roughly 1 per 1,000 per year. Then, from around the year 2009, that rate of improvement accelerated to roughly 2 more children surviving per 1,000 per year! This will almost certainly be the *fastest improvement ever experienced* in human history because, if it does not slow down, by 2031 not a single infant on the planet will die (which really is impossible). Across all of Europe by 2015, 10 per 1,000 were dying and the lowest rates in the world then reached around 2 per 1,000.[5] In Africa, on average, the infant mortality rate was 55 per 1,000 live births.

You could say it is better to give birth in a rich country than in any poor country today, and in terms of child survival this usually is true.[6] However, you must again choose carefully. The rates of infant deaths per 1,000 live births in Iceland and Japan – two of the most equitable affluent countries – were a third of those in the US in 2015.[7] This suggests that two-thirds of all the infants dying every year in the US are dying unnecessarily, as a result of the great levels of inequality tolerated in that country and the social ills associated with that inequality. In fact, in 2016 it became apparent that infant mortality rates were actually rising rapidly in parts of the US, especially Texas, following a cut in funding for maternity clinics.[8] That is especially shocking when compared to what is achieved in other affluent countries.

Even more worrying is the maternal mortality ratio in the US – the proportion of mothers dying in childbirth – which has doubled since the early 2000s to stand now at around 28 per 100,000 live births, compared with 8 in the UK, 6 in Japan and 4 in Iceland.[9] The rise in the number of women dying in childbirth in the US shows that it is very possible to see progress rapidly reversed.[10] Rising economic inequality in the US has led to greater ignorance there of what is possible and of why equality of access to healthcare in particular matters so much.

Many people in the US are unaware that it is so much safer to give birth in other countries with better public health systems and more equitable economics. They do not know that by 2015 the maternal mortality ratio in China had been reduced to 32 per 100,000 – only just above the US ratio – and was still falling. By the time you read these words a woman will be more likely to die in childbirth in the US than in China – and that is according to World Health Organization projections that do not yet include the most recent 2016 evidence of deterioration in the US.

Infant mortality may not be a high priority to you at the moment because it is so much lower now than when you were born and very much lower than when your grandparents were born. However, the unnecessary death of any baby or young child is highly distressing for the family involved. Regrettably, the media in countries with high economic inequalities only rarely recognize such deaths as unnecessary. Geographical comparisons help us to realize how often, in countries with high levels of inequality, such deaths should be classified as unnecessary. It is also a quantitative way of assessing how compassionate a society is, or whether an elite within it think that a large section of people are not as deserving as others of their basic human rights – in this case the right to life for expectant mothers and for babies in their first year of life.

Iceland and Japan have suffered great economic hardship in recent years – an economic crash associated with a foolish foray into finance in the former and decades of very low growth and a huge debt overhang in the latter. Yet their more equitable societies are better placed to absorb the effects of this – the average family in these two countries is far better off, on many measures regarding quality of life, than the average (median) family in more unequal affluent nations, such as the UK and US. However, in most countries, quality of life is now much better than it was in the recent past. This is also down to the greater equalities that were won almost everywhere not so long ago: in the US, in Iceland, as well as half a world away in India. Wherever there have been improvements in the most basic life chances, underlying those improvements were changes in thinking about people that predated them. Those changes involved beginning to see everyone as valuable, and all lives as being worth saving, as well as realizing that infant mortality and the deaths of women giving birth were not acts of god, but were affected by human action or inaction.

Just over a century ago, in 1909, Britain was the richest country in the world. Nevertheless, the infant mortality rates suffered by the newborn children of the very richest people in Britain stood at around an enormous 100 per 1,000 live births. These were the people with high-enough incomes to be able to pay servants to cook and clean for them. By 2015 only two of the very poorest countries of the world still suffered rates anything like that high – infant mortality was highest in Angola at 96 per 1,000 live births and in the Central African Republic at 92. In many ways it is much better to be born poor now than to have been born rich a century ago, because so much progress has been made, because greater equalities have been won so often and led to healthcare, education and housing improving across so much of the world.

In aggregate the global infant mortality rate continues to fall and it is now falling fastest where it used to be highest. The absolute fall in the number of grieving parents has, moreover, been even greater than the fall in the worldwide infant mortality rate. Between 1970-74 and 2005-09 world population increased by 67 per cent, but the number of children the average woman in the world was giving birth to (in her lifetime) fell from 4.45 to 2.52 babies, or by 43 per cent. Combining the falls in fertility and rise in population reveals that there were 28 per cent fewer babies being born by the end of the first decade of this century than there were in the early 1970s and far fewer of them were dying.[11] So, in absolute terms, there are much less than half the number of grieving parents in the world now than there were in the early 1970s, even though world population is now much larger. Fewer babies are now born and far fewer of those then die in their first year of life. That is real progress.

Singapore: the national equivalent of a country mansion

There is one exception to the general rule that, among affluent countries, infant mortality rates are lowest in those nations that are more equitable. That exception is Singapore which, according to the UN, had a very low rate of two infant deaths per 1,000 born alive in 2015. How then does Singapore manage to maintain very high income inequalities – by some measures the highest amongst the 26 richest nations of the world[12] – but also have one of the lowest infant mortality rates?

Some of the poorest people in Singapore are the 'maids', the servants who work for one in five of all middle-class households. The maids act as personal cleaners, shoppers and child-carers. Most of the maids are guest workers from abroad. They have no right to remain in Singapore. In more economically unequal countries the poor tend to have fewer legal rights. Every six months they must take a pregnancy test and, if they are found to be pregnant, they are deported.

Migrant workers make up about a quarter of the population of Singapore and are mainly at the bottom of the income range, where you would expect infant mortality to be highest. This section of the population is effectively removed from the picture by deportation and the threat of it. Poorer women trying very hard not to become pregnant is one way in which infant mortality rates can be reduced. The babies who would have a greater chance of dying are never actually conceived, or are aborted, or are born and possibly die elsewhere.

In some ways the nation-state of Singapore acts like a very large Victorian British country house. In these country houses, servants were expelled if found pregnant. Aristocrats didn't want servants' children cluttering up the place and servants could not afford to pay others to care for their children. So naturally, if a domestic servant became pregnant she had to leave. There was, of course, nothing natural about this; which is why, in Britain today, the idea of working 'in service' is still so resented.

Many maids in Singapore do have children back home but return to work, leaving their child with its grandmother or another relative. The money they send home ensures the survival of both. But is this a sensible way of living for the rich as well as the poor?

Where inequalities are great and poverty is widespread, the short-term incentive grows ever greater for the rich to segregate and cut themselves off in great country estates or smaller gated communities. In Brazil the rich and poor live parallel lives despite the slums often being so near the wealthy enclaves. The rich then have to live behind enormous barred gates. In India, most of the rich work hard to insulate themselves from the poor. They do not want to see them, often not even to acknowledge their existence. Wine bars in Mumbai skyscrapers are so high up that people on the streets below appear smaller than ants. But those ants will be the siblings, parents and children of the servants of the rich.

From the spread of infectious diseases that feed on poverty, to the fear of armed insurrection occurring one day, maintaining high levels of inequality within a country for decades is very damaging to wider public health and well-being, as well as very hard to achieve politically. However, a few countries have seen economic inequalities rise rapidly from the late 1970s all the way through until the time of the global financial crash of 2008. The countries where this was most apparent, the US and the UK, were also the affluent countries that experienced the slowest improvements in infant mortality over that period.

One way to begin to answer the question as to whether the perpetuation of inequalities in a place like Singapore is sustainable, is to ask: does it also harm the rich? Would you be better off being brought up by a servant with no long-term commitment to you, or by your own parents? Would you rather sort out your own food to eat, or always have it presented to you? It is rumored that Prince Charles, the heir to the throne in Britain, has a servant who dresses him each day. But wouldn't you rather pull up your own trousers? Once you become reliant on servants for everyday activities, it is easy to become increasingly incompetent.

Being brought up by a woman who is naturally preoccupied with the child she has had to leave behind is not something to be envied. The Victorian English rich were not a joyous bunch. They were an historical aberration. The citadel of Singapore may be too, sitting, as it does, at the crossroads of world cargo-ship trade that has boomed in recent decades only because so many trinkets as well as more necessary goods are now made in China and transported by sea.[13]

Some 900 years ago, the city of Merv on the Silk Road was claimed to be the largest city in the world. Its ancient ruins are

**Figure 3.1: The take of the best-off 1% in
South Korea and Singapore, 1933-2012**

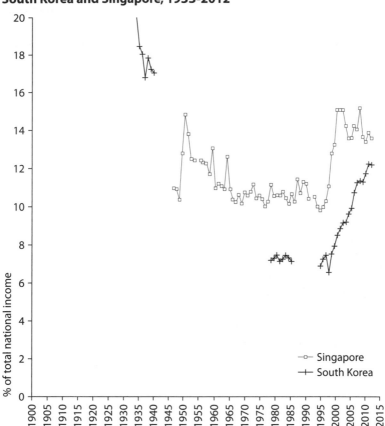

Years of consecutive data connected by a line. Where no data is shown it is missing for that year.

Source: World Wealth and Income database – accessed March 2017: http://wid.world/

now a 'world heritage site' and yet you probably have not heard of it.[14] It came and it went. Places that become very unequal often do so just before a great change. European countries were at their most unequal just before the First World War, which was called a world war because it changed so much. In Britain it was in the years just before that war that infant mortality rates peaked. Following that war people began to begin to see each other as more deserving of respect – more equal, and all their fates as being intertwined. Good public health and

Inequality in South Korea

"Korea's income inequality is the worst among 22 countries in the Asia-Pacific region with the top 10 per cent of the population receiving 45 per cent of the total income, the International Monetary Fund (IMF) said Wednesday...

'Korea shows a surprisingly large increase by 16 percentage points since 1995 and records the highest level among the available countries with the top 10 per cent earning 45 per cent,' said the report.

Korea suffers from widening income inequality between haves and have-nots. Generational income inequality also poses problems in Asia's fourth-largest economy, as young jobseekers have trouble landing quality jobs due to sluggish growth. The nation's youth unemployment rate hit a record high of 12.5 per cent in February, up from 9.5 per cent the month before; while the average jobless rate in surveyed countries reached 4.9 per cent.

The organization attributed this trend to rapid ageing, the wage gap between regular and non-regular workers and gender occupational inequality. It also said that social mobility is declining in the country, referring to recent studies.

Singapore came second in the table, with the top 10 per cent owning 42 per cent, followed by Japan with 41 per cent. New Zealand also marked relatively high income inequality, as its top

the reduction of poverty became a national priority. And in Britain's overseas colonies and 'interests', such as Singapore and Korea, inequalities also fell, especially after the Second World War.

The trend towards greater equality in Singapore after the Second World War can be seen in Figure 3.1: the take of the richest one per cent fell from almost a sixth of all income to around a tenth by the 1970s and early 1980s. After that, inequalities in Singapore rose rapidly, following the US and UK model, but they fell shortly after the millennium and fell again more recently in the three years up to 2012. Inequality in Singapore is still extremely high, but twice in the most recent decade its rise has stalled. People in Singapore may be beginning to take note of their extreme differences from one another. Recently the government in Singapore introduced

10 per cent own 32 per cent of the total income.

In terms of the top one per cent's income shares, Singapore topped the list with 14 per cent, followed by Korea with 12 per cent, up from 7 per cent in 1990. The top one per cent in Japan, Australia, Malaysia and India also owned around 9 per cent of the total income, showing high levels of inequality.

The IMF said that countries in the Asia-Pacific region need to address inequality of opportunities by broadening access to education, health and financial services...

The organization said that elevated levels of inequality are harmful for the pace and sustainability of growth, leading to suboptimal investment in health and education. The IMF also pointed out that widening inequality can weaken support for growth-enhancing reforms and may spur governments to adopt populist policies and increase the risk of political instability...

'Expanding and broadening the coverage of social spending is critical for more effective redistribution,' it said. 'This includes improving low-income families' access to higher education and adequate health services as well as a better targeting of social benefits, which can also finance an expansion of their coverage.'"

Source: Kim Jae-won, 'Korea worst in income inequality in Asia-Pacific', *The Korean Times*, 16 March 2016.[16]

capital controls to prevent very rich overseas buyers investing in premium property there.

For South Korea there is a large gap in the data, from before the start of the Second World War though to the 1970s, but there was clearly an enormous gain in equality during that period, as the take of the best off one per cent fell from a fifth to just over a fifteenth of all income. However, since the mid-1990s, economic inequalities in South Korea have been rising relentlessly, only pausing for breath at two points and then only for a single year at each time. However, those two points are the same very recent years when inequalities in Singapore fell. It may as yet be premature to believe that inequalities in Korea will continue to rise as they have in recent years. Not least because by 2016 even the International Monetary Fund was warning against any further rise and suggesting remedies (see box above). In late 2016 half a million protesters marched in South Korea where 'the underlying cause of frustration among protesters was due to a variety of social issues including economic inequality, lack of career prospects and social mobility, and the sky-high cost of living in the city [of Seoul].'[15] South Korea's president was impeached in March 2017.

Extreme inequality and Apartheid

In very recent years more and more data on historical trends in income inequality has begun to be made available for more countries. Figure 3.2 shows the trends in income inequality in South Africa and Malaysia, from around the time of the First and Second World Wars respectively, as this is when each of these data series began.

Inequality was so high in South Africa in the past that at times the best-off one per cent of the population received almost a quarter of the sum total of all personal income there. Furthermore, unlike in Europe, inequalities in South Africa did not fall during the Second World War; they rose to a peak in 1946. Many poor Black migrants from nearby countries were drawn into South Africa during that war to work in the cities and the mines. The global price of gold had fallen during and after the First World War but increased rapidly after 1930 to a maximum in 1933, coinciding with Hitler's rise to power in Germany. It did not fall substantially until 1946 and 1947 when global stability looked more likely.[17]

Profit from gold matters greatly to the income of the richest people in South Africa. In 1948 Apartheid was introduced to prevent greater equality being won and then gathering pace there, though following Apartheid's introduction the income of the one per cent did fall as a little more was then shared out within the white minority. After the end of apartheid, in 1994, inequality did not fall but rose dramatically when measured by the take of the top one per cent, which was cornering 18 per cent of all income by 2007. Simply winning greater equality by ethnicity or race does not ensure greater economic equality. But in recent years inequality has begun falling again in South Africa. Again, this adds to a worldwide picture of a potential recent turning point having been reached and suggests that global as well as local

Figure 3.2: The take of the best-off 1% in South Africa and Malaysia, 1914-2012

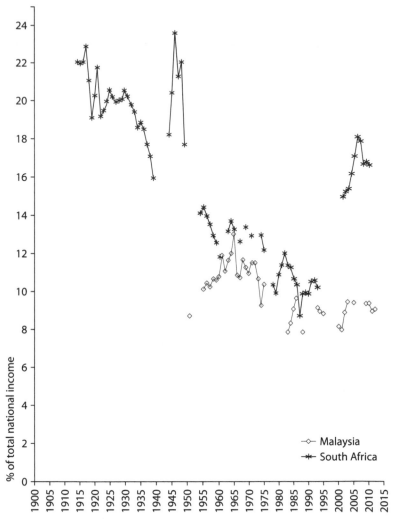

Years of consecutive data connected by a line. Where no data is shown it is missing for that year.

Source: World Wealth and Income database – accessed March 2017: http://wid.world/

events can strongly influence trends in economic inequality in any country.

Contrast the experience of South Africa with that of Malaysia, another former British colony. Malaysia gained independence from Britain in 1957 and Singapore separated from it in 1963. By then Malaysia and South Africa appear to have had similar levels of economic inequality as far as the take of the top one per cent was concerned. But without Singapore to skew it Malaysia began to appear a little more equal as each year passed from the 1960s to the 1990s. Malaysia still makes a great deal of its income exporting oil, rubber and palm oil, but it also has a thriving electronics industry and by 2014 was the world's third-largest manufacturer of solar panels after China and the European Union. A more diverse economy tends to concentrate money in fewer hands.

The gulf between these two countries in terms of inequality that is shown very clearly in the graph above is reflected in other key statistics. The infant mortality rate, for example, was 34 per 1,000 live births in South Africa in 2015 compared with just 6 in Malaysia (lower than in the US). In Malaysia 29 women died in 2015 for every 100,000 live births, compared with 140 in South Africa. Malaysia ranks 47th in the world for happiness, in contrast to South Africa, which ranks 116th.[18] Malaysia is no Utopia, and is only ranked 68th out of 167 countries in the Democracy Index,[19] but these are very substantial differences in terms of quality of life, and they emerge from its greater levels of equality.

Sustainable Development Goals – and why British children are unhappy

In September 2015 the United Nations adopted Sustainable Development Goals (SDGs) for the year 2030. The goals do not include a commitment to increase happiness, but they do aim to promote both health and wellbeing, and to end hunger and poverty, as well as meet a range of other targets in terms of 'development', environment and peace. The first health target of the SDGs is to reduce global maternal mortality to below 70 per 100,000 live births. The second health target is to reduce neonatal mortality (babies dying in the first month of life) to below 12 per 1,000 births. The goals also include a commitment to reduce economic inequality: that the poorest 40 per cent of people should see their incomes rise by more than the national average by 2030 in each country.

Inequality and health are clearly linked. Quite why they are so strongly linked is harder to determine, especially in terms of how economic inequality between adults might affect children, so to begin to understand that we need to think a little more widely. And, if we are concerned about progress, then we need to worry about the problems of people in the richest countries of the world as well.

In March 2016 a World Health Organization study revealed that, of 42 affluent countries investigated for child well-being, the UK did particularly badly.[20] The study reported that 15-year-olds in England and Wales were among the *least likely* to report high levels of satisfaction with their lives, with only children from Poland and Macedonia feeling less satisfied, while 80 per cent of 15-year-old girls in Scotland reported feeling pressurized by school work. Fewer UK children are drinking and smoking now but, as the BBC put it at the time: 'Children in England are among the unhappiest in the world, behind countries such as Ethiopia, Algeria and Romania'.[21] And the BBC interpretation of the results blamed schools in the UK in particular for being 'exam factories'.

Economically unequal countries such as the UK put children in a very pressurized environment where they are encouraged to compete with each other at school and often suffer in terms of their mental health as a result. They also do not generally become better at learning through such competition and fear. English schoolchildren fare badly when compared in international tests with children in other affluent countries, especially after they have left school, as cramming for exams often means that in the long run much is forgotten. In a very unequal society, parents and teachers are justifiably fearful of what will happen to their children if they do not do well. All this is then exacerbated by the media environment in unequal countries that tends to promote competition above co-operation, to be unsympathetic about the real reasons why children do not enjoy school or learning, and almost always to look for reasons to blame the victims or their parents.

The UK government is supposed to monitor the well-being of children. The extent of this monitoring appears in section 15 of

a report titled *'Measuring national well-being: Life in the UK: 2016'* and has only three paragraphs which, in essence, tell the reader to download the spreadsheet. The latest report was published on 23 March 2016 and the spreadsheet reveals that, in the most recent year for which the government collected data, the number of babies born with low birthweight had risen from 2.8 per cent to 2.9 per cent; the proportion of children who were obese rose from 29.5 per cent to 31.2 per cent; the number who had symptoms of mental ill-health rose from 12.4 per cent to 13.5 per cent; and the number who attained 5 GCSEs at grade C or above (standard 'good' examination results), including mathematics and English, fell from 53.4 per cent to 52.8 cent.[22] Many other factors appeared to improve slightly, but often these were all less important than being born too small, becoming mentally ill, obese, or being labeled as a failure at school. Most importantly, although the government still collected these statistics, it did not take any note of them, let alone decide to act on what they revealed. In late 2016 a former president of the British Medical Association (BMA) explained in concise terms what UK government policy under Prime Minister Theresa May now entailed:

'It is government policy to increase inequality, and to make things harder for families with children. And that will have an adverse impact on the health of the children, the health of those children when they become adults, and the health of the parents who are trying to make ends meet.'

Professor Sir Michael Marmot, former President of the British Medical Association, speaking at the organization's 2016 special representative meeting[23]

The US also appears not to be especially concerned about its poor child health record. Every so often an article appears in the US media that reports how 23,000 infants die there each year and notes that the country has a far higher infant death rate than its peers. Reading these American articles is a little like travelling back in time when it comes to the attitudes they reveal.

As mentioned in passing above, in the September 2016 issue of the journal *Obstetrics and Gynecology* it was reported that, between the years 2010 and 2014, the maternal mortality rate in Texas nearly doubled from 18.6 to 35.8 per 100,000. The pregnancy-related death rate, which includes deaths more than 42 days after giving birth, rose even faster. Black women in Texas account for only 11 per cent of all births in the state, but by 2014 they suffered 29 per cent of all pregnancy-related deaths. In 2011 the Texas legislature had cut its family planning budget by two-thirds, resulting in the closure of 82 clinics. Amazingly a: *'Department of State Health Services spokesperson told the* Houston Chronicle *that it's "a complex problem" and "there is no evidence" to conclude that the clinic cuts caused the increase in maternal mortality rates'.*[24] Of course there is also no evidence that they did not and a very high likelihood that the cuts were the immediate and direct cause of the rise, considering that no other explanation was proffered.

When countries become very unequal, it becomes easier to view other human lives as being less valuable. This can lead to people thinking it is fine if Medicaid care for mothers ceases 60 days from delivery, even though 60 per cent of pregnancy-related deaths in

Figure 3.3: Pregnancy-related deaths in Texas, US, 2006-2014

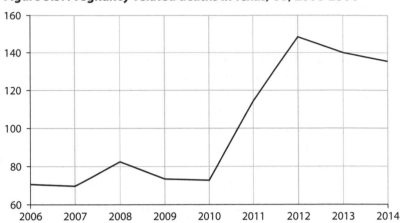

Source: 'Recent increases in the US maternal mortality rate: disentangling threads from measurement issues' (*Obstetrics and Gynecology*, September 2016) nin.tl/Texasdeaths

the US occur *more than* 42 days after delivery. This callousness about the lives of others does not just apply to the poor within the US, but also to people living in other countries.

Children are more easily influenced than adults. I was born and brought up in the English city of Oxford. As a teenager I knew that in the surrounding countryside were American nuclear cruise missile bases. One day I went to hear a debate in a church hall outside one of these bases – it could have been Upper Heyford in the north of Oxfordshire, or Greenham Common in Berkshire to the south. These bases had pleasant-sounding names because they were named after the nearest village, but they weren't villages – they were airstrips surrounded by razor-wire fences through which the concrete bunkers could just be made out in which the missiles were held. When 'needed', the cruise missiles were to be driven out of each base on huge trucks and hidden in secret locations in the countryside to be fired when the US president chose. The American bases made where I lived a target for Russian nuclear missiles.

The debate I had traveled to hear was between the commander of the base and the then head of the Campaign for Nuclear Disarmament, Bruce Kent. The American commander spoke first, about the need to be strong and how the weak never win.

Bruce spoke second and began his reply by saying, *'I don't think the man above your head would agree about the weak'*. Above the base commander's head was a small statue of Jesus being crucified. You didn't have to have any religious belief to realize what a devastating put-down this opening line was. It was also said in a kind way, to try to explain to the American base commander why others might not agree with him and his country's weapons being placed in Europe to fight a war between the US and what was then the USSR. Europe was to be crucified in the continental annihilation for which these missiles had been designed. For me, Bruce had won by the end of his first sentence.

Russia and the US still have thousands of nuclear missiles, but the cruise missiles kept in bases named after ancient rural English villages are now long gone. It turned out that they weren't as vital as had been claimed by the Cold Warriors. Today the Americans and Russians rely almost entirely on intercontinental ballistic missiles to plan and play their war games. However, a teenager growing up in Oxfordshire today would have heard the unelected Prime Minister, Theresa May, say she would not hesitate to kill 100,000 men, women and children with a nuclear weapon. They would also have heard US President Donald Trump, elected with a minority of US votes in 2016, say that he would happily use nuclear weapons. I don't think they would be any more reassured than I was at their age by the arguments still being put forward for keeping and hence potentially using such weapons.

Today's teenagers are less concerned by nuclear war than I was, although they should know that the few large nuclear powers in the world still hold enough weapons to destroy humanity many times over (see Figure 2.1 in Chapter 2). Now their fears are more personal – more about themselves. This is no criticism of today's youth. It is an example of how increased economic inequality can lead to individuals worrying more about their immediate fate and being less concerned about our general sustainability and survivability. I grew up in more economically equitable times.

Consider just one example of why today's teenagers and young adults often end up worrying more about themselves than I had to. In May 2016 a recent university graduate in the UK, Simon

Crowther, discovered that his student loan had grown by £1,800 in one year due to the interest accrued – it now stood at £41,976 (at the time of writing around $52,000) and was rapidly rising. He wrote: *'I was still in sixth form at school when I agreed to the student loan. I had no experience of loans, credit cards or mortgages. Like all the other thousands of students in the UK, we trusted the government that the interest rate would remain low – at around 0%-0.5%.'*[25] The actual interest rate applied by government diktat was the rate of inflation with an extra three per cent on top. At a time when the Bank of England was bringing the rate banks have to pay to borrow money down to 0.25 per cent this was extortionate.

The UK has copied the US in introducing high-interest student loans. More equitable affluent countries simply don't do that (and almost always don't tolerate or try to build nuclear missiles). In the UK the children of very rich parents pay their student fees up front and so a minority of children never have to take out a loan. But the vast majority will be in Crowther's situation. One recent graduate posting on Facebook below Crowther's letter said she had *'nearly passed out'* when her statement arrived, while another wrote: *'I wouldn't have taken out my maintenance loan if I'd known. They essentially targeted children, lured them in, and then screwed them over!'*

So, if universities are such a rip-off in the UK due to the loan system, why do so many parents try so hard to get their children into one? The obvious answer is that the alternatives are worse. Low-paid and precarious employment is today often the best you can hope for if you do not secure a university degree. Even if you do secure a degree, such employment is still a very likely outcome, but a child is told that to reduce their chances of that fate they should go to university. In August 2016 the most popular tabloid newspaper in the UK, *The Sun*, also told some of its readers who were parents what many others had known for a few years before: that even if their children do well and get a job paying £40,000 (currently $50,000) a year, rising gradually to £67,000 a year after 30 years, they will still have to repay £105,145 over 27 and a half years, and that is after they have paid tax and rent and bought food and other necessities. *The Sun* quoted the vice-chancellor of the UK's largest private university as saying *'There is a real risk it will very soon not be seen as financially worthwhile to go to university.'*[26] But, of course, whether it is worthwhile depends on what the alternatives are. This is because not going to university significantly increases your chance of only finding precarious and low-paid work, at least in recent decades, whereas in the 1950s, 1960s and 1970s people enjoyed near full employment.

Aside from poorly paid work in retail or other services, there are not many other 'options'. A young adult in the UK who does not have a job has received £73.10 (around $90) a week to live off since April 2013. If they happen to be living in a flat with two bedrooms then they will have to pay up to £20 a week of this in 'bedroom tax'. The rest of their rent might still be paid by what is called housing benefit, as long as they live in a poor city, but they then only have £53.10 a week to live on. They will also now be asked to pay a local council tax; this might be £8 a week, leaving them with £45.10 a week. Food for an adult in the UK, for the minimal diet that does not lead to malnutrition, costs £43 a week if very carefully purchased. That leaves £2.10 a week for any other items.[27] It is no wonder, in such circumstances, that many young adults commit crime, and that so many others are so anxious.

At the very bottom of the heap, below even the homeless, are those who have lost their freedom. Britain's prisons are now bursting with young people, mostly young men. As the number of youngsters who are incarcerated increases, the amount spent on prisons per person has also fallen, and many attempts are made to cut the costs. By 2016 the starting salary of a custody officer in Thameside Prison (now run by the private company SERCO) had fallen to £17,350 (currently $21,700). The pay rate for the equivalent job in the nearest state-run prisons was £24,500 ($30,600). UK prisons are being privatized partly to try to cut costs, and partly out of a neoliberal commitment to shrinking the state. But there is a clear tension between running a business for profit and making a decent job of providing a public service. Towards the end of 2016 it became clear that almost every single privatized probation service in England and Wales had become loss making, while at the same time only providing a service that was *'mixed and patchy, when it is not chaotic and inadequate'.*[28] 2016 had started with reports that deaths of mental-health patients had increased by 21 per cent over the previous three years, including a rise in suicides. An insincere NHS England spokesperson suggested that the rise was simply due to more reporting, as if many suicides had occurred before, but not been recorded.[29] There was also an unprecedented increase in suicides in prisons at the same time.

As economic inequality grows in the UK it is not just prisons, mainly catering for those in or just out of their teenage years, that are being privatized. University privatization is also under way. In April 2016 the *Sunday Times* announced that US companies such as Apple, Google and the education publisher Pearson will soon be allowed to award *'cut-price degrees to British students'*. The proposals were announced in a white paper a month later but were leaked earlier to soften the public response. A student currently studying at a private Pearson college (soon to be called a university) in London explained that her course: *'really focuses on things like presentation skills and working together in small teams, things that you need to know in the workplace.'*[30] Universities in the UK are in many ways becoming training centers for learning banal techniques – how to look good

Social mobility at the bus stop

using the latest version of PowerPoint and how to pretend you are co-operating while actually competing in a cut-throat world.

Learned ignorance

It is often assumed that the minority of children who attend a very expensive private school in a very unequal country must be getting a 'good education'. However, because these children are almost always mixing only with other very wealthy children, what they actually get is a very peculiar education in which they are taught how to get high exam marks. They can often confuse such expertise in taking examinations with real learning and conclude that people who do not gain high marks are not as bright. They are also taught in a privileged context where issues about inequality cannot easily be raised, which can lead to their finding it difficult later in life to deal with such issues.

Living in a country with high economic inequality alters what people in that country come to believe and how they behave. This is seen in everything from the kinds of questions children in school ask, and what they think might be possible, through to how children are treated by their parents and others. At the extreme, child abuse and neglect is more common in countries that tolerate greater inequalities. The amount of economic hardship in a rich country is determined by the degree of inequality in that country, and: *'the greater the economic hardship, the greater the likelihood and severity of child abuse and neglect'.*[31]

Reducing economic inequality between people and households is the only way to reduce family poverty in a rich nation. The alternative of suggesting that eventually more and more economic growth will eradicate that poverty is now clearly a mirage, as demonstrated by the current extent of poverty in some of the more unequal rich countries. It is not just the poorest children who suffer in unequal societies: better-off children are also more likely to suffer from bad parenting in countries where parents are more conscious of and fearful about their status. It is the daughters of 'aspiring parents' who are most likely to self-harm. Across the population as a whole, research suggests that reducing economic inequality is likely to have a positive effect on reducing both the extent and severity of child abuse

Figure 3.4: The take of the best-off 1% in Argentina and Indonesia, 1921-2004

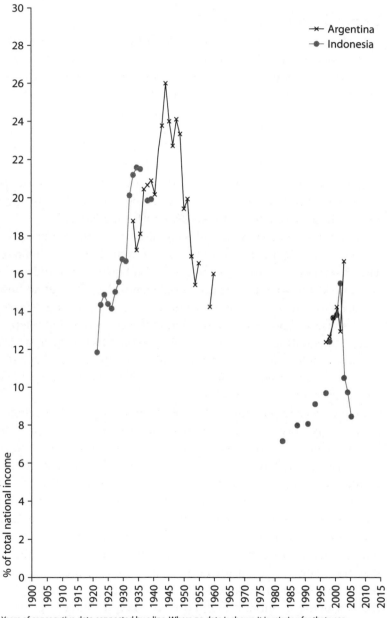

Years of consecutive data connected by a line. Where no data is shown it is missing for that year.

Source: World Wealth and Income database – accessed March 2017: http://wid.world/

World Bank: why Indonesia needs to reduce inequality

'Jakarta, 8 December 2015: Inequality in Indonesia is climbing faster than in most of its East Asian neighbors, raising the concerns of many Indonesians, says a new World Bank report.

'According to a 2014 survey on public perceptions of inequality, most Indonesians see a "very unequal" income distribution and urge government action to reduce inequality. Over the last 15 years, the Gini coefficient – a measurement of inequality – has increased sharply in Indonesia, climbing from 30 in 2000 to 41 in 2013, where it remains now.

'With the potential of creating social tensions, inequality constrains a country's growth potential, according to the report *Indonesia's Rising Divide*.

'"Despite impressive economic growth and poverty reduction, equity in growth has been more elusive in Indonesia. With the affluent racing ahead faster than the majority, in the long term Indonesia risks slower growth and weakened social cohesion if too many Indonesians are left behind. Their lost potential is Indonesia's lost potential," said Rodrigo Chaves, World Bank Country Director for Indonesia at the report launch attended by policymakers.

'Concern about the long-term implications of inequality influenced 60 per cent of survey respondents to say that they are willing to accept lower economic growth in exchange for lower inequality.

'In response, the Government is targeting to lower the Gini coefficient to 36 by the year 2019, and the example of countries such as Brazil show that public policy can help reduce inequality, particularly if the policies address the main drivers of inequality in Indonesia: inequality of opportunity, inequality in the labor market, high concentration of wealth, and unequal resilience to shocks.'

Source: World Bank press release, 8 December 2015[32]

and neglect in childhood. Greater equality results in reducing the consequences of child abuse and neglect in adult life and then for the next generation.

Even in states that are not among the richest in the world, such as Argentina and Indonesia, reducing inequalities is now seen as the next step towards reducing poverty and the recent experiences of both these populous countries demonstrates just how quickly the situation can change. Argentina had among the greatest inequalities ever recorded in the world in the 1930s. Indonesia was not far behind it in the 1920s. During and after the Second World War inequalities in both countries fell, but they then rose in the 1980s and especially in the 1990s. However, inequalities fell in Indonesia after the turn of the millennium. And although Figure 3.4 does not show it, they also fell very recently in Argentina (as Table 1 in Chapter 1 made clear, using different data). In recent years the World Bank has warned Indonesia of the need to reduce economic inequalities and has mentioned Argentina's neighbor, Brazil, as a positive example (see text box above). This may be a little premature, as Brazil does not yet release the data needed to know if there have been any recent falls in inequalities there. Although the take of the richest one per cent fell in the most recent years for which we have data for Indonesia, the overall Gini index of income inequality continued to rise after that. So we need better data and more scrutiny to be sure of what is going on before concluding that any turn in Indonesia toward greater equality has actually begun.

Sewers as cathedrals of the commons

This chapter began by making the point that no country, even the very poorest in the world, now sees as many of its infant children die as died in Britain a century ago. In Britain early on, and in many less affluent countries a little later, rates of infectious diseases (those diseases which still kill most infants globally) had been brought down enormously by immunization and better sanitation. It was the introduction of better sanitation for all in Britain, most importantly the introduction of sewers, which did most to protect all children, rich and poor.

Sewers are a public good: they make us all more equal. If you look around the world today, at the megacities especially, you can see great public works being undertaken almost everywhere. Because sewers run underground they are not as visible as the great mosques, palaces, temples and cathedrals of the world and yet, in the last few decades, we have built (underground) more cubic meters of sewer and storm drain worldwide than have ever been constructed as majestic public buildings above ground. And whereas only a select few are allowed in each palace, the sewers are for everyone's waste.

Our eyes are more often drawn to new slums, and not to where former slums are turning into poor but permanent neighborhoods. Rulers sanction the building of sewers because they are as much in their own interest as in that of their subjects, but they are quicker to do this where the gap between them and those they rule is narrower. Greater equality makes it easier for the elite to realize that the rest deserve proper sanitation, and easier for the rest to demand it. Next comes better education, better healthcare, better housing, and better jobs; but the route towards all of this requires falling income and wealth inequalities.

Often huge numbers of poor people are unfairly evicted from areas that are being gentrified. Slum clearance is rarely a fair form of progress. The poor frequently turn out not to have legal rights, which is another source of great inequality. And among the poor it is often children who suffer the most. Children especially depend on the quality of the 'commons', on what is commonly provided, from sanitation and healthcare, to schooling, to having public places to play in for free. The commons become depleted in countries that tolerate increasing inequality and consequently more power in the hands of the wealthy. Public places are privatized and children are excluded. Then there are calls, often through the media, to reduce taxation and state expenditure. Public services are then further run down and that hurts children more than adults, other than the most frail of adults. But these cases are the exception rather than the rule. In general the frail are now cared for better than they were cared for in the past in most places worldwide, and children are far better cared for than was the case just one or two generations ago.

In the world as a whole we have been becoming more equal for quite some time. Gaining greater equality is not some fantasy: it has been the real-life experience of most of our parents and grandparents. This is so if you look within the countries that are home to most people, and if you take the long view and are not mesmerized by what has happened most recently in strange countries such as the UK and the US. But we only become more equal if we constantly complain about inequalities and highlight the worst current examples and trends.

The commons have expanded in terms of education free at the point of delivery. In the recent past huge numbers of older children, and especially older girls, were denied access to school education. In affluent countries access to university has also expanded greatly in comparison to what was on offer to our parents' generation, and in most cases worldwide this education is still either provided for free or very heavily supported by the state. An 'information commons' has been created in the era of the internet with Wikipedia being the clearest example, trumping the public provision of libraries as a source of free information. Worldwide, health services have expanded. Treatments are available now that were either simply not provided or severely rationed in the past, including mass vaccination. But it is true that increasingly a few seek to encroach on these commons by erecting paywalls to access for education and health, and by filling the internet with advertisements, and that they have to be beaten back again and again.

The past is one good guide to how greater equality can be gained. Experiences of countries that are more equal are another guide. In addition, new ideas and aspirations for greater equality are constantly being created and these too are possible good guides. Old ideals have to be defended: pensions, social benefits, free education, healthcare, decent housing. In poorer countries the list is often a little shorter, but it has tended to be lengthening.

In many ways much has been improving in international terms. However, the vast bulk of the large reduction in global poverty between 2000 and 2015 trumpeted by the Millennium Development Goals was accounted for by China's surge in living standards. Elsewhere there was much less change – and Africa is still being left behind despite the advances of individual countries within that continent that have oil or other commodities to interest international markets. There has recently been a huge growth in interest from Chinese elites in particular parts of the African continent. Whether that interest helps or hinders in future may well largely depend on the extent to which the Chinese themselves begin to view economic inequality as a threat, not just internally in China, but to sustainability worldwide.

The future of our children and issues of equality and sustainability are all closely linked. Those who argue against greater equality are arguing against a good future for most children in the world and against an environmentally and economically sustainable future for them and their own children. The next chapter of this book presents very new evidence that has only recently emerged to show just how detrimental to our shared environment high rates of economic inequality can be. The equality effect is one of the main mechanisms we have to secure a better future for all, not just for those that live within our own countries, but to help usher in a more stable future in which we need not fear others who live elsewhere as much as we currently do. The equality effect is the genie in the bottle waiting to be released. If you had three wishes, would you ask for great wealth, health and happiness for yourself in a world where so many lived in fear, or would you wish that we could all be healthier and happier in future?

1   J Sachs, 'Facing up to income inequality', *The Boston Globe*, 2 Oct 2016, nin.tl/SachsGlobe
2   S Laville, 'Pacifist white poppies: record sales this year', The Guardian, 16 Nov 2016, nin.tl/whitepoppies
3   All of the evidence on this is neatly summarized in Richard Wilkinson and Kate Pickett's book *The Spirit Level: Why equality is better for everyone*, Penguin, London, 2010 (second edition). See equalitytrust.org.uk
4   By quintile-group comparisons the Chinese are more equitable than the Indians, but still suffer from high rates of income inequality which, compared to the countries of the Global North, are only to be found in the US.
5   Global Health Observatory (GHO) data from the World Health Organization accessed in Aug 2016: nin.tl/GHOneonatal See also: nin.tl/GeobaGazetteer
6   Giving birth is not always safer in richer countries. Compare, for example, the infant survival rates of Cuba and the US. In Cuba, income inequalities as measured between decile groups are almost five times lower than in the US.
7   UNICEF, *The State of the World's Children 2016*, unicef.org/sowc2016
8   Danny Dorling, 'When policy makers act like scientists, the result can be inaction', *Nature Human Behaviour*, vol 1, article 9, 10 Jan 2017.
9   US figures: nin.tl/WHOUSdata Japan figures: nin.tl/WHOJapandata UK figures: nin.tl/WHOUKdata Iceland figures: nin.tl/WHOIcelanddata The actual figure for Iceland may be even lower than this given its very low population; the rate has to be calculated from the last time any woman died in childbirth there.
10 A Rutkin, US pregnancy-related deaths are rising and have doubled in Texas, *New Scientist*, 23 Aug 2016, nin.tl/Texasdoubling
11 We can work out that fewer babies in absolute terms are born now than in the 1970s by calculating the drop as: 28% = 100 minus (100 x 1.67 x 0.43). We also know that half as many of those babies now die in their first year of life.

So the number of parents who grieve the loss of a baby is now less than half the number it was in the 1970s.

12 See Table 5 (page 124) of the 25 largest rich nations sorted by income inequality. Here I include affluent countries with a population of at least two million. Singapore may mostly be a small island, but it is home to over four million people.

13 If you want to know more about Singapore read Chris Brickhill's book, *Singapore's Avaricious Oligarchy*, published by CreateSpace on 8 Jul 2016: createspace.com/6409160

14 Look it up on the Web – that way you can learn as much or as little as you like. For those who have internet access, it is a wonderful leveller of knowledge. For those who don't, a new hurdle has been erected.

15 C Tai, 'South Korea's umbrella movement?' *This Week in Asia*, 17 Nov, nin.tl/slavedemocracy

16 K Jae-won, 'Korea worst in income inequality in Asia-Pacific', *Korean Times*, 16 Mar 2016, nin.tl/Koreaworst

17 Macrotrends, Gold Prices – 100 Year Historical Chart, accessed Feb 2017, nin.tl/historicalgold

18 See Figures 2.2 and 2.3, the ranking of happiness 2013-2015 and change since 2005-2007 in the 'World Happiness Report 2016 Update: worldhappiness.report

19 nin.tl/Democracyindex

20 *Growing up unequal*, Health Behaviour in School-aged Children (HBSC) study: international report from the 2013/2014 survey, nin.tl/HBSC2014 Also see UNICEF Innocenti Report Card 13, which also details the inequality in child well-being within countries: nin.tl/RC13unicef

21 BBC, 'Children in England "among unhappiest in world"', BBC education news, 19 Aug 2015, nin.tl/unhappyEnglish See also: S Weale, 'British teenagers among least satisfied in western world', *The Guardian*, 15 Mar 2016, nin.tl/leastsatisfied

22 ONS, Children's Well-being Measures, dataset, London: Office for National Statistics, 23 Mar 2016, nin.tl/Childwellbeing

23 BMA, 'Health in all policies: health, austerity and welfare reform', 5 Sep 2016, nin.tl/BMAausterity

24 'What's causing Texas' alarming spike in women dying after childbirth?' *Dallas Morning News*, 29 Aug 2016, nin.tl/Texasspike

25 H Osborne, 'Graduate whose loan grew by £1,800 in one year says students were misled', *The Guardian*, 25 May 2016, nin.tl/misledgraduate

26 A Tolhurst, 'Graduates with student loans could end up paying back £100,000 for their degrees thanks to crippling interest rates', *The Sun*, 21 Aug 2016, nin.tl/Sunstudentloans

27 P Nicholson, *The welfare benefits uprating bill*, Zacchaeus, 2000, nin.tl/2mZfVTa

28 According to the September 2016 report of the UK Public Accounts Committee as cited in R Garside, *Let them Fail*, Centre for Crime and Justice Studies, 27 October 2016, nin.tl/2lZoQin

29 D Campbell, 'Spike in mental health patient deaths shows NHS "struggling to cope"', *The Guardian*, 26 Jan 2016, nin.tl/2mmIdpd

30 *Sunday Times*, 24 Apr 2016, http://archive.is/jGUjS

31 P Bywaters, L Bunting, G Davidson, J Hanratty, W Mason, C McCartan, & N Steils, *The relationship between poverty, child abuse and neglect: an evidence review*, Joseph Rowntree Foundation, p 4, 3 Mar 2016, nin.tl/2n71p8S

32 'Indonesia: Rising inequality risks long-term growth slowdown', World Bank press release, 8 Dec 2015, nin.tl/2lZbTVU

4
Equality and the environment

Equality matters in terms of health and happiness – this much has been clear for some years. But it is also better for the environment – and this chapter charts new territory in beginning to bring together data establishing the evidence for that. In the more equal rich countries, people on average consume less, produce less waste and emit less carbon. They are also, believe it or not, better at mathematics. Almost everything associated with the environment improves when economic equality is greater.

> 'We cannot afford to be slowed by the climate skeptics or deterred by the defeatists who doubt America's ability to meet this challenge. That's why as president, I will make combating climate change a top priority from day one, and secure America's future as the clean energy superpower of the 21st century.'
>
> Hillary Clinton, unsuccessful Democratic Party candidate for the US presidency, December 2015[1]

The most important benefit of the equality effect may be how our lives and behaviors are improved when we are more equal, and how that then leads us to behave in ways that are less environmentally damaging. Chapter 3 discussed sustainability and the future for our children more widely. Now this chapter considers the environment in a little more detail in relation to a particular group of affluent countries. It also shows how inequality affects us all by impacting on education, crime and transport in ways that make it harder for us to protect the environment.

The public provision of goods is more favored in more equal countries. A key example is public transport, which tends to be greater in quantity as well as higher in quality in more equitable countries, making it far less necessary to use a car to get around. Private air travel is also far more unusual, partly because the most affluent people are not quite rich enough to be able to afford to run their own plane, but also because the public provision of railways is often so much better that it makes little sense to fly between cities when you can travel between their centers almost as quickly by rail.

Furthermore, in a more economically equal society the actual need to make particular journeys appears to be questioned more and 'throwing money about' is less acceptable when it might be used to pay the poorest more. There may also be less 'grandstanding' – less 'posh' traveling to a meeting to keep up appearances – since this kind of thing matters so much less as equality grows. The word 'posh' has become linked to 'Port Out Starboard Home' – referring to the most prized cabins on ships leaving Southampton for India. Apparently such cabins had the best views, since they always faced the land rather than the open ocean, but booking those cabins was more about status than comfort.

In more equitable times and countries, firms can concentrate more of their energies on enhancing the lives of their workforce, as well as producing goods that last and are of practical value. In more unequal societies there is a proliferation of products that are designed not to last so as to allow greater profits to be made. Producing endless must-have new versions exploits the higher levels of emotional insecurity that living with great inequality generates.

The success of the clothing industry is an interesting example to consider. People buy far greater quantities of cheaper clothes and throw them away more frequently in the most economically unequal countries. This results in much higher levels of waste, and it is questionable whether it is good for you to worry so much about your appearance that you find it necessary to keep buying more clothes. A recent UK survey of 2,000 women suggested that the majority of clothes are bought because they are seen as fashionable and are worn, on average, just seven times before they are discarded. A third of women see them as old after they have been worn three times. However, the survey also suggested that in almost half of all cases, women discarded clothing in the UK because of a change in their weight and thus over-consumption of clothing and over-consumption of food (as well as repeated dieting) may be linked. The survey was sponsored by a charity that would like women to donate more of their 'used' clothes to its shops. The argument that we should make better-quality clothes and wear them out is rarely made; so too is the argument that our societies should be arranged so that there is less need for people to rely on charities to help them survive and clothe themselves.[2]

The rich and the planet

In October 2016 we learnt that the world's 1,397 billionaires had each lost, on average, $215 million of their wealth in the previous 12 months. Global wealth inequality was falling. It had fallen a little before, in the immediate aftermath of the financial crisis of 2008, and then quickly recovered and grew rapidly, but now it was falling again, and more strongly. In total their wealth fell from $5,400 billion to $5,100 billion within the year to the end of 2015.[3] A more equal world is not only just possible, we may actually be at the tipping point of moving towards it as I write – you need hindsight to be sure. The super-rich waste money on luxuries rather than spend it on necessities, and they are much less careful with their money than the rest of us.

So what might the environmental benefits of a more equal world be? To study that we need to look at those countries where the rich have more and the poor have less, and compare them to more equitable affluent countries. We will confine ourselves to just 25 of the world's wealthiest countries in this chapter, as measured using 2015 data, and order those countries according to the 'Real 90:10 ratio' which is the ratio of the sum total of incomes of the best-off 10 per cent of households in each country

Table 5: Inequality ratio of the best-off tenth of households to the worst-off tenth (real 90:10 ratio), richest countries, 2015

1 United States	20.3	14 Australia	8.8
2 Singapore	18.5	15 Netherlands	8.6
3 Israel	17.4	16 New Zealand/Aotearoa	8.2
4 United Kingdom	17.4	17 France	7.4
5 Canada	14.5	18 Japan	7.3
6 Spain	13.6	19 Austria	7.0
7 Greece	12.7	20 Switzerland	6.7
8 Italy	11.3	21 Sweden	6.3
9 Ireland	11.1	22 Norway	6.2
10 Germany	10.4	23 Belgium	5.9
11 Portugal	10.1	24 Slovenia	5.5
12 South Korea	10.1	25 Denmark	5.2
13 Finland	9.2		

Source: various official sources combined in late 2015, latest data available and consistent.[4]

to the worst-off 10 per cent. The most recent Real 90:10 ratios for 25 countries are shown in the table above.

These are the countries with a population of at least two million people that also had the highest GDP per capita in 2015. We are comparing them with each other in this chapter because they are home to the majority of very rich people in the world. And if you are an inequality statistics obsessive you may note that these most recent data show the US to have become even more unequal than Israel very recently based on a comparison with the data from a year or two earlier that appeared in Table 1 in Chapter 1. The two tables don't just refer to slightly different dates but also use slightly different sources so they are not strictly comparable, but it is always the same countries that top and tail the table. The countries at the top and bottom are very similar in terms of overall affluence but they are now very different countries in terms of their levels of inequality.

It is sometimes claimed that the rich are environmentally friendly because they save and invest money that the rest would otherwise spend on more consumption with its concomitant pollution. If that were the case then the United States, with the highest real-inequality ratio, of 20.3 to 1, would be one of the least polluting countries per head and Denmark would be one of the most polluting ones with its ratio of just 5.2 to 1. Comparing these countries allows us to see whether claims that the poor simply waste money, if given more, are true.

The ratio is called the 'real 90:10 ratio' because it includes the really rich and the really poor. It is very important not to confuse this measure with an alternative 90:10 ratio that only compares the household that is at the 90th percentile with that at the 10th percentile of the national income distribution. For statisticians the latter is a much easier ratio to compute – these are normal people doing normal jobs and the super rich and very poor can be ignored – but it is not a good measure of the full extent of income inequality because it ignores the incomes of almost all of the households in the best-off 10 per cent and all but the very best-off of the poorest 10 per cent. In other words it does not show up the excessive takes of the top 1 per cent or 0.1 per cent, let alone the extraordinarily wealthy 0.01 per cent.

It is much harder to compute the real 90:10 ratio because the very richest households are not normal.[5] Just as it is not normal to sleep rough on the streets or to have to go to food banks, it is not normal to live in locked estates with private security guards, to send your children to exclusive schools, to get bonuses larger than your annual salary, to own expensive yachts or even private jets. Many of these very rich people view taxation as theft, and do everything they can to hide their (often unearned) income from the taxation authorities. Even when using the real 90:10 ratio, the figures for the very rich are probably an underestimate because so much income and wealth is hidden by the richest, especially in the most unequal countries.

When we use the real 90:10 ratio, even in equitable Denmark, the mean income of the best-off tenth of households is (at least) 5.2 times as high as that of the worst-off tenth. You may need to think about that for a minute. Even in equitable Denmark, if the best-off tenth of households were, on average, to give up slightly less than a fifth of their annual income then the incomes of the worst-off 10 per cent of households could all be doubled! Even so-called equitable countries today are far from being as equitable as they could be.

So what is the apparent environmental effect of living in a country in which households are very economically unequal as compared to living in one in which the economic differences between people and their families are far smaller?

First, a note of caution: just because an environmental indicator is correlated with income inequality does not mean that it is the inequality that is directly affecting or determining the level of that environmental indicator. It could happen by chance, although that is unlikely if a clear pattern is formed. There could be another factor that affects both inequality and the amount of environmental damage such as 'trust', or the lack of it – trust tends to be lower in more economically unequal countries. Or it could even be that unequal environmental behavior is driving the income inequality – although to believe that takes some impressively creative thinking. The richest countries of the world matter greatly in environmental terms because they consume and pollute the most.

At this point it is also important to add another word of caution, this time about data quality: comparing data from different countries can be problematic because of different methods and reliability of data collection and because methodologies change over time. It is not just that it is hard to collect data on income inequality between households in rich countries. It is even harder to collect data on many environmental indicators and often a subsequent set of data shows sudden changes, suggesting that one or other figure was an error, or at least misleading. So please bear in mind these caveats when looking now at some environmental behaviors and how they might be related to economic inequality.

The meat-eating problem

We will start with eating meat and the latest data we can get on that which is shown globally in the maps below (Figure 4.1). It is the richest countries that consume the most excessive amounts of meat. All the countries colored the darkest shade in the three maps below are those in which people consume at least three times more meat (200 per cent more) than the average world citizen. The first map is a conventional map, the second uses an equal population projection, but it is the third that is most telling, in which all countries of the world are sized by how much extra

Figure 4.1: The global map of who eats too much meat, 2011[6]

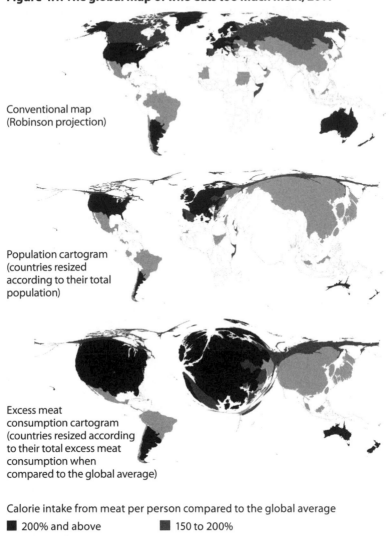

Conventional map
(Robinson projection)

Population cartogram
(countries resized
according to their total
population)

Excess meat
consumption cartogram
(countries resized according
to their total excess meat
consumption when
compared to the global average)

Calorie intake from meat per person compared to the global average

- ■ 200% and above
- ■ 150 to 200%
- ■ 100 to 150%
- □ below global average

meat their inhabitants consume compared with the consumption of the average world citizen.

Eating a lot of meat is not very good for you. It is also not very good for the planet. The amount of crops that have to be grown and transported to feed the animals that we eat is far greater than the amount needed if we just ate the crops themselves – if we ate less meat and more cereals, pulses and vegetables. So, the more meat per person that is eaten in a country, the less environmentally friendly the people of that country are.

By weight (if we ignore insects and fish) most of the animal life on our planet is now intensively farmed for our own consumption. Those animals produce enormous amounts of greenhouse gases during their short lives, with cattle being the worst polluters of all in this respect. Intensively farmed animals require antibiotics as diseases spread between them so easily, and sometimes to us. New diseases and antibiotic resistance emerge far more frequently when many animals are farmed in such great concentrations. The most common bird on the planet is now the domestic chicken, reared solely because so many of us in the rich world have become so used to eating cheap chicken.

Our great-grandparents did not each much meat at all, and chicken was often for Christmas Day and the occasional Sunday.

unintended consequences

Increasing meat consumption has not made us healthier. In some countries we are now eating so excessively that it is making many of us obese. Obesity rates are much higher in affluent countries that are more economically unequal. One theory as to why is that the poor in such countries have to resort to cheap fast food, which is advertised to them aggressively. Fast food often includes meat. Another theory is that people eat more meat in unequal countries for reasons of self-esteem – because in the past it was better-off people who ate more meat.

In more equitable countries the population tends to be better educated and so can more easily see through the folly of fast-food advertising and gluttony. All these theories remain unproven, but what we do know is that people in more economically unequal countries – where there tend to be more fast-food takeaways, more cheap meat for sale in supermarkets, and a greater weight of food consumed – in general eat more meat per person by weight.

We also know that the average is not being pulled up just by the richest people in these countries because that would require too massive a meat intake. The 2004 film *Super Size Me* graphically illustrated the effects on the body of eating that amount of meat. What is considered normal, how much meat it is considered reasonable to eat, varies over time but also between countries, and is affected by how economically unequal or equal a country is.

In Figure 4.2 (and all the other graphs in this chapter), the size of each country's circle is proportional to its population. It demonstrates how meat consumption tends to be higher in more unequal countries. The relationship only appears so strong because meat consumption per person is so high in the US, more than twice as much is eaten per person as in Japan, one of the rich world's more equal countries.

Without the US in the diagram the relationship would not look strong at all, but if the 50 separate states of the US were all shown as separate circles, with their areas in proportion to their populations, then the relationship would look even stronger, especially as meat consumption tends to be higher in the more unequal US states, such as Texas. It is worth remembering this point when considering all the graphs shown in this chapter.

Figure 4.2: Economic inequality and meat consumption (excluding fish), 2011

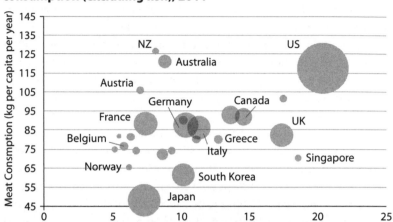

A value of 82 means = eating approx. one beef steak a day every day all year

One reason why the relationship between economic inequality and meat consumption is not stronger is that inequality is not the sole (or possibly even the main) determinant of over-consumption in a particular country. Tradition and availability may be an issue and hence consumption is very high in New Zealand/Aotearoa and Australia, where a great deal of sheep and cattle are raised, both for export and for internal consumption. However, when I drew the first version of this graph a few years ago, one of the countries with the highest per-capita meat consumption was Denmark, famous for its bacon. The latest data for Denmark show much lower meat consumption, which better fits the overall distribution. It is unlikely that both statistics could have been correct and that meat consumption in Denmark has fallen this fast or was so high in the very recent past, so there could well be errors in these official estimates.

The data used to draw the graph came primarily from the United Nations Environment Programme Environmental Data Explorer, which in turn drew them from the Food and Agriculture Organization (FAO) of the United Nations.[7] The data contained a wide range of 'most recent years' and where figures were missing they had to be estimated from another source.[8] If you find these statistics interesting or useful, it would be worth looking up the original sources yourself and seeing what the numbers are by the time you read this – because data quality tends to improve significantly over time. I give more than the usual level of detail about sources and definitions in this chapter as the relationship between inequality and the environment is a very recent area of social-science research and much more work on it is needed.

Meat consumption refers to the total amount of meat produced that is available for human consumption expressed in kilograms per person per year. It covers horsemeat, poultry and meat from all other wild or domestic animals, including camels, rabbits, reindeer and game animals. The FAO has a separate dataset measuring fish and seafood consumption. A value of 82 means eating approximately one beef steak a day, every day of the year. The UK is currently at around that level – a huge amount of meat to be eating every year. Because this scale of meat consumption is not good for health, we should expect meat consumption to fall in future, although the equality effect suggests that it would be far easier to sustain and achieve such reductions if very unequal countries were to move towards becoming more equal more quickly.

Knowing the precise mechanisms that are at work here is important, but it is not essential to know them before concluding that there does appear to be a relationship between economic inequality and eating too much food – more specifically, eating too much meat. It may be that more equal countries better protect children from bad food advertising. It may be that people are better informed in general. It may be that those who seek to make a profit out of selling meat try to do it more through quality rather than quantity in more equitable countries. It may be that sales tactics are less aggressive in more equitable countries. Whatever the reason – greater equality is associated with less obesity and less meat eating.

The world needs human beings to eat less meat if we are to avoid depleting our soils, increasing greenhouse gases and also reducing the biodiversity of the planet to such an extent that monocultures prevail and we lose habitats. In addition, the animals that we currently farm for meat live a pretty short, brutal and miserable life – and more and more of our meat is factory farmed each year.

Finally, there are many warnings that we are already part way through one of the planet's great mass-extinction events. The previous ones were caused by natural events, by very large asteroids from outer space hitting the earth or by many volcanoes erupting at once and the consequent dust blocking out the light and cooling the planet. In great contrast, the current mass-extinction event is being caused purely by us. For the first time a single species of animal is responsible – humans. By breeding such a small variety of animals for us to eat, in such enormous numbers, we have been crowding out the space that the 99.99 per cent of other species need. We have been destroying forests and jungle to make space for our farms, and have polluted watercourses and aquifers in the process. If we ate less meat we would need to use so much less land.

Using too much water

One of the main ways in which we speed up the extinction of species is through degrading the environment they live in, and one of the key ways in which we do that is by extracting so much water from rivers and underground aquifers that areas become dried up, desertification spreads, or the water table in a region is no longer high enough to support rainforests or other increasingly rare habitats.

We mainly extract water for agricultural uses, to water the crops that we then feed to the animals, but we also use water for industries that produce more stuff and more packaging for that stuff than we actually need. How many plastic containers does the world really need? Can't we transport food and other goods in something more easily recyclable?

The final use we have for water is for ourselves, for domestic use, and here, just as with meat, we can see huge variations between countries that are otherwise similarly wealthy. And again the variations appear to be related to economic inequality. In more unequal affluent countries people, on average, consume more water for personal use – or are far more wasteful over their use of water. Figure 4.3 measures domestic water consumption against

Figure 4.3: Economic inequality and water consumption (domestic), 2009-13

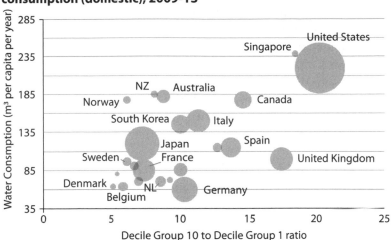

economic equality for the 25 most affluent countries in the world.

Again the excessive use in the United States stands out: the consumption per person is around three-and-a-half times higher than in Germany. It is not as if the US has ample rainfall. You can look at the US Drought Monitor any week of the year to see their ongoing problems.[9] The relationship between water consumption and inequality seems clear from the chart, though there is quite a lot of variation. The UK may use a little less water than might be predicted from its levels of economic inequality, partly because the climate of the UK makes it less useful to have private outdoor swimming pools if you are rich. You can still see a great many private swimming pools in gardens from the air in southern England but they are not ubiquitous. In contrast, more water is used per head in Australia than might be expected from its level of inequality, presumably because of its warmer climate – the building of swimming pools in gardens is much more usual there.

So why are people in Canada, Singapore and the US using so much more water for domestic purposes than those in Germany, France or Japan? It has nothing to do with rainfall or the availability of water from underground sources or the rivers flowing into each territory. Possibly there is a lot less concern about wasting water in the more unequal countries. Toilet cisterns may be less 'eco-friendly', people may worry a little less about watering the garden with a chlorinated supply designed for human consumption, not for plants.

It is not that people are cleaner and wash more often in the more inequitable countries (per person the Japanese buy the most soap worldwide), and it is certainly not that they are drinking more water. What is happening is that they are wasting more, and that may be related to a more general ethos that people should be free to do as they wish and damn the consequences for others – an ethos that appears to be far more prevalent in more inequitable countries.

It is not that how much meat people eat or how much water they use (and numerous other things as we proceed through this chapter) is directly determined by the level of economic inequality in a country, but that the level of inequality influences it sufficiently for that to be detectable when you compare the most affluent 25 large countries. So, in general, why does inequality appear to affect so many apparently unrelated things – what is the common factor?

How much you earn and how wealthy you are reflects how much you are valued in the society you live in. The greater the difference in income within a society, the stronger the implication that people in that country are valued differently, and that less respect is accorded to those who are 'worth very little'. This lack of respect for each other creates a degree of selfishness that appears to spill over into a lack of respect for the environment or a lack of concern about how our own behavior impacts on other things as well as other people, especially people we see as 'not counting'.

The relationship with water consumption is not incredibly strong, but it is evident in the graph, especially if you imagine the US circle being replaced by 50 smaller circles representing its states. Again issues of data matter and can add to the uncertainty. The Real 90:10 ratio may not be the best ratio of inequality to use when trying to find a measure that best reflects 'not giving a damn', if that is the key factor at play here. And the data on water use is far from perfect as well. As with food consumption, it often varies too much between statistical releases for us to believe the figures are very accurate, compatible or comparable. There could, for example, be problems over exactly what is included under 'domestic consumption' and whether many people have unmeasured private water supplies. Different countries often have very different methods of data collection and proxy measures and estimates are sometimes needed. The source of the data used here is the Food and Agriculture Organization of the United Nations, and in particular its AQUASTAT database.[10] Data are from the latest year available spanning the 2009-2013 period.

The intended measure here is municipal water consumption by the general population, as opposed to industrial or agricultural use. It will not include people collecting rainwater from their roofs to water their gardens. Water consumption is mainly reduced simply by being less wasteful, but also by using more water-efficient washing machines, and perhaps by families sharing bath water. Try it – it's not as bad as you might think! And perhaps the Germans more than any other group understand what is meant (regarding toilets) by 'if it's yellow let it mellow, if it's brown flush it down" (*Wenn es gelb ist, bleibt es stehen, wenn es braun ist, darf es gehen*).

World leaders in waste

So far we have considered two specific items people can choose to consume and waste in greater or lesser quantities, but what about general consumption? How could we measure that? There is, luckily, one easy way. If we want to know how much stuff people buy every year we simply need to look in their bins or, more efficiently, measure the weight of what they throw away each year.

Almost all of what you buy ends up in the bin. Much food is wasted. We can only store a finite amount of possessions in our homes. We buy far more stuff than we can store for any great length of time. Increasing numbers of people in more unequal countries are persuaded to rent commercial self-storage units for their not-actually-needed-now possessions. There is all the copious packaging to throw away, often the item it is replacing, and also the ever-constant need for a clear-out. That is why our bins are so full every week and why they are much larger (240 liters or more in size) than the 90-liter galvanized metal dustbins our grandparents had. Those grandparents almost always threw away much less because they bought much less and reused and repaired so much of what they did buy before eventually disposing of it. Think of how older people tend to store many items, from jam jars to plastic bags, in case they find a later use for them. Those older people almost all grew up in more equitable, less wasteful times.

When you buy an item, you don't think about throwing it away. But you will eventually throw away almost everything you buy, most immediately the packaging – tins, cartons, cardboard, expanded polystyrene, plastic, bubble-wrap etc. Some of it you may recycle, but if you had not bought it in the first place you would not need to recycle it, and recycling is never fully efficient; it also uses a great deal of energy and hence generates pollution itself. Not buying things you do not need is far better, but in a world where the main function of advertising is to get you to buy things that you could live without, that is hard.

The less something is advertised, the more necessary it is likely to be – people don't need to be persuaded to buy it. In economically unequal countries the pressure to buy items to

Figure 4.4: Economic inequality and waste production (domestic), 2009-2013

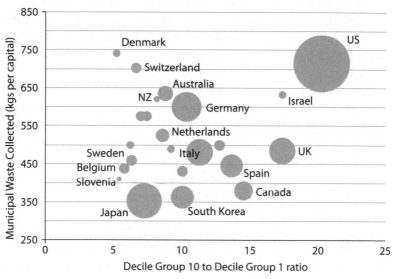

keep up with your peers, with 'people who count', is enormous, especially when it comes to clothes, fashion, new cars and other status symbols. We are encouraged to be aspirational, to better ourselves, not for the greater good, but for selfish reasons – ultimately to be able to get all that stuff. A good job is no longer one that involves doing good, which benefits society, but has to be one that pays you well. Some recent estimates for the consumption of clothes by 2,000 women living in the UK were mentioned earlier in this chapter. There are many similar studies and surveys available which all tend to point in the same direction: in more equal countries people buy fewer clothes of greater quality that they tend to keep much longer.

The higher consumption in more unequal affluent countries does not apply just to clothes: almost everything apart from jewelry ends up in the bin after a few years or even a few months of use. In Japan people on average buy and throw away half as much as people in the US – of everything! And again it is the US data that are vital in demonstrating the relationship, especially if you imagine the US represented by 50 smaller circles showing waste in each of its states. And then, even if there were no pattern within the US, the overall pattern between the (now) 74 circles would be far more obvious.

All the graphs here show correlations, some of which would be statistically significant if tested, especially if the US were split into its 50 states. I could have drawn the line of best fit on these graphs to make the actual trend appear much clearer. However, it would be wrong to do that if some of the data points themselves could be wrong or misleading, and should be treated with caution. For example, some particularly environmentally conscious countries might make a far better job of collecting data on waste and hence on consumption. This could include Denmark and Switzerland and might explain why they are outliers in Figure 4.4. Perhaps they include some office waste as well because when we throw away our drinks cans and junk mail at work, rather than at home, we are still individually creating waste.

If you are interested in trying to sort out all these conundrums, then a good place to start is the source of the data for the waste graph: the OECD StatsExtracts Database.[11] The graph shows the 'latest year available' as of June 2015, spanning the period 2009-13. For Singapore (deliberately not plotted) it was necessary to rely on the United Nations Statistics Division Environmental Indicators.[12] These provide a measure that includes industrial waste and so would probably have unfairly elevated that circle in the graph. Singapore has very little industry. It is essentially a port – and the more we buy and throw away, the larger and larger are the ships that pass through that port.

When it comes to waste you have to worry about definitions, and of course some waste is far worse than other waste, but here all waste is included as equally important by its weight. Municipal waste consists, to a large extent, of waste generated by households and as such is distinct from measures of agricultural and industrial waste, but it may also include similar waste generated by small businesses and public institutions and collected by the municipality. For areas not covered by a public municipal waste collection scheme, the amount of waste generated has to be estimated by the statistical authorities from other sources and those estimates have also been used here.

Carbon dioxide and consumption

The most damaging form of pollution (in terms of absolute effect) is the carbon dioxide (CO_2) we are responsible for releasing into the atmosphere. We have only discovered this to be the case during current lifetimes and so have to come to terms rapidly with the harm this gas causes through its contribution to global warming. CO_2 is not the most damaging greenhouse gas, but by weight there is far more of it produced by us than any other pollutant, and so it is the most important to restrict. Alongside water vapor, which increases in the air as the oceans warm, it accounts for the bulk of current global warming.

As Figure 4.5 shows, residents of the US contribute more emissions of CO_2 than any other of the 25 rich countries featured. US emissions per person are almost twice those of the Japanese, and more than three times those of the French. As these are all large countries by population, the total emissions they produce per capita are especially important. In general, the more economically unequal a rich country is, the more CO_2 it emits.

Figure 4.5: Economic inequality and carbon dioxide emissions, 2011

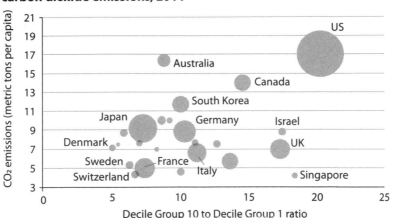

There are exceptions of course: the UK is a relatively low emitter because it currently has access to natural gas from the North Sea to burn in its domestic heating boilers and some power stations. That gas is less polluting than burning coal. France's per-capita emissions are especially low on the chart because 75 per cent of its electricity production derives from nuclear power, which emits less CO_2 but creates much longer-lasting radioactive waste. In contrast, Australia mines and burns a great deal more coal (and also, incidentally, mines a large amount of uranium). Finally, the UK has relatively low emissions per capita because it has mined and burned all of its most accessible coal but we should remember that in historical terms the UK is responsible for more carbon dioxide in the atmosphere per person than any other country.

Because so many other factors are important, including having exhausted easily accessible reserves of coal, there is not a simple relationship between current carbon pollution and inequality. Singapore appears to pollute little because all the pollution caused by the ships that visit its ports to be refueled is not included as consumption in Singapore. Again, if you find the graph above unconvincing, try to imagine including every US state as a separate set of circles centered around where the United States as a whole currently sits in the graph. If you can do that, you will better understand why what this graph shows matters.

Figure 4.6: Global income deciles and associated carbon dioxide emissions, 2015

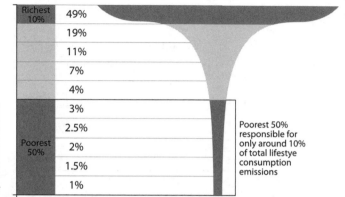

Oxfam: 'We conservatively estimate that the average emissions of a person in the poorest half of the global population are just 1.57 tCO₂ – that equals 11 times less than the average footprint of someone in the richest 10%. The average emissions of someone in the poorest 10% of the global population is 60 times less than that of someone in the richest 10%.'

The source of the data in Figure 4.5 is the World Development Indicators Database.[13] In turn these are based on estimates produced by the Carbon Dioxide Information Analysis Center in the Oak Ridge National Laboratory based in Tennessee, in the US. The data are drawn from 2011, which was the latest year available for all countries when the database was accessed in 2015. CO_2 emissions are those stemming from the burning of fossil fuels and the manufacture of cement. They include CO_2 produced during consumption of solid, liquid, and gas fuels and gas flaring.

In 2016 the charity Oxfam reported in detail on why emissions from some countries were so much greater than others (see Figure 4.6). Oxfam, collaborating with economists such as Thomas Piketty, discovered that what drove excess consumption in any particular affluent country was economic inequality because the best-off in a country tend to waste more energy, heat their homes more than they need to, drive more than they need to in bigger gas-guzzling cars, take more flights and, occupying more space, require more cement and other materials to be made to construct their larger-than-needed buildings, while at the same time buying and throwing away more items. In short, if you are very rich, money is no object and you want to be seen spending your riches. In a more equitable country people are, in general, more careful, public transport is better, and the need to keep up with those above you and mimic their behavior is far less acutely felt.

Oxfam concluded that we should concentrate on the richest countries because even in those poorer very unequal countries where pollution has been increasing in recent years the rich do not pollute as much as they do in wealthier countries:

> Comparing the average lifestyle consumption footprints of richer and poorer citizens in a range of countries helps show that while some 'emerging economies' like China, India, Brazil and South Africa, have high and rapidly rising emissions, the lifestyle consumption emissions of even their richest citizens remain some way behind that of their counterparts in rich OECD countries, even though this is changing and will continue to do so without urgent climate action. The lifestyle emissions of the hundreds of millions of their poorest citizens, meanwhile, remain significantly lower than even the poorest people in the OECD countries.[14]

Globally, half the CO_2 emissions associated with individual lifestyles are due to the actions of the richest tenth of humanity, who disproportionately live in the more unequal of the world's most affluent 25 countries.

Gasoline (petrol) consumption

Our excessive use of motor vehicles contributes not only CO_2 but also other damaging gases such as carbon monoxide and nitrogen oxides as well as pumping particulate matter into the air we all have to breathe. Among the most affluent 25 countries three stand out as extreme: the US, Canada and Australia. These three are among the least densely populated countries in the rich world and driving distances between homes and workplaces are often long, but they have chosen to arrange their cities in this

The carbon billionaires

Oxfam: 'Multinational fossil-fuel companies are some of the most profitable on earth – and behind the well-known brands is a club of carbon billionaires. These are the mega-rich super-elite who have made their wealth from the business of driving climate change – for which the poorest and most vulnerable pay the highest price.

'Between the Copenhagen and Paris climate conferences, the number of billionaires on the Forbes list with interests in fossil-fuel activities has risen from 54 in 2010 to 88 in 2015. Over these five years, the size of their combined personal fortunes has expanded from over $200 billion to over $300 billion.

'The fossil-fuel industry has a lot to lose from ambitious climate regulation – and so it is not surprising that the sector spends millions of dollars every year lobbying to try to influence and delay government action – buying more years to pollute and protect their profits.

'Fossil-fuel interests declare spending $44 million a year on lobbying the EU in Brussels – around $120,000 a day. In the US in 2013, the oil, gas and coal industries spent almost $157 million on lobbying – over $430,000 per day, or $24,000 per hour. By comparison, the entire alternative energy sector spent the same amount on lobbying in one year as just the top two spending

way. That choice was again affected by economic inequality and the beliefs associated with it, such as that individual aspirations should trump the collective good, that 'the car is king' and that pollution doesn't matter much when the wind will take the pollutants away.

Relatively low gasoline use in the UK, Singapore and Israel shows that very unequal countries need not necessarily use huge amounts. In these three cases there are large dense urban areas that can only function with good public transport such as underground trains, buses and trams. That is a part of the reason why these three countries are outliers in the graph below. A car is pretty useless for getting around in London compared with the underground or the buses, and you have to be able to park it

oil giants, according to the Overseas Development Institute and Oil Change International. As these are self-reported figures in Washington DC and Brussels alone, they are clearly just the tip of the iceberg.

'All this investment clearly buys results. One clue is in the subsidies and tax breaks awarded to the fossil-fuel sector, which, as the OECD shows, far outweighs support to the renewables sector. The US government provides $5.1 billion each year in tax deductions for exploration. In each annual budget, President Obama has attempted to repeal some of the most egregious tax breaks, but has been blocked by Congress – many of whose members rely on campaign donations from the fossil-fuel industry. The US is now the world's largest producer of both oil and gas, ahead of Saudi Arabia and Russia."[15]

Jeffrey Sachs talks of: '...the historic role, for more than a half century, of Royal Dutch Shell in Nigeria's oil-sector corruption... While there is enough top-level political corruption to go around – from Afghanistan and Nigeria to Malaysia, Brazil, South African, FIFA, and many more places – the channels of corruption and secrecy havens are largely owned and operated by the big boys – the United States and the UK – and depend absolutely on the gross impunity that prevails at the highest reaches of power and finance in the United States.'[16]

as well. But look at Figure 4.7 and note that no relatively equal affluent country consumes more than half as much gasoline as people in Canada and the US do each year. All of us will have to consume far less fuel in the near future and those reductions will be far more easily achieved in a country that sees the provision of efficient, low-polluting public transport as a collective good rather than a dangerous precedent.

The low consumption of petrol in France, Germany and Italy is particularly impressive, if it is true, and again data quality is a worry as these are all quite new statistical series. However, we do know that car use has been declining in Japan for several decades so it is interesting that its use of petrol is not lower. If you are interested in rechecking the sources of these data then

Figure 4.7: Economic inequality and gasoline (petrol) consumption, 2012-13

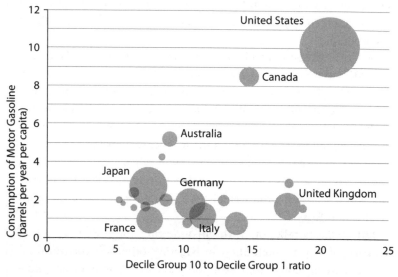

one place to start looking is the International Energy Statistics of the US Energy Information Administration.[17] The data used here were from 2013 for all countries except Singapore where they were from 2012. Finally, behind the data there is the politics, as Oxfam and Jeff Sachs made clear, both writing in 2016 (see box on pages 142-3).

The equality effect is most evident when we look within countries. In its 2016 report, quoted from at length in the box, Oxfam found that the greatest polluters of all were the most affluent 10 per cent of US households. Each emitted, on average, 50 tonnes of CO_2 per household member per year, largely through their excessive use of cars, planes, and (occasionally) yachts. The Canadian top 10 per cent were the next most polluting followed by the British, Russian and South African elites, as shown in Figure 4.8. In more equitable affluent countries such as South Korea, Japan, France, Italy and Germany, the rich don't just pollute less, but average pollution is lower because the bottom half of the population in those societies also pollute less (despite being better off) than the bottom half of the population in the US, Canada or Britain. The equality effect is clearly also an environmental effect.

Figure 4.8: Emission of pollution by income group in selected rich nations, 2015

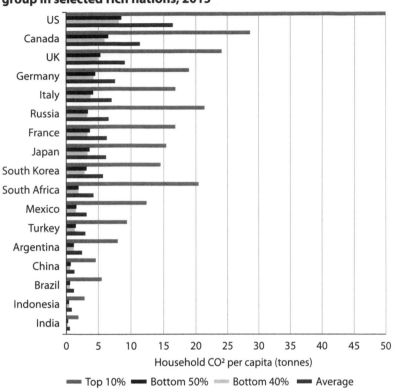

Household CO² per capita (tonnes)

━━ Top 10% ━━ Bottom 50% ━━ Bottom 40% ━━ Average

Source: oxfam.org/en/research/extreme-carbon-inequality

The poor pollute less when less poor and the rich pollute less when less rich.

Wasting young lives

In Chapter 3 of this book a great many words were devoted to the recent spectacular overall improvement in infant mortality rates worldwide, but also to the inequalities in infant mortality between rich countries, how infant mortality rates are not currently improving in the US, particularly in some of its most economically unequal states, and how the apparently low infant mortality rate in Singapore is something of a chimera.

Figure 4.9 shows infant mortality rates drawn in the same style as the environmental graphs above. Countries in which

Figure 4.9: Economic inequality and infant mortality rates in affluent nations, 2015

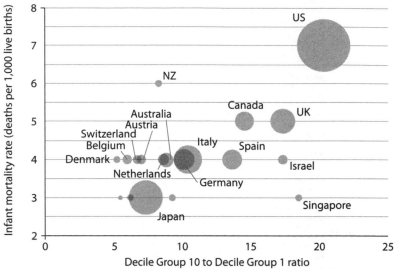

people care less about polluting are also countries in which they care less about the lives of others, including children born into mostly poorer families who are most at risk of dying within their first year of life. All the rates in Figure 4.9 above are historically low, but again the US reports rates more than twice as high as in Japan and this cannot be unrelated to environmental behavior and the general heightened selfishness that great inequality encourages.

The source of these data is again the World Bank's 2015 World Development Indicators database.[18] In 2016 even lower rates were reported for some of the most equitable affluent countries in the world, but there was little improvement among the most inequitable affluent countries.

Half a century ago doctors investigated if cigarettes caused lung cancer by studying themselves – comparing what happened to those who smoked with what happened to those who did not. Their research kept on revealing other harmful effects of cigarettes on health, to the point where they wondered if they were making some bizarre statistical error. There was no mistake. It was possible to see the effects clearly because the group studied (doctors) were well off but varied greatly in their smoking habits from not smoking, to occasionally smoking, to being heavy smokers. A similar thing is happening now in research regarding economic inequality within affluent countries.

Economic inequality unexpectedly appears to be contributing to numerous social ills that many never dreamed it might impact upon. We can only see these effects clearly because the group studied (the most affluent countries) are all well off but differ greatly in their degrees of inequality. If that had not been the case, many results would have been inconclusive. A more equitable society turns out to be one that cares more about all its children and also to be one that cares about the environment.

More economic equality appears to have multiple wider benefits than simply preventing so many people from being poor. When this is more widely understood then the clamor to reduce economic inequality will grow, just as the clamor to reduce cigarette smoking has grown. At the moment we are still at the stage of looking at the very first graphs that suggest there is a relationship to be explained.

Ecological footprints

Not everything lines up as neatly by inequality as do infant mortality rates or excessive water and food consumption. As always, one suggestion is that the data may not be good enough for us to be sure we are seeing the real picture. Figure 4.10 shows what appears at first sight to be something very peculiar. One estimate of the overall ecological footprint is shown – the crude ranking of the 25 countries by how ecological they are considered to be. Although the positions of the US and Japan help to suggest that the overall trend seen above is still important, a few countries such as Denmark, Belgium and Sweden are clear, but unexpected, outliers.

When these data were released, the Danish spokesperson for the World Wildlife Fund (WWF), which had produced them, explained that part of the problem was that:

'It is the way we live and the way we have arranged our society that gives the big ecological footprint. Our country consists of roadways, cities and crop fields with hardly any nature. On top of that, we consume way too much meat, among other things.'

However, as shown above in this chapter, the Danish consumption of meat appears to have fallen greatly since the data used in the WWF study was collected. Furthermore, the reporting of the spokesperson's comments was accompanied by the news that in 2014 Denmark had managed to produce 41.2 per cent of all its electricity using wind power.[19] A country's ecological footprint is improved if it gives over more land to biodiversity, which is easier when population density is low, but it should also improve if it is generating so much of the energy it needs so sustainably.

It is very possible that more economically equitable countries are more conscientious when collecting environmental data. This point was made above in relation to data on waste collection. It is very likely the case that in a few years' time a very different ranking of these countries will emerge with the more economically equitable countries reporting lower figures, not least because countries like Denmark continue to increase their wind-power capacity, whereas the US continues to exploit its use of fracking, and its leaders continue to show very little concern about the environmental damage caused by its current rates of very high

Figure 4.10: Economic inequality and ecological footprints in affluent nations, 2014

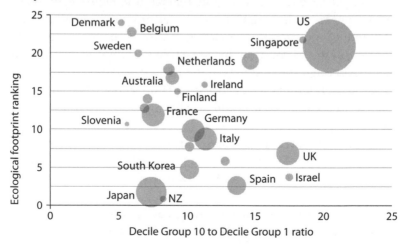

consumption and pollution. Hillary Clinton, if her quotation at the head of this chapter was to be believed, might have been more concerned. But she lost the presidential election partly because US voters are, on average, not that concerned about the environment. People in very economically unequal countries tend to have fewer such concerns.

If you want to know where we are heading, then look up the original WWF Living Planet Report from 2014.[20] This in turn relied on original data from the Global Footprint Network. The ecological footprint measures the amount of biologically productive land and water area (biocapacity) required to produce the resources an individual consumes and to absorb the carbon emissions they generate, given prevailing technology and resource management. This area is expressed in global hectares (hectares with world average biological productivity). The calculation is far from simple and perhaps Figure 4.10 demonstrates that the current method leaves a lot to be desired. For instance, in future, the effects of the British finance industry could be included. When British financiers invest money abroad in schemes that harm the environment in other places, should that environmental damage be attributable to Britain or to the country in which it occurs?

Air travel

One way in which the residents of affluent countries can pollute less is by flying less. Many of the flights we undertake are unnecessary, but we take them because we can. Of course, most people – even in affluent countries – will not fly in any given year, while a few will fly often. Those who pollute the most (per person) are executives flown around in private jets. It is at take-off that aircraft use most fuel and so Figure 4.11 shows the average number of airplane take-offs per person per year in each country. Again there is a relationship with inequality. Again a few of the outliers can be explained by the presence of many remote settlements, or by a country being an island (in the case of New Zealand/Aotearoa). Yet again the US dominates and if circles for all its separate states were drawn the overall pattern would look even more obvious.

Figure 4.11: Economic inequality and aircraft flights taken in affluent nations, 2014

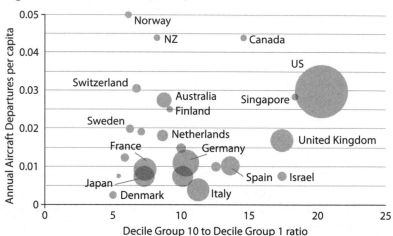

The US provides the world-leading model for how to pollute the most. It could have chosen to develop a series of high-speed rail lines across its land, as other affluent countries have done and as even less affluent ones such as China are now doing. The US is notable for the number of people living there that have never left their own country, so most of its air flights are internal. It is also well known for preferring free enterprise and competition to social planning. High-speed rail lines require planning. They require timetabling. Only a fool would try to run trains that competed with one another. The UK has recently done this and shown the world what a foolish idea it is.

In the majority of the 25 countries, less than one plane takes off per year for every hundred people living there. In the UK it is nearer two planes, in the US three, in Canada four and in Norway five. Norway is famously equitable, but it is also remote and has access to relatively cheap aircraft fuel from its oilfields. Being more equitable is no guarantor of better environmental behavior, but it tends to be associated with it.

Note how Denmark, chastised above for having one of the highest ecological footprints on the planet, appears to have the least flights taking off per person. You can see why writers like me who work with these statistics sometimes worry about their overall reliability. They cannot all be true! But Denmark is also well established within the European rail network. Live on much of the European mainland and your first thought when thinking of traveling far is to get a ticket for a train rather than a plane. In more equitable countries fewer people have so much 'spare money' that they can think of taking several holidays by air a year. More people have holidays in such places, but they more often take them without flying. More equitable countries also ensure that rail travel is cheaper than air travel. Business meetings are held more often over the Web rather than face to face because they are less about trying to make deals that have to be made in person, almost in secret, and more about practically getting on with the work. And, of course, in more equitable affluent countries people tend to be more concerned about the environment in general and less willing to fly as a result.

Figure 4.11 could certainly be improved by working out total pollution from flights rather than simply tracking the number of flight tickets purchased. The data used to draw it came from the latest World Bank Indicators.[21] These were in turn derived from the International Civil Aviation Organization's statistics and estimates. Multi-stage flights are counted as a single flight if they have the same registered flight number throughout, unless it includes both international and domestic stages, in which case it is counted twice.

Crimes committed

Our environment is a far wider set of circumstances than the natural world we live in, the pollution in our air and water, the transport systems we develop, our housing, or even the quality of healthcare we provide for each other. It is about everything that surrounds us and affects our lives. Crime is one aspect of our wider environment that affects people's sense of well-being, their level of anxiety and their freedom to move about without fear.

Comparing international crime rates is notoriously difficult, partly because what is deemed to be a crime in one country may well not be a crime in another. In some countries regimes are so authoritarian that crime rates appear low because people live in fear of the authorities. In Singapore, for example, dropping chewing gum on the floor is a crime punishable so severely that almost no gum is ever dropped. Countries like Finland record all speeding offenses as crimes, which markedly increases the number of crimes reported (see Chapter 6 for more on equality and crime). However, overall, crime and imprisonment rates are far more prevalent in more unequal affluent countries. The gulf between the US and Japan is enormous and these two countries matter most because they contain such a large proportion of the population of these 25 affluent countries. Large populations carry more weight. They are less likely to be affected by idiosyncratic reasons, which is why we excluded countries with populations under two million from these comparisons.

There is less need to commit crime in a more equal country where fewer people are impoverished and everyone is less desperate about their financial situation. Burglary and robbery are rarer, people are more considerate when driving and less aggressive in general. There is also far more empathy evident in more economically equal countries. People find it easier to understand each other and are more aware of the consequences of their actions for others. Even the richest people in more equitable societies are less likely than their peers in unequal countries to

Figure 4.12: Economic inequality and crimes committed in affluent nations, 2004-2013

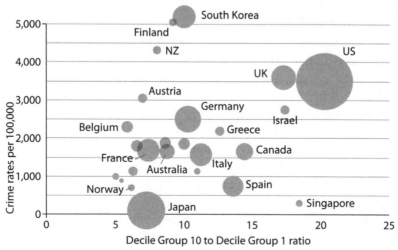

exploit others, far less likely to commit fraud or to ignore the speed limit in their souped-up cars, or even to own or drive such cars. In more equal societies both rich and poor don't feel the need to break the law to make an extra buck, or to behave in many other anti-social ways.

The source of the data for Figure 4.12 above (which illustrates the relationship) was the United Nations Office on Drugs and Crime: Statistics on Crime.[22] The creators of this dataset ask users to note that, when using the figures, any cross-national comparisons should be conducted with caution because of the differences that exist between the legal definitions of offenses in countries, or the different methods of counting and recording crimes. Data are from the latest year available spanning 2004 to 2013.

Education and environment

The environment in which we live includes our educational system, political systems and our media. In June 2016 the UK Parliament's public accounts committee said that ministers lacked a sense of urgency in making sure schools had enough teachers, despite teacher-training targets having been missed for four successive years. A Department for Education spokesperson replied to complaints of lethargy by claiming that:

'Teaching remains an attractive career and we have more teachers entering our classrooms than those choosing to leave or retire... Teacher retention has been broadly stable for 20 years and the annual average salaries for teachers in the UK are also greater than the OECD average, and higher than many of Europe's high-performing education systems like Finland, Norway or Sweden."[23]

Housing costs in Finland are far lower than in the UK, so the same salary for a teacher goes far further. Teachers in Finland are actually considered very well paid as a result and because there are far fewer people earning ridiculously high salaries due to the greater economic equality of Finland. This is also the case in Norway and Sweden. I suspect the UK spokesperson realized this. In a more unequal society it is normal to try to put a good

Figure 4.13: Economic inequality and the mathematics ability of children at age 15, 2004-13

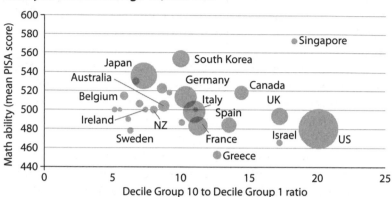

face on everything rather than to admit to a problem or failing for which you are responsible. It is common to be 'economical with the truth'.

It is also possible that the British spokesperson was just very poor at interpreting statistics (see Figure 4.14 below on young adult numeracy). In the UK in general we are very bad at mathematics and so for most of us understanding numbers is harder than it is for people who live in the Scandinavian and other more equitable countries. Figure 4.13 (above) illustrates this. The trend is in the opposite direction to the other graphs in this chapter as higher scores are better in this instance and (with the exception of Singapore) the scores tend to be higher in those countries where families, and hence children, are less separated from one another in economic terms. Although statistically significant, the picture is not straightforward, but Japan and the US again stand out. What you are seeing here is achievement at age 15, the age at which most children take their first formal exams or are preparing for them.

The source of the data used in the graph above is the mean score for mathematics in the 2012 PISA survey. A new survey was undertaken in 2015 but it did not include the data needed to produce Figure 4.14 (opposite) and so here we use the 2012 data. PISA (Programme for International Student Assessment) is the world's global metric for quality, equity and efficiency in school education.[24] It assesses the extent to which 15-year-old students have acquired key knowledge and skills in the mathematics that is considered essential for full participation in modern societies. Around 510,000 students completed the assessment in 2012, representing about 28 million 15-year-olds in the schools of the 65 participating countries and economies: all 34 OECD member countries and 31 partner economies. But PISA doesn't just test at age 15. They have also tested a subset of young adults, often up to eight years after they were last taught mathematics and when we look at these later results we see something very interesting: suddenly the circles line up far more clearly in order of their countries' level of inequality, as Figure 4.14 shows.[25]

A little of the very neat ordering of the circles in Figure 4.14 may be due to chance but the lining up could also be telling us something very important about the educational environment to which children growing up in each of these countries were being exposed. And very similar results are produced when measuring other skills, such as literacy and problem solving.

So what is going on here? Why do the circles now line up so well in Figure 4.14? One interpretation is that in more economically

Figure 4.14: Economic inequality and the mathematics ability of young adults up to age 24, 2012

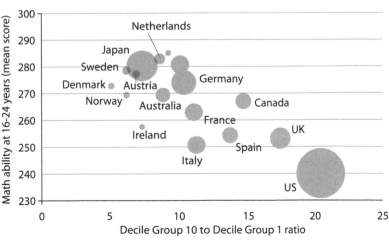

unequal countries, such as the UK and the US, children are taught mathematics with the emphasis on getting the highest grade they can on the day they take the test at the age of 15 or 16. They don't tend to enjoy mathematics and have not really learned it well because they have not been enjoying it. But they live in such unequal societies and will be going on to do jobs that are so differently rewarded, depending on their results, that their teachers and parents are desperate to try to get them the highest mark on the day – rather than making the subject fun to learn and hence better taught. In contrast, children in Japan, France and Germany learn mathematics in such a way that they are still able to give good answers when tested up to the age of 24. If this means that they are more numerate then their whole society benefits, including by having the ability to understand somewhat complex arguments about inequalities and correlations.

These last two graphs make a further point. With better data or slightly different data, correlations can become much clearer and you can get further insights into what might really be going on. For simplicity we have used a single measure of inequality, but it will not always be the best one in the circumstances. In a few years' time, how many more graphs will it be possible to draw that show even clearer correlations than those in this book? This is the first time these graphs have been drawn in any book on economic inequality. Richard Wilkinson and Kate Pickett's book *The Spirit Level* book considered many social issues, but not many environmental issues, and not issues such as educational attainment.

Should you be interested in looking into the above statistics you can find the data behind these trends in OECD Skills Outlook (2013) Table A2.7;[26] the original source being the Survey of Adult Skills (PIAAC) (2012). Educational statistics are amongst the hardest to interpret. For instance, the latest UNDP (2015) *Human Development Report* suggests that tertiary education rates, in effect enrolment rates in universities and their equivalents, are 94 per cent for the US, 71 per cent for Ireland and 62 per cent for the UK.[27] These are the rates of people who have attended some post-18 education by a certain age (or ever) as a proportion of the school-age cohort. This does not mean that the US is doing best – just that its tertiary education sector, some of which is for profit – is very good at getting people to sign up for a qualification at some point. Many are never awarded the qualification they enrolled for, and sometimes the qualification is 'not worth the paper it is written on'. Donald Trump is well known for having set up a university that raised such controversies: *'Trump University was only interested in selling every person the most expensive seminars they possibly could.'*[28]

In contrast, Finland sends 94 per cent to university or equivalent – and no university there is allowed to exist simply to make a profit. So which country might be producing the more able university graduates: Finland or the US? If university graduates are ever tested several years after they have graduated, and the results compared, the effects on the reputations of many so-called leading US and UK universities could be very telling.

Cycling and walking

All the graphs presented in this chapter show that there can be marked differences between the environments of affluent countries – for example the amount of pollution, of crime, of car and plane use – that correlate, at least to a certain extent, with the level of economic inequalities that are tolerated in each country.

Figure 4.15: Healthy behavior and economic inequality: walking and cycling 2006-10

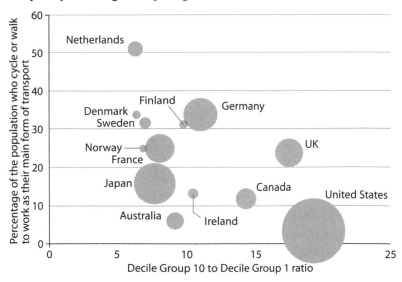

We end with something as simple as the proportion of people who cycle or walk to work in each country. This varies from 50 per cent (in the Netherlands) to less than 5 per cent (in the US). The proportion in Japan would be higher but a great many people put down the train or subway as their main form of travel despite walking or cycling to reach it each weekday morning.

Everything is connected. People are fatter in the US because they eat more food, because they sit in cars more often and for longer, because they are exposed to more advertising and eat more and buy more cars as a result, because they live in greater fear of crime and so are afraid of not driving, and because they are surrounded by other obese people and therefore don't feel so unusual if they are obese. But behind all of these factors lies the basic difference in how human beings are ranked.

Ranking really matters to people. Rank them sky high by paying them many times more than other people and they can become so conceited that they more easily treat others who are less well-off poorly, with no respect and with little empathy. When pay differentials are less and no-one's income is out-of-this world, people realize that they have far more in common with others. They then argue for cycle routes, pavements, good public transport, and to be able to afford to live near where they work.

The equality effect influences almost everything we do and so much about us. Had you been born and brought up in a different country, you would almost certainly be a very different person despite having the same genes, the same parents, the same body, the same looks and good or bad luck in your life. A majority of people in the US are the descendants of migrants who left Europe. They are not another race, but they have changed their attitudes by living under such high and rising inequality for so many recent decades. They could change again. None of us are prisoners of our pasts.

Even in the US there is still much hope – new learning occurring and new understanding growing – but it is now happening locally rather than nationally. Progress on making roads safer and moving towards better use of public transport and cycling and walking is steadily growing around the planet. In Seattle a 20-miles-per-hour (mph) limit was agreed in 2016 for all residential streets in

the city. The downtown arterial roads in that city will now be limited to 25 mph, making it far safer to cycle along those roads and to cross them as a pedestrian. Such measures also encourage people not to believe that their car will get them from place to place much more quickly than others can traveling by bus or, where it is available, by light rail.

Many cities around the world are currently making even greater progress than Seattle. All of the following cities are either now committed to or have introduced 30 kilometers per hour (19 mph) as the default speed limits on their residential roads: Dublin in Ireland, Grenoble and Paris in France, Valencia in Spain, and Milan in Italy. In November 2016 the Dutch government committed a further 40 million euros of public spending to providing more parking spaces for bicycles at train stations.[29] The Netherlands performs even better on this indicator than its low levels of economic inequality would predict (see Figure 4.15 above). However, even in the UK where progress is sometimes a little slower, a quarter of the population now lives in areas where 20 mph is becoming the normal limit on most residential roads.[30]

Lake Suwa

In 1443 Shinto priests who lived on the edge of Lake Suwa in Japan began recording the day when the lake froze over in winter and when the temperature changes created a ridge of ice across the surface. They believed that the ridge was formed by the feet of the gods as they walked over the lake and so they carried on recording the day the ridge was formed each year after that, to the present day.[31]

In the first 250 years of the priests' recordings the lake only failed to freeze over three times. Between 1955 and 2004 it failed to freeze over 12 times. Between 2005 and 2014 it failed to freeze over five times, every other year. Since 2014 it has never frozen over. There are many different records of global warming, but the Lake Suwa records are the longest and most striking.

In Europe our oldest similar records date back to 1693 and the recording of the date when the ice broke up on the River Torne, which constitutes the Swedish/Finnish border. But it was much more recently, in the US state of Hawaii, that CO_2 levels were first measured so accurately and repeatedly that it became clear what was driving global warming – as the pollutant levels rose, so did average worldwide temperatures.

There are huge differences between the cultures and histories of the 25 separate countries that have been the focus of this chapter but between them they can show us what matters and hint at why and how it matters. It has only been since the late 1970s that these countries have really begun to diverge widely to arrive now at very different levels of economic inequality. Because they have done so, a set of natural experiments has been set up which today allows research into the effects of these differences.

The preliminary conclusion based on these natural experiments is that the more economically equitable countries tend to be far more environmentally friendly across a wide range of environmental measures. There are many exceptions to this general rule, but in years to come the data will get better and more and more of these exceptions will be explained. We can anticipate that the results will be even more conclusive because there is not just one thing that appears to correlate with inequality but many, and that cannot be chance. Society affects attitudes, but people can also change society. Once we know what the driving forces are, and become fully aware of the damage that is done by inequality in environmental as well as social terms, we will know how necessary it is to embrace change.

1 A Doyle, 16 quotes from world leaders on the Paris climate agreement, World Economic Forum, 12 Dec 2015, nin.tl/leadersonParis

2 M Morgan, 'Throwaway fashion', *Daily Mail*, 9 June 2015, nin.tl/Binningclothes

3 R Jones, 'World's billionaires lose £215m each as global economy struggles', *The Guardian*, 13 Oct 2016, nin.tl/billionaireloss

4 N Stotesbury and D Dorling, 'Understanding Income Inequality and its Implications, *Statistics Views*, 21 Oct 2015, nin.tl/statsviews

5 The data underlying these estimates come from several sources and are the work of many people. Natasha Stotesbury brought the data together, drawing on the New York Times (NYT) Income Distribution Database (2014) assembled by Janet Gornick of the Luxembourg Income Study (LIS), Thierry Kruten (LIS), Branko Milanovic (LIS), David Leonhardt (NYT), and Kevin Quealy (NYT). To get a little more technical, the ratio is the fraction of mean equivalized household income (measured in 2005 PPP $) of the top divided by the same for the bottom decile. Natasha also used the OECD Income Distribution Database that was published by the OECD (2015): see 'Overview of inequality trends, key findings and policy directions' in *In It Together: Why Less Inequality Benefits All*, OECD Publishing, Paris, nin.tl/OECDdatabase . Japanese data on equivalized household disposable income shares is from D Ballas, D Dorling, T Nakaya, H Tunstall and K Hanaoka, 'Income inequalities in Japan and the UK', *Journal of Social Policy and Society*, 13,1, pp103-117, 2014. Note that the OECD Database obtained a value of 10.7 for Japan and UNU-WIDER database obtains a value of 7.9 – it all depends on how you equivalized for household size and the original source survey.

6 B Hennig and D Dorling, 'The global map of who eats too much meat', in B Kateman (ed), *The Reducetarian Diet*, Random House, 18 April 2017.

7 Accessed Feb 2017. Accessible from: http://geodata.grid.unep.ch/

8 FAOStat, http://ede.grid.unep.ch Data are from 2011 except Singapore, where the 2002 estimate is from Guardian datablog: nin.tl/meatperhead

9 USDA, United States Drought Monitor, Lincoln, Nebraska, accessed Feb 2017, droughtmonitor.unl.edu

10 FAO Aquastat, fao.org/land-water/databases-and-software/aquastat/en for world map: chartsbin.com/view/1455

11 OECD nin.tl/UNwastestats

12 UN municipal waste nin.tl/citywaste

13 World Development Indicators database, databank.worldbank.org/data/home.aspx

14 T Gore, 'Extreme Carbon Inequality', Oxfam, 2 Dec 2015, nin.tl/Oxfamoncarbon

15 Oxfam, op cit, Box 3, drawing on E Bast et al, 'The Fossil Fuel Bailout', Oilchange International, 2014, nin.tl/Priceofoil

16 J Sachs, 'The age of impunity', *Boston Globe*, 13 May 2016, nin.tl/ageimpunity

17 US Energy Information Administration, nin.tl/intenergystats

18 World Development Indicators: Mortality, wdi.worldbank.org/table/2.21#
19 'Denmark's ecological footprint is fourth largest', *The Local*, 30 Sep 2014, https://nin.tl/Denmarkfourth
20 *Living Planet Report 2016*, World Wildlife Fund, https://nin.tl/WWFLivingPlanet2016
21 World Bank data, nin.tl/WBairdata
22 UNODC, nin.tl/UNODCcrimedata
23 S Weale, 'Almost a third of teachers quit state sector within five years of qualifying', *The Guardian*, 24 Oct 2016, nin.tl/teachersquit
24 OECD PISA results, nin.tl/OECDPISA
25 N Stotesbury and D Dorling (2015), op cit.
26 OECD Skills Outlook, nin.tl/skillsOECD
27 UNDP, *Human Development Report*, 2015, Table 10, p 242, nin.tl/HDR2015table10
28 J Cassidy, 'Trump University: The Scandal That Won't Go Away', *The New Yorker*, 7 Sep 2016, newyorker.com/news/john-cassidy/trump-university-the-scandal-that-wont-go-away
29 E Baltatzi, 'Dutch government to spend 40 million euro on bicycle parking at stations', European Cyclists Federation, 3 Nov 2016, nin.tl/Dutchcycleparking
30 See: www.20splenty.org/seattle and www.20splenty.org/winningcouncilmotions
31 M Nijhuis, 'Japanese Monks Recorded the Climate for 700 Years', *National Geographic*, 26 April 2016, nin.tl/LakeSuwa

5
Population, housing and migration

This chapter begins with babies, continues with migration and ends with housing. All these issues are interconnected. There is currently a very rapid slowdown in fertility – since 1990, the absolute number of babies born has fallen in most years. Rich countries with low fertility levels need migrants to support their ageing populations – though immigration is lower to places with greater equality because there are far fewer jobs at the bottom of society to be filled. A person moving from Syria to Europe on average reduces global fertility and benefits everyone. People in refugee camps will have little to do and will have more children. If they come to Europe their children will often go to university and will delay having children themselves. Everyone who moves from one home to another is a migrant, but some migrants are seen as more deserving of equality than others.

'As long as the general population is passive, apathetic, diverted to consumerism or hatred of the vulnerable, then the powerful can do as they please, and those who survive will be left to contemplate the outcome.'

Noam Chomsky, 2011[1]

The connection between fertility, migration and equality may not be immediately obvious but they have been intertwined for a very long time.

In the country famous for declaring in 1776 that all men are created equal, the idea that all infants are equally worth saving has, as was noted in Chapter 3, become open to question. Almost a century after the US Declaration of Independence, back in the heart of the country that had been the primary colonial oppressor, a much smaller, but in its own way just as great, declaration was made by a woman in a courtroom in London in 1876. Annie Besant stood alongside Charles Bradlaugh. Both were accused of propagating obscenity because they had together published a pamphlet on birth control that explained the function of a condom.

A number of eminent Victorians opposed knowledge of contraception becoming more widespread for the reason that it would prevent supposedly brighter people being born, because it was the more knowledgeable parents who would be more likely to use it. At Annie and Charles' trial, '...some experts, including Charles Darwin, feared that as contraceptive information became widely available at low cost, it would be used by the wrong sorts of individuals and not by others, so that the salutary effects of natural selection on human perfection would be suspended'.[2]

Besant and Bradlaugh lost the trial and were found guilty of obscenity. What they had done was to make available information that the US birth-control campaigner Charles Knowlton had published 44 years earlier. He had also then been put on trial, but the greater equality of rights within the US at that time had made publication possible. Fertility, equality and migration have been intertwined for a long time.

In hindsight, we know now that as a result of the Besant-Bradlaugh trial, hundreds of thousands of people in Britain began to use birth control. It was already more commonly used in parts of the European mainland before then, but contraception quickly spread from Britain to its empire. Birth rates fell rapidly, from almost precisely nine months after the trial, and – as a result – more women had more time to work for greater rights. Emigration from Britain to the rest of the world also began to quickly decline. Britain and the rest of Europe had been the source of the greatest number of international migrants in the world before then.

Annie and Charles were not trying to increase equality in particular, and certainly did not plan to be taken to court and found guilty, but they were moved to act and their acts had huge consequences. Not long after the London trial, fertility also began to fall in India. And the number of migrants leaving Europe for the rest of the world, and especially the Americas, also began to fall. Migrants left Europe for a better, more equal life in the Americas, and at first that is what they usually found. Alexis de Tocqueville described a remarkably equitable country (at least for the settlers) in his books on democracy in America, which were published in Europe in the 1830s and 1840s.

Two European countries with some of the greatest out-migration rates to the US were Ireland (two million between 1820 and 1860) and Italy (four million between 1880 and 1924). Fertility was a little higher in these countries than in the rest of Europe even after contraceptive use became widespread because the Catholic Church tried to forbid its use (it still does). As a result the US has relatively more people who can trace their origins back to these two countries, given their initial population sizes, than from most other European countries. Today we often forget that places now in receipt of many migrants (in these cases from Eastern Europe and Africa respectively) were themselves not many generations ago the source of very high numbers of migrants.

Migration out of Ireland, Italy, and much of the rest of Europe, reduced as fertility fell and equality rose; all from just over a century ago. People have fewer children, not just when they have better access to contraception, but also – and despite religious opposition – when they begin to gain the security that means they no longer need to rely on their children to look after them in their old age.

Records on inequality in Italy and Ireland before the 1970s are very sparse, as they are for much of the world today, but we know from many sources that both countries had very unequal distributions of land ownership, wealth and income in their recent past. However, Figure 5.1 shows how, by the 1970s, those inequalities had been largely overcome, with the best-off one per cent taking only just over six per cent of all income in both Ireland and Italy in that decade.

Inequalities then rose in both countries, but more slowly in Italy. In Ireland a different model was followed in which taxes were cut and the rich were allowed to make ever-greater profits. Companies were attracted in from abroad to Ireland in the 1990s on the promise that they would be taxed at very low rates. This created the so-called 'Celtic Tiger' economy and resulted in a local economic boom and concomitant housing bubble that, when it burst in the global economic crash of 2008, hurt Ireland far more than Italy. Both countries suffered, but Italy remained a little

Figure 5.1: The take of the best-off 1% in Ireland and Italy, 1933-2009

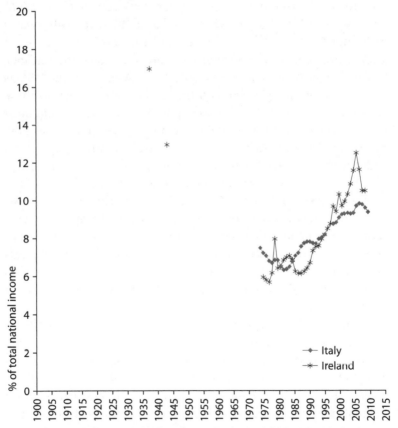

Years of consecutive data connected by a line. Where no data is shown it is missing for that year.

Source: World Wealth and Income database – accessed March 2017: http://wid.world/

more equal. And in both, in the most recent years for which there is data, inequality, as measured by the annual take of the richest one per cent, has fallen.

In Italy today fertility is very low, averaging around 1.4 children per woman; in Ireland it is just over 1.9 children, but following the financial crash in that country it fell to its lowest rate in a decade and it has fallen each year since 2008 (when it was nearer 2.1 children per woman).[3] Fertility in Ireland was a little higher in 2008 partly because an economically booming and increasingly unequal Ireland attracted poorer migrants, many from Eastern Europe. Migrants tend to be young adults of the ages that can be expected to have children. When migrants arrive in a country fertility rates can rise a little. This is currently happening in Germany, but the fertility rate there, even with such great recent migration from Syria, remains extremely low.

The period from the 1970s until now, the period in which inequalities have increased in many affluent countries such as Ireland and Italy, has been the first period in recent centuries in which there has been a worldwide deceleration in population growth. Fewer and fewer babies are being born each year in almost every country in the world. The main reason for this is the increased power of women in almost every part of the world to be able to choose to have fewer or no children, which rises relentlessly even as economic inequalities in some places grow.

When population growth slows, there is less profit to be made by older richer people. The wealthy can become less willing to share. The old model of making ever-greater profits from an ever-growing customer-base cannot work when population growth slows. Firms try to diversify, for instance selling toys around the world rather than in the most affluent markets. But as the appetite for more material goods also falls when people realize that there is a limit to how many toys a small child needs, that model also becomes less and less sustainable. You cannot make ever-greater profits selling toys to fewer and fewer children; especially as their parents become more environmentally aware and aware of what actually makes children happy. And, as Chapter 4 demonstrated, consumption per head of optional items in large quantities is already lower in the more equal affluent countries.

There is a danger of stereotyping when national statistics are used, but here is an interesting example of a toy company using new stereotypes to try to sell more toys. In 2016, in order to diversify its range of trains, Mattel (the copyright owners of 'Thomas the Tank Engine') introduced 13 new 'international' engines. These included: Carlos from Mexico, who, they said, was always 'proud and wearing a smile'; Ashima of India, who showed no fear and was happy to help out; Yoong Bao of China, a little engine apparently 'driven to achieve and make progress'; and Raul from Brazil who is 'feisty, strong and agile.'[4] As these are all countries with large populations of children, it perhaps makes sense that Mattel targeted them.

As they are also all inequitable countries, affluent parents there may be more susceptible to advertising, but as people in these countries began to have fewer and fewer children (which is still happening now) these markets also started to shrink. The most unequal of the world's very large countries is Brazil, where the

A rising tide lifts all boats?

best-off one per cent currently take somewhere between 20 per cent and 25 per cent of all income[5], more even than in South Africa. Raul needs to be 'feisty, strong and agile' just to survive in such a country. If Raul is average then he is poor. Raul lives in a country where how dark your skin is and to whom you are born affects your life chances far more than almost anywhere else in the world today. However, I suspect Mattel will not be telling his true story.

The Thomas the Tank Engine story was widely reported in the press over fears that Thomas and his friends were being made less white. There is said to be a 'crisis of whiteness'[6] at the moment. That 'crisis' is especially acute in countries such as the UK and US where people who might have been relatively poor, but felt themselves superior to others because they were white (or, earlier on, not Irish or Italian) are now being encouraged to blame their unjust poverty on other, even poorer people, especially migrants.

The plight of the 'white working class' is wrongly attributed to migrants, not to growing inequality. Migrants, it is pointed out, are willing to work for less. The same argument was made earlier about women working – that it would harm men. Behind all these arguments the problem is economic inequality, not women or migrants, or members of an ethnic minority, or a lack of respect for one particular 'white' group who feel they have indigenous rights despite so often having had immigrant forebears – as is especially the case in the US.

The right to equal treatment

In any history of equality, the position of women should be a key issue. If you live in an affluent country you will in recent years have begun to see more statements in job advertisements suggesting one organization or another is pro-diversity, including ensuring that more senior staff are female. If you live in the US you can read studies that find that such statements result in a 'more diverse applicant pool'[7], but not necessarily in more successful applicants from diverse backgrounds.

One reason why there are still fewer women 'at the top' in the US is because in more unequal countries men are often much more aggressively competitive. Also in those countries being older and white and male is more often perceived by the small minority in power as trustworthy, and as a safer pair of hands in a senior position. Upset the status quo and *anything* might happen, they say – that suggestion can be used to spread fear.

In the US today – where people at the top are paid so much more than in any other large country worldwide – there are more Chief Executive Officers named David (4.5 per cent) than there are those who are women (4.1 per cent). David is not, by the way, the most common name for a US Chief Executive, which is John (5.3 per cent). The chances of women being appointed to senior positions in the US only improve when at least two women are shortlisted for a job. The chances of someone from an ethnic minority being appointed only improve when two or more people who are not white are shortlisted. It is only on the rare occasion when that occurs that the appointment patterns actually begin to change.[8]

Women are more often to be found in senior positions in more equitable affluent countries. Views about women and people deemed to be from ethnic minorities are usually far less hostile among men from the ethnic majority in more equitable countries. Co-operation, not competition, is the order of the day when the gap between you and the person above you in terms of pay and wealth is so much narrower. There is less concern about not being promoted if promotion only brings a little extra financial reward, but a great deal more 'admin' – so naturally you then only apply because you want to do the job, not for the pay packet. How different the atmosphere is when the winner takes the lion's share and people apply for promotion mainly to increase their salaries!

To appreciate how greater equality is being won in many areas other than by securing a fairer distribution of income and wealth we first need to recognize how much and how quickly the divisions between men and women have changed in recent years, and that these changed most quickly in those most affluent countries of the world where fertility rates fell earlier. There are many links between population, migration, mortality, fertility and equality. One key clue is in how many children we now each have, or don't have.

Until very recently, worldwide, most women who survived long enough would give birth to six or more children, most of whom

Figure 5.2: Median income and average number of children per household, countries, year 2000

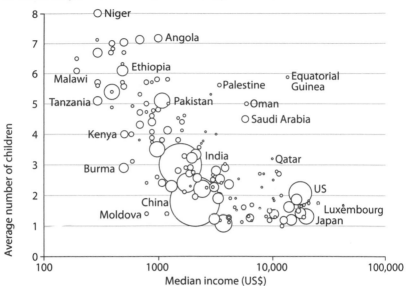

Note: The Y axis is average numbers of babies per woman and the X axis is median income in comparable US$ per year on a log scale. Circle area is proportional to the population of each country.

Source: United Nations Human Development Report and Worldmapper. Figures are for around the year 2000, as data from some regions is often very out of date.

would die before they themselves could become parents. Figure 5.2 shows that such high fertility is still the case in a few very poor countries, but the fact that it is not the case in the vast majority of places is due to the winning of greater equality between men and women, and between rich and poor across almost all of the world during the past century.

Today, across the vast majority of the world, including India, it is now much more normal to have three or fewer children; but there is still surprising variation among the populations of most affluent countries. Or perhaps it is not that surprising given how greatly such countries now differ in terms of economic inequality. And just as it is useful to examine the most affluent countries when looking at environmental inequality, it is also useful to compare them when considering the relationship between equality and demography.

In Figure 5.2 every circle represents a country, and each circle has an area proportional to that country's population. Circles are placed towards the right-hand side of the graph when average annual incomes are larger, while they are placed higher in the graph if the average woman in that country has given birth to more children. The data come from the year 2000 and so the children being measured are now approaching adulthood today. If more recent data were used the graph would look a little different (we'll come back to this later) but it would not look hugely different.

Imagine almost all the circles in the graph above being in the top left hand corner of the graph, the space where average incomes are low and fertility is high. That is where most of them were a century ago. As median incomes rose and equality increased, the circles moved towards the right. Then education became more widespread, infant mortality was reduced, women's rights were won and use of better contraception became more common. As a result, fertility fell, and the circles all began to fall, some more rapidly than others.

A very strong contemporary argument for the benefits of greater equality is to consider how it has altered the life chances of women in recent decades. Those gains may have partly been made following other emancipations, including liberation from formal slavery, winning greater employment rights and free secondary education for all children. Almost all the circles (apart from a few of the very lowest) are still moving downwards and doing so far faster than the circles move rightwards. Median incomes only rise slowly and in a few cases fall, while most people in the world now live in countries that are below the two-children-per-woman line. The large majority of young adults in the world were born into larger families than the families they will have themselves.

Except where there is a short-lived and poorly shared out oil bonanza, such as in Equatorial Guinea, it was winning more rights that made it possible for a country to have a median annual income in excess of $10,000 per person a year. But when median incomes are higher than that, as Figure 5.2 shows, greater wealth does not necessarily result in further falls in fertility. In the more unequal US, women had (until very recently) almost twice as many children as in Japan, and many more on average than in Europe. This is because, after a certain point, the effect of reducing inequality becomes more relevant than affluence in terms of reducing fertility.

Why women's rights change everything

A gain in equality in one area can lead to unanticipated progress elsewhere. Greater rights for women, for instance, almost always result in fewer children being born and often in more equality within the subsequent smaller generation. This is one reason why this chapter will keep returning to fertility as a quantitative example of the benefits of greater equality. It is a complex issue because fertility can also fall when people delay starting families because of economic recession and housing shortage but, in general, when we are more equal, we reproduce more sustainably.

Many worry about there being too many people in the world, but it is those in more equitable affluent societies who have the fewest babies. Greater equality is partly greater freedom from fear. In a more equitable society, you need have less fear for the future of your children and about your own capacity to prosper in old age. In a more equitable society, far fewer children are very poor, have hopeless prospects and very few die in childhood. But there are also better collective pension systems, better old-age care facilities, better health services and better housing for the elderly. Greater equality results in more stability and could well be one reason behind the recent rapid global decline in human fertility. Income *equality* in most of the Western world rose as family sizes *fell* from 1910 to 1980. Across North America, the average number of children per woman had fallen to a minimum of 1.79 by the end of that period, but rose thereafter as social inequalities increased.

Table 6 shows the average number of babies born worldwide and in each continent every five years from 1950 onwards. It shows how fertility is now lowest in the most equitable of affluent continents (Europe) and highest in the second most unequal and the poorest of continents (Africa). Thus one of the widest benefits of egalitarianism can be a world more quickly approaching human

173

Table 6: Total fertility (children born to each woman on average), 1950-2010, by continent

Region	1950 -55	1955 -60	1960 -65	1965 -70	1970 -75	1975 -80	1980 -85	1985 -90	1990 -95	1995 -2000	2000 -05	2005 -10
World	4.95	4.89	4.91	4.85	4.45	3.84	3.59	3.39	3.04	2.79	2.62	2.52
Africa	6.60	6.66	6.71	6.68	6.67	6.57	6.38	6.07	5.62	5.23	4.94	4.64
Asia	5.82	5.58	5.58	5.61	5.00	4.05	3.69	3.43	2.97	2.65	2.41	2.28
Latin America/ Caribbean	5.86	5.91	5.96	5.53	5.02	4.47	3.93	3.42	3.02	2.73	2.53	2.30
North America	3.33	3.64	3.36	2.55	2.05	1.80	1.79	1.87	1.96	1.93	1.99	2.03
Europe	2.65	2.64	2.56	2.35	2.17	1.98	1.89	1.82	1.57	1.42	1.43	1.53
Oceania	3.81	4.02	4.00	3.57	3.30	2.74	2.57	2.49	2.49	2.45	2.41	2.49

Source: United Nations, Department of Economic and Social Affairs, Population Division: World Population Prospects DEMOBASE extract, 2011

population stability. The continent of Africa is still recovering from the forced migration of millions of people taken during the centuries of slavery and the damage done to traditional societies over the course of the generations in which slave-taking occurred. It is also recovering from the colonialism that was then imposed. How everything fell apart subsequently – as independence *without* order, *without* fair terms of trade, and *with* continued exploitation – has repercussions for generations.

Chinua Achebe's 1958 novel *Things Fall Apart*, which was published during the first decade of data shown in Table 6, gained its title from the lines in Yeats' poem 'The Second Coming': 'Things fall apart; the center cannot hold; Mere anarchy is loosed upon the world'.[9] Increased anarchy resulted for a time in rising fertility in Africa in the 1950s and early 1960s. It has been falling ever since.

Had greater equality not been achieved over the course of most of the last century in most countries of the world then it is very doubtful that families would have felt confident enough about their futures – and that women would have been powerful enough to express their wishes – to have fewer children. In most couples the woman on average favors having fewer children than the man.

The most recent preliminary figures for the 2010-15 period,[10] and the most recent revisions made to the 2005-10 estimates, suggest that the worldwide fall in fertility is continuing at least as strongly as before, but that it had not previously been falling as fast as we thought it was in 2011. The 2005-10 total global estimate was revised upwards to 2.56 in the latest UN statistical release which illustrates how tables such as that above (Table 6) show a picture of much less certainty than they appear to show; but the 2010-15 estimates do show a continued fall to 2.51 children per woman worldwide.

This small change in the figures in that table have resulted in the current (2015-based) UN estimate for the population of the world in 2100 to be 11.2 billion people – it had previously been lower, nearer to 10 billion people. An extra billion is added in future if the average women in 2005-10 had 2.56 children rather than 2.52 children (as in the table above). That is because of the children they themselves will most probably have. However, these projections are extremely volatile and are very likely influenced by not taking into account previous baby booms. More importantly, given the relationship between winning greater equality and having fewer children, if greater equality continues to be won then 11.2 billion is surely a considerable overestimate. Therefore the very recent evidence presented earlier in this book, especially in Chapter 1, that increases in equality might be spreading faster than we had thought in 2011 suggests that the future total worldwide human population might be lower in 2050 and 2100 than is currently predicted – possibly much lower, reaching nearer 9 or 10 billion people rather than 11 billion. It may all depend on how much more equality is won in the coming years.

According to the latest, 2015-based UN population revisions, fertility rates in Africa continue to fall by about four per cent every five years; in Asia by the same, to now stand at just 2.20 children per woman across that enormous continent, and still falling fast (just over 2 means stability, less than 2 means decline); across Latin America and the Caribbean the total fertility rate is now estimated to be 2.15; in North America 1.86; in Europe 1.60; and in Oceania 2.42. Among the continents only Europe has had a slight rise in fertility very recently, but it still has the lowest rate. In Africa the most recently revised rate is 4.71 children per woman, slightly higher than the estimate published in 2011 used in the table above, but still representing a rapid fall from a few years earlier. It is in Africa that the greatest increase in equality is needed if global population is to stabilize earlier than currently predicted by the UN. It is in Africa where the center needs to begin to hold more strongly and where any increases in equality that resulted from this would have the greatest worldwide effect.

Any table containing very recent data will always be subject to revision, but the revisions that have been made suggest no fall in the rate of progress towards population stability and even a suggestion that European rates might be stabilizing at a very low rate of between 1.4 and 1.6 children per woman, rather than falling ever further or rising back to 2.0, and that this is partly due to in-migration. The situation shown in the table above has improved so much because, with the exception of Africa, inequalities between continents have improved. Living standards are rising in the poorer continents faster than in the richer ones (although inequalities within countries and continents can and often are still growing).

As well as worrying about what the very latest figures might mean, we should also be careful still to celebrate the gains in equality that have recently been made. Far more is written on the global rise in income and wealth inequality and the growing gaps between different social classes of people than, for example, on the closing gap in income inequalities *between* countries in recent years.[11] If more equitable richer countries in future years begin to exploit poorer countries less, and if more inequitable richer countries become more equitable and behave a little more like other affluent countries, then achieving greater equality and rising living standards in poor countries is a far less daunting task. It seems very likely that a world in which more women have more power might be one in which very antisocial behavior, including greed, is less tolerated.

Women form the largest group of people to have recently won much greater equality in most countries of the world. Of course there is so much further yet to go before women are treated as equal to men. However, only a century ago, in most of the newly industrializing world, the position of women was little different to that of slaves. We so easily forget how quickly we can and have changed.

Figure 5.3 contains two graphs. The top one shows each continent of the world again with a circle drawn in proportion to its population. Three low-fertility countries are also shown: Germany, Sweden (the smallest circle) and Japan. The highest circle in the top graph is Africa; this is because the vertical axis of the graph is the average number of children each woman gives birth to. The circle drawn furthest to the right is Latin America and the Caribbean because the horizontal axis is of income inequality, which here is the ratio between the income of the best-off tenth and the worst-off tenth of households.

All countries are shown in the bottom graph in Figure 5.3. In general, the more equitable a country or continent is, the lower the fertility. A slowly declining human population would have a fertility rate of around, or just under, two children per woman. A slowly declining population is stable, especially as we continue to live longer and want on aggregate to consume and pollute less overall.

In Japan, as most recently recorded, the total fertility rate had risen from 1.30 children per woman in 2005 to 1.40 by 2015. It appears to no longer be falling, but that rate still implies great population declines to come. In Germany the total fertility rate rose from 1.35 to 1.39 over the same time period, again no longer falling so fast and in the case of Germany we expect it to rise a little higher due to the recent arrival of many migrants. In Sweden it rose from 1.67 to 1.92 over this 10-year period; again, migration helped (as recent migrants had more children), but there were also progressive policies introduced to make it easier for all women to have children, Most importantly, in none of these countries is fertility at all likely to reach replacement levels in the foreseeable future, if ever again.

In the two European countries of Germany and Sweden in-migration helps slow down the falls in population that would otherwise happen and also reduces the extent to which the population would otherwise be ageing. In Japan there is very low in-migration, mainly due to the lack of low-paid jobs in a country that is so equitable, but that low rate of in-migration is also due to language barriers and some racism. It is not impossible to imagine Japan taking more migrants in future, just as Sweden

Figure 5.3: Total fertility and income inequality in the year 2000, by continent and country

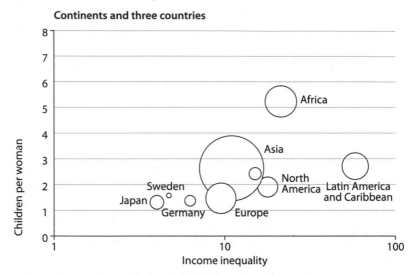

Continents and three countries

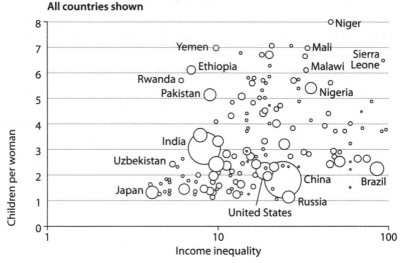

All countries shown

Note: According to the United Nations' Economic Commission for Latin America, the decile ratio (share of total income for the top 10 per cent of wage earners divided by the bottom 10 per cent) in Latin America was 45 to 1, whilst that of Cuba was only 4 to 1. (en.wikipedia.org/wiki/EconomyofCuba)

Source: Data is from UNDP report 2004 and worldmapper using table 14 of the UNDP report. Income inequality is the ratio of the income of the richest tenth to the poorest tenth and is drawn on a log scale as the horizontal axis of each graph. The vertical axis of each is average lifetime number of live babies born per woman.

and Germany have done. While robots are a great substitute for humans when it comes to assembling cars, they are a very unlikely substitute for humans when it comes to providing care.

Migrants moving to Japan are likely to adapt quickly to the fertility patterns of their new country. This happens with almost all migrants in the world and so their own fertility would be lower than it would have been had they not migrated. In June 2016 the prime minister of Japan announced the introduction of the world's '...fastest permanent-residency cards for skilled migrants.'[12] Of course, Japan needs migrants with many different kinds of skills, not least the skills required to look after very elderly people, of which it has so many because it became so equal in the immediate aftermath of the Second World War (people in more equitable countries tend to live longer).

There is a wide range of fertility amongst economically unequal countries, but more equal countries all appear to have low fertility. The US, which makes up most of North America (by population), is partly obscured on the bottom graph. China, which is a similarly unequal country, has lower fertility than the US, partly through coercion (although that is now largely ending). The bottom graph shows that very economically *equal* countries never have high fertility, but that low fertility is possible when economic inequalities are great, as demonstrated by Russia, and to a lesser extent by Brazil.

It is now not just in some of the richest countries on earth, but also in some of the poorer (but also more equitable) countries, that women have the fewest children. In Figure 5.4 affluent countries are colored the lightest grey, and the poorest countries the darkest. Countries are divided into six groups according to their levels of income inequality, not their wealth. In the first group, for example, people with an income at the bottom of the top 10 per cent receive around six times the income of those at the top of the bottom 10 per cent. In these most equitable countries fertility is on average well below replacement rate (2.1 children per woman) or only just above in the poorest of these more equitable countries.

Fertility in the world is lowest – at around 1.3 children per woman – in those very affluent countries that are most equitable.

However, as we have seen above, in many of those it has recently risen again to around 1.4 children so greater equality does not mean *ever* fewer children – but it does mean stability, as we need fewer children to compensate for the population increase that results when we all on average live longer. What Figure 5.4 makes most clear is that if we wish to live on a planet with a stable human population then we cannot tolerate gross inequality decile ratios (top 10 per cent measured against bottom 10 per cent) within countries of over 20, or inequalities between countries that result in average incomes being below, or as low as $12 to $23 a day.

Very poor countries tend in most cases to be very unequal and to have high fertility rates. Greater prosperity and greater equality tend to be accompanied by lower overall fertility. When women win more rights, more education and are paid more or are otherwise better off in other ways, fertility falls and overall equality rises. You may feel I have already made this clear but it

Figure 5.4: Income inequality and average number of children per woman by median income, 2000

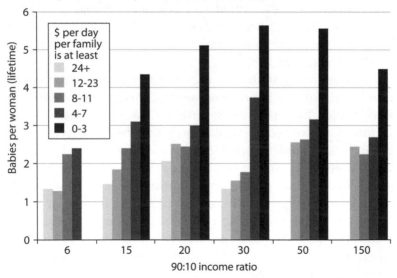

Source: Data is from around the year 2000 from United Nations sources. Height of each bar is the average number of children born to all women living in those countries with the median income indicated by the shade of the bar and with the inequality range shown at the base of the bar.

is necessary to keep repeating it because it is such a vital point. It is important environmentally, because a stable population is far more sustainable than one that is forever growing. It is also important economically because a stable, better-educated and ageing population is harder to exploit by firms that are solely seeking to maximize their profits (the old are wiser and less susceptible to advertising). And it is important politically because people should be free to choose the number of children they have and not be forced by circumstance to have more to be secure, or to have fewer because gross inequality means that they cannot afford to become parents, as has been increasingly the case in Russia and Brazil but also, more recently, for many young couples in the UK and the US.

Winning greater equality may be a precursor to achieving higher living standards. The American Revolution is a key example that has been mentioned at several points in this book: it led to substantial rises in living standards in the US from the late 18th century through to the mid-20th century. However, losing a war is as effective as winning a revolution when it comes to gaining greater equality, as Japan and Germany have demonstrated. This is because wars are extremely costly and much of the money to fight them has inevitably to be gathered from the wealthy. Subsequently the victors have no vested interest in recompensing those wealthy people in the countries they vanquished. In contrast, if the status quo is not challenged for decades, then inequalities can slowly but inexorably grow. However, nowadays no greatly inequitable country has ever become well off: note that the best-off bars are missing from the two right-hand groups in Figure 5.4 because no countries qualify to be in those categories. Countries became better off when they were more equal.

Of the most *equitable* group of countries in Figure 5.4, none have median incomes of under $4 a day and of the most *inequitable* groups of countries, none have median incomes over $24 a day. More equitable countries tend to have both better-off citizens and more sustainable birth rates. When combined with higher living standards, greater equality appears to be driving the slowdown in the growth of global human population. That slowdown will be sustained and possibly enhanced if we secure greater equality in the immediate decades to come. If we want to live on a planet that is home to fewer people in future and if we want our grandchildren to be living in a better environment, then we need greater economic equality for our children.

Health and equality

Countries that are more economically equitable tend to place more emphasis on funding for health and social care. When the UK introduced its National Health Service in 1948 it was becoming rapidly more equal in economic terms. Part of the reason for the introduction of the health service was that the upper middle classes were no longer so well off as they had been before the 1930s and fewer of them could afford to pay for adequate private healthcare in the aftermath of World War Two.

Today the UK National Health Service remains one of the most efficient and accessible healthcare systems to be found anywhere in the world, but it is now being starved of cash. All other affluent countries in Western Europe spend a higher proportion of their GDP on public health than the UK does. Greece and Italy spent slightly less in some years immediately after their extreme post-2008 austerity, but by 2016 the planned cuts to health spending in the UK were greater again and so those two countries will now again be spending more per head. As a result of the health funding cuts since 2010, hospital deficits in the UK have soared and spending is set to increase by only 0.2 per cent per year from 2016 until 2020 whereas annual rises of 4 per cent would be needed just to maintain the current service, given the growing elderly population.[13]

In contrast to the UK and the US (which is far worse than the UK when it comes to public healthcare), more equitable affluent countries routinely dedicate a greater share of their national income to collective healthcare and to improving public health, rather than to ineffective private healthcare. Enormous rises in public spending would be required to bring the funding of the UK health service up to the level at which government-supported health services in Germany and Switzerland are funded. For instance, to compete with the Swiss, health funding per person in the UK would have to double.[14]

It is no coincidence that the top one per cent in Switzerland take only about half of what their equivalents in the UK do each year in personal income. In Switzerland people are paid more equally, and hence have a higher median income, and they are also taxed more so as to provide better healthcare for everyone. You can never know when you might need healthcare. Luckily most of us don't need much but it makes sense to ensure as good a general provision as possible rather than simply attempt to insure yourself with privately provided, often limited, care via a premium that depends on your age and previous claims.

Accepting gross inequality as normal in the UK does not just mean living with a depleted and deteriorating health service.[15] State social care in the UK (help in old age especially) is also quite miserly for an affluent country. The number of people assessed as eligible to access such social care fell by 26 per cent between 2009 and 2014 in the UK despite a rise in the elderly population – the government moved the goalposts partly because it dislikes public provision of services anyway and partly because it wanted to avoid the cost. The number of nurses available to help people, especially the elderly in the community, has been reduced and there are now fewer care workers being employed in care homes per increasingly frail elderly resident. This has happened partly because the majority of British care homes are now privately run for a profit. The UK is a good case study to demonstrate the converse of the equality effect as it shows what happens when you allow inequality to grow and who then suffers.[16] The elderly fare especially badly in such circumstances, including many who were once quite affluent in their own middle age.

In September 2016 it was predicted that at least one of the private providers that local authorities in the UK currently use to deliver social care would soon go bankrupt and fail to operate as a result of state funding cuts and, it has to be said loudly and repeatedly, as a result of the inefficiency of allowing shareholders to profit from providing such care. It is anticipated that by 2019 in the UK there will be a funding gap of around £1.25 billion (currently around $1.6 billion) for adult social care and one of £1.9 billion for children's services. If these cuts are not rectified – by increasing taxation on the rich and ensuring that more care is provided publicly rather than privately – the currently inadequate and overstretched services will have to be reduced even further.[17] Grossly unequal affluent countries, such as the UK, see many of their residents now with a quality of life similar to that experienced in far poorer countries. So what did the government of the UK do, the one that oversaw the cuts that led to this situation? It decided to measure how happy people were from the point it began to cut their public services! In 2010 the (then) UK Prime Minister, David Cameron, announced that he would ask his statisticians to create a happiness index, measuring 'personal well-being' via questions such as: 'Overall, how satisfied are you with your life nowadays?'; 'Overall, how happy did you feel yesterday?'; and 'Overall, how anxious did you feel yesterday?'. Presumably they did not want to risk asking about the whole of the past week, month or year!

In 2014 statisticians compared such measures with others taken across the rest of Europe and discovered that the UK was the European country where people were both least likely to know their neighbors and also least likely to have friendships on which they could rely in a crisis. The UK was named the 'the loneliness capital of Europe' by *The Telegraph* newspaper.[18] If you consider the four graphs in Figure 5.5, you can see one of the reasons why that might be.

Within the UK a key component of David Cameron's happiness index was a measure of self-reported health. This particular measure became a national statistic each year in an obscure report. In every year from 2010 onwards the key self-reported health component of the measure worsened, as Figure 5.5 below illustrates. Fewer and fewer people in the UK declared that they were completely satisfied with their health. The proportion that said they were most dissatisfied doubled after 2011.

In March 2016 the worst-ever sets of statistics on UK self-reported health were revealed. These are not shown in Figure 5.5 as they were not disaggregated in the same way, but the total measure for health satisfaction was the lowest recorded in a long time series dating back to 2002.[19] Most of those saying their health had declined were elderly. Within a few years of these falls in self-reported health occurring, actual mortality rates among the elderly in the UK began to rise significantly for the first time since the Second World War.

Figure 5.5: Trends in self-reported health used by ONS in annual UK well-being reporting 2009-13

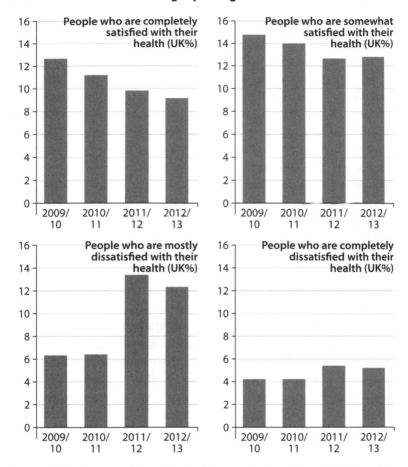

Source: D Dorling, Comment on: New statistics for old?—measuring the wellbeing of the UK, *Journal of the Royal Statistical Society*, vol. 180, issue 1, pp.3-43, 2017, nin.tl/statscomment

It is not just the elderly who suffer in the UK, although their suffering is more easily measured once their death rates rise.[20] In 2016 UNICEF's executive director in the UK identified the urgent need to reduce income inequality between families across Britain and Northern Ireland because the UK had the largest difference in children's health outcomes by social class of all the many countries that UNICEF reported on that year. In particular, many parents' low income affected their children's chances of eating fruit or vegetables, as well as creating one of the largest gaps in access to physical exercise and activities. Inequalities in education were also flagged, '...with the UK being ranked 25th out of the 37 countries – behind Slovenia, Poland and Romania – in reading, maths and science. Denmark was ranked first overall by UNICEF.'[21]

So, in a very unequal affluent country, such as the UK, spending on health, social care and education can easily be cut, and many privatized services become subject to the risk of 'market failure'. It is not only the privatized care services that now more often risk bankruptcy, including those care homes for the elderly. Personal bankruptcy in England and Wales increased by seven per cent between July and September 2016, but the overall personal bankruptcy rate is still slightly less than it was a year earlier. The reason being that far more insolvent people are opting for IVAs (Individual Voluntary Arrangements) with their creditors instead of bankruptcy. Such IVA insolvencies rose by 11 per cent between July and September 2016, and were up by 29 per cent on a year before, more than outstripping the slight fall in bankruptcy.[22] At the same time, 2.5 times as many private tenants are being evicted from their homes than was the case seven years ago in the UK. This is not always because they cannot pay the rent but sometimes just because their landlord wishes to sell their home and reap the profit. The landlord can evict tenants with just two months' notice under UK law.[23] So often the equality effect is best demonstrated by its converse, by highlighting just how many things go wrong for a population when greater inequality is tolerated.

A few years after people's health began to decline in the UK the population became more desperate, especially in those areas where the declines in health had been greatest. There was a close link between areas that voted most heavily to leave the EU in the Brexit referendum of 2016 and where the elderly lived. The elderly were the group who saw their health deteriorate the most after 2010, and they were promised that an extra £350 million a week would be spent on the NHS if they voted to leave. That promise turned out to be a lie. Then, just a few months later, almost exactly the same phenomenon was seen in the US, where

**Figure 5.6: Poor rates of health closely predicted
the swings in votes to Trump in the US in 2016**

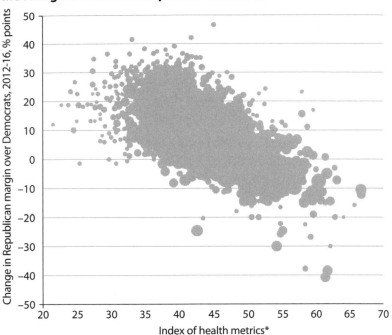

Sources: Atlas of US Presidential Elections; Census Bureau; IPUMS; Institute for Health
Metrics and Evaluation; *The Economist*. Note – each circle is a US county.

*Weighted index of obesity, diabetes, heavy drinking, physical exercise and life expectancy, 2010-12

one of the strongest predictors of whether an area saw an increase
in the Republican vote and hence helped usher in the election of
Donald Trump was whether health had been deteriorating more
greatly there, as Figure 5.6 makes clear. [24] Trump also promised to
improve health services. That too was a lie.

Housing: building equality

In the UK the year 2016 began with Will Self, a writer famous for
producing elaborate fiction, explaining in the *Financial Times* the
non-fiction of how the financial system and the role of housing
within it worked for bankers:

'The current housing crisis is not so much emblematic of a
transmogrification from a social market economy to a neoliberal

one. It is constitutive of that process: the asset transfer from the state to the rich; the pump-priming of the value of those assets; the forcing of the poor into more expensive private rental accommodation – all of which measures are underpinned by a financial system heavily dependent on mortgage lending. Of all British bank loans, 76 per cent are for property, and 64 per cent for residential property alone. Any radical reform of the system entailing a fall in land and house prices would, ipso facto, result in a fundamental destabilization of the banking system.'[25]

The housing crisis in the UK is now so bad that despite its recent criminalization, squatting in England is on the rise, especially in London. The Metropolitan Police say that most buildings that squatters live in have been abandoned or are otherwise empty, but still such sensible actions are deemed criminal.[26] When people's only choice is criminalized, the legality of the law itself is discredited. In the two years since the law in the UK was changed to make squatting a criminal offense, at least 588 people have been arrested for squatting, mostly in winter. Some 200 of these were actually prosecuted but only 51 were then convicted. The law has effectively been used to harass homeless people.[27]

During 2016 report after report lamented the state of housing in the UK and especially in London; not only its physical state but its cost, which rose both due to rising economic inequalities (with a minority of landlords becoming very rich) and also then caused those inequalities to rise even further and faster because of rents depleting any disposable income. Researchers at the Centre for London explained that *'London's housing crisis is by now infamous: it is the top issue for London voters and for London businesses, who are increasingly worried about recruitment.'*[28] There were calls for capital gains tax to be increased to end speculation. John Healey, the UK Shadow Housing Minister in 2016, explained to public audiences that *'by wealth the top 10 per cent of households have 877 times more than the bottom 10 per cent.'*[29] He was saying this because he too could now see the need to tax high housing wealth.

The UK law is designed to criminalize people simply seeking shelter while it protects investors, including many from countries

Concrete canyons

such as Kuwait, Russia and Saudi Arabia, who often buy property to leave it empty. In 2016 London estate agents were promising such investors '...*expected cumulative capital growth of 19.1 per cent over the next five years*'.[30] Eventually even the rich will lose out as inequality increases because there will come a day when housing prices can no longer rise any higher. Investors trying to pre-empt that will start selling and be the trigger for a housing price crash. London would have done better had it followed the example of Paris, where only 3 per cent of the overall 150-per-cent increase in housing prices between 1993 and 2008 was attributed to 'overseas investors'.[31]

Evictions from private rented accommodation in London doubled in the year to 2016. The rise began shortly after the financial crash and is accelerating at the time of writing.[32] The rising line in Figure 5.7 shows how, from 2010 to 2015, loss of an AST, an Assured Shorthold Tenancy, most often through being unable to pay the uncontrolled rent, became cited three times more often as the reason why a family with children became

Figure 5.7: Reasons families find themselves homeless in England, 1998-2015

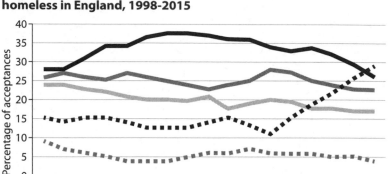

■■■ Loss of an AST   ▬ Relative/friend ceased accommodating

■■■ Mortgage/rent arrears   ▬ Relationship breakdown   ▬ Other

Source: K Webb, Bringing homelessness to the forefront of the political agenda in England, London, Shelter, 7 October, 2016, nin.tl/katewebb

homeless. ASTs are now the most usual form of tenancy in the UK. These figures are only recorded for families with children. Such families are the main vulnerable group for which the government in the UK (outside of Scotland) believes it has any housing responsibility.

For other Europeans, the UK again serves to illustrate the inequality effect, and what happens when the laws of a country are changed in favor of the affluent because they have become so rich that they can effectively buy the interest of political parties – often through obtaining media support – and hence politicians, and then, by getting the laws they want, they control the judiciary. But rising economic inequalities are only sustainable for a relatively short number of years and the anger now building up in the UK testifies to that. Public support for politicians when there is great inequality relies on finding scapegoats to blame, diverting the blame from the politicians and businesspeople who are maintaining the existing inequalities.

Migrants have long been a favored scapegoat. But we should remember that the poor do not have a monopoly on migration, despite 'migrant' often being associated with poverty. The rich, and especially the extremely rich, migrate more than anyone else in the world. They just do it in such a way that they are often not viewed as migrants. They have more holidays than anyone else, they own more homes than anyone else, they move between countries more than anyone else and they send their children away to schools, sometimes in other countries, more than anyone else. The powerful, in the US and internationally, send their children to universities such as Harvard. The average household income of parents at Harvard University is now $450,000 per year.[33]

If there are not enough migrants you can blame the poor, the supposedly feckless, you can distract your local population by taking part in foreign wars, but eventually you run out of excuses for why so many residents of a country find it so hard to cope but know there was a time when their parents were able to find a home and start a family much more easily.

In June 2016 the UK voted to leave the European Union mainly because of a campaign that blamed all the country's woes on EU membership and particularly on the migrants that arrived from the rest of Europe as a result. Having had that vote, who will be blamed next? Migrants were not the reason housing was so hard to come by in the UK in 2016. Housing had becoming increasingly unequally shared out since the late 1970s, too much public housing had been privatized and too much was being primarily used as an investment. Underused housing, uncontrolled rents and insecure tenancies had created a toxic mix.[34]

In countries and times of greater equality there tends to be more public house-building as private individuals can rarely all house themselves given the expense of building a home, just as private individuals cannot set up and run their own schools or hospitals. Because houses last so much longer than people, there is no need for all individuals to be able to raise the full initial cost of their housing or to pay much more than that over their lifetime in rent. Homes need to be built when immigration is adding to overall population numbers, but also to renew housing stock and because people everywhere will soon need more user-friendly apartments for the growing elderly population.

Rent regulations in more equal European countries

Almost all European countries both have lower income inequality than the UK and also ensure by law that tenants who rent their homes enjoy much longer tenancies. To be able to do this, they have to give tenants a degree of certainty about how much rents can rise during the time they live in a property; otherwise the landlord can easily evict them simply by raising the rent. This is why rent regulation is so important. It is the only defense against arbitrary eviction.

- In Germany half of all householders rent privately. Often they are renting via very standard leases, which are offered over their lifetime. 'You can live in the property until you die,'[35] according to Kath Scanlon, a researcher at the London School of Economics interviewed in 2016 by *The Observer*. This compares to standard tenancy agreements in the UK that at most give you a right to stay for the first 12 months and allow your landlord to evict you at just two months' notice. Tenants in Germany often furnish their home and also decorate it, fit kitchens and cupboards and live very much like people with a mortgage live in the UK. Rent caps are enforced so that landlords cannot set whatever rent they wish for new tenants. Rents are also not permitted to rise at all quickly. Tenants' groups organize to complain when landlords are not penalized for breaking the law.

- In Sweden private-sector rent levels are set through negotiations between representatives of landlords and tenants in a very similar way to how trade unions and employers negotiate over pay levels, rather than encouraging individuals to try to bargain individually about their pay. In 2014, the whole of Stockholm was limited to increasing rents by only 1.12 per cent as a result of this. Just as in the UK, there are shortages of properties available in Stockholm, but of course the rent caps do not cause these shortages, just as not having rent caps in the UK doesn't result in

If the equality effect is to be employed in the field of housing then we need a new, more inclusive model of public home-building. In countries such as the UK and US new public housing is also needed in areas of high population turnover. However, where people don't come and go so quickly a new form of social

a great increase in the supply of high-quality rental housing at reasonable cost.

- In the Netherlands the rent charged for any property is fixed by government. Government officials inspect it for quality and then fix the rents permitted depending on its quality. The factors involved in assessing quality include the amount of space both inside and outside the property and the quality of the building, such as whether it has double-glazing. Location is not a factor in assessing quality. For prime properties that are large, well built and also very well maintained by the landlord, no rent regulation is imposed.

- Denmark has two forms of rent regulation, one for properties built before 1991 and one for those built afterwards. Again worries are raised about whether rent regulation restricts the supply of housing but, when Denmark is compared to the UK or the US, it becomes clear just how much better its housing is. This is one of the reasons why children in Denmark fare so well relative to children in most other affluent countries. Denmark also does not suffer homelessness on the scale of countries with a supposedly more 'free market'. 'Free' housing markets merely give a free rein to those with most money.

- In France a new set of rent regulations came into force in the capital, Paris, in August 2015. These regulations state that private rents 'must be no more than 20 per cent above or 30 per cent below the median rental price for the area'. Of course the rules prompted anger among property agencies and landlords, who claimed they would deter investment. But the evidence of more unequal countries is clear: being able to charge whatever you like does not result in enough housing being made available. The Paris controls should also help reduce rent inflation there when financial and other firms move parts of their workforce to that city during the Brexit process.

housing might be possible that is managed at a very local level – rather like the way a village green is looked after, or a local primary school. It could be called 'local housing'.

Progressive politics always comes up with new models. At first in the UK it was housing associations, and then it was council housing, which was more democratic but still controlled by the local authority. Local housing would be owned and managed more locally – with a 'use it or lose it' allocation of money. Tenants would be far more involved in the running, as parent-governors are with local schools. The local authority would still have oversight, as it does with schools – or used to, as unfortunately schools are also being semi-privatized in the UK today through being turned into academies. Given the high percentage of more numerate university graduates now, the UK population should be able to manage such local housing in a way that it could not have done in the 1930s.

The UK does not have to embrace any particular notion in order to solve its housing problems – but it does need an idea that is as radical as council housing was in its day. National government could make available funding for more new homes to be built. Local authorities would have to help with the identification and planning of sites. But then the housing would be maintained and the lettings allocated at a smaller geographical scale and often the sites would be much smaller than the council estates of the 1950s. Between April 2015 and March 2016 there was an increase of 11 per cent in the number of homes in England, mainly because 12,824 offices were converted into flats for people to live in.[36] There is a better future for those impersonal open-plan office blocks – but that better future will not involve being run by unregulated private landlords.

Before inventing new schemes it is worth looking at what more equitable countries already do. Germany, Sweden, the Netherlands, Denmark and France already all have better models than the model currently in place in the UK and the US (see text box on pages 192-3 above).

It does not have to happen all at once

In times and places of greater equality, people are better housed, their housing costs are lower and the quality of their homes is higher. Women are treated more equally although still nowhere are they treated as well as men in terms of pay and power. Children are happier and healthier where equality is greater. Migrants are blamed less for local woes, partly because there are fewer local woes to blame them for. People have fewer children and are looked after better in their old age, enjoy better health and live longer. The rich mix far more with the rest of society because the rich are less rich and the poor are less poor and everyone has a more similar lifestyle. In an unequal society, the rich find mixing with the poor scary, and the poor rightly fear the rich.

If you think it is *not important* for everyone to be able to secure a nice home, to not have to worry about being evicted, to have children who are able to look forward to a future with less anxiety, to have your elderly population not living in fear that their care will not be a priority – then greater equality is *not for you*. But if you care about those around you and are not certain of your own prowess in a survival-of-the-fittest competition in which the winners take almost all, then you would be better off living in a state of greater equality. If you live in the UK or the US and think that the ideas presented in this book are all very well and good, but virtually impossible to implement where you live, remember this: it does not all have to be done in one go, but can be taken little step by little step. It is not reaching your goal that is most important, but knowing that you are going in the right direction. We are all happier as soon as we know things are getting better for us, for our children and especially for our grandchildren. You push and others will push with and after you. And it is so much easier to know what direction to go in when people in other countries have shown you the way. It would be sensible for people in the US to look beyond that country's borders for ideas, and for the UK *not* to turn to the US for inspiration so frequently, ignoring what is being achieved in the rest of Europe.

As fertility continues to fall worldwide, as incomes slowly rise in newly affluent countries, people across the planet will begin to look more closely at the lives and experiences of the residents of the world's most affluent countries and will ask themselves which models work best. It is very doubtful that many people in 2017 will be impressed by what the US has achieved in social terms or by where it appears to be heading. But even the US may not for much longer be able to afford to be as unequal as it currently is, regardless of who currently holds most power there.

1 N Chomsky, 'Is the world too big to fail?' *Aljazeera Opinion*, 29 Sep 2011, nin.tl/ChomskyAlJazeera

2 See SJ Peart and DM Levy, 'Darwin's unpublished letter at the Bradlaugh-Besant trial: A question of divided expert judgment', *European Journal of Political Economy*, 24, 2008. A free abstract of the piece can be read at: nin.tl/BradlaughBesant

3 See table 1.3 of: Department of Health, *Health Ireland, Key Trends 2015*, Dublin: Government of Ireland, nin.tl/Irishhealth

4 E Stewart, 'Thomas the Tank Engine is becoming more diverse...', *The Independent*, 28 Mar 2016, nin.tl/TankEngineThomas

5 Personal communication, Jan 2017: Pedro Herculano G Ferreira de Souza, IPEA Brazil, ipeadata.gov.br

6 A Taub, 'Behind 2016's Turmoil, a Crisis of White Identity', *New York Times*, 1 Nov 2016, nin.tl/whiteidentity

7 S Kang, K DeCelles, S Tilcsik and S Jun, 'The Unintended Consequences of Diversity Statements', *Harvard Business Review*, 29 Mar 2016, nin.tl/diversitystatements

8 SK Johnson, DT Hekman and ET Chan, 'If There's Only One Woman in Your Candidate Pool...', *Harvard Business Review*, 26 Apr 2016, nin.tl/onlyonewoman

9 Chinua Achebe, *Things Fall Apart*, Anchor Books, New York, 1958 and en.wikipedia.org/wiki/Things_Fall_Apart

10 UN, *World Population Prospects, the 2015 revision*, esa.un.org/unpd/wpp

11 This claim was first made in 1999. Whether it is true depends almost entirely on how accurate current income estimates are for China, and to a lesser extent in India. See G Firebaugh, 'Empirics of World Income Inequality', *American Journal of Sociology*, 104, 1999.

12 P Landers and Y Koshino, 'Japan Moves to Lure More Foreign Workers', *Wall Street Journal*, 8 June 2016, nin.tl/WSJonJapan

13 Mission Health, *Underfunded, underdoctored, overstretched: The NHS in 2016*, Royal College of Physicians, 2016, nin.tl/underdoctored

14 All the statistics used to calculate these figures are given in D Dorling, *A Better Politics*, London Publishing Partnership, 2016, An open-access pdf is available for free here: dannydorling.org/books/betterpolitics

15 L Hiam, D Harrison, D Dorling & M McKee, 'What caused the spike in mortality in England and Wales in January 2015?' *Journal of the Royal Society of Medicine*, 17 Feb 2017, dannydorling.org/?page_id=5946

16 L Hiam, D Harrison, D Dorling and M McKee, 'Why has mortality in England and Wales been increasing? An iterative demographic analysis', *Journal of the Royal Society of Medicine*, 17 February 2017, dannydorling.org/?page_id=5942

17 R Humphries, P Hall, A Charles, R Thorlby, H Holder, *Social care for older people*, The Kings Fund, 15 Sep 2016, nin.tl/socialcareforold and A McNicoll, 'Adult and children's services "face £3.2bn funding gap"', Community Care, 20 Oct 2016, nin.tl/CCfundinggap

18 J Bingham, 'Britain the loneliness capital of Europe', *The Telegraph*, 18 June 2014, nin.tl/lonelinesscapital

19 D Dorling, 'Public health was declining rapidly before the Brexit vote', *Public Sector Focus*, Jul/Aug 2016, pp 20-22 nin.tl/preBrexithealth

20 D Dorling, 'Brexit: the decision of a divided country', *British Medical Journal*, 354, 2016 nin.tl/Brexitdivide and dannydorling.org/?page_id=5639

21 B Quinn, 'Unicef criticizes UK's failure to tackle child inequality as gap grows', *The Guardian*, 14 Apr 2016, nin.tl/UKchildinequality

22 'Number of insolvencies jumps by a fifth in England and Wales', *The Guardian*, 28 Oct 2016, nin.tl/insolvencyjump

23 L Silver, 'New study shows house price rises linked to private tenant evictions', *BuzzFeed News*, 31 Oct 2016, nin.tl/evictionshouseprices

24 ' The presidential election, illness as indicator', *The Economist*, 19 Nov 2016, nin.tl/illnessandTrump

25 W Self, 'A rentier nation's fading dreams of home', *The Financial Times*, 16 Jan 2016, nin.tl/rentiernation

26 Persons Unknown, *Options for dealing with squatting*, Dog Section Press, 2016, nin.tl/2mXz7h4

27 Persons Unknown, *'Homes, Not Jails' – SQUASH's latest report*, Squatters Action for Secure Homes, London, Apr 2015, nin.tl/homesnotjails

28 N Bosetti, S Sims, and T Travers, *Housing and Inequality in London*, Centre for London, 4 Apr 2016, nin.tl/Londonhousing

29 In his Mansfield College (Oxford) lecture of 29 April 2016 in which he referred to ONS, Total Wealth: Wealth in Great Britain, July 2012 to June 2014, *Wealth and Assets Survey*, ONS, 5 Jan 2016, nin.tl/wealthWave

30 H Osborne, 'Gulf investors plan to "buy to leave" London property, survey shows', *The Guardian*, 20 June 2016, nin.tl/buytoleavehouses

31 *London the global powerhouse*, Greater London Authority, Feb 2016, p 185, nin.tl/Londonpowerhouse

32 A graph showing this sudden change can be seen here: K Webb, 'Rising homelessness: Too much welfare reform and not enough rental reform?' *Shelter Policy Blog*, 26 Mar 2015, nin.tl/norentalreform

33 S Collini, *Speaking of Universities*, Verso, 2017, p 29.

34 A great deal more is said about this here including a graph of inequality from 1911-2011 which illustrates how the current under-use of housing began during the 1980s and has accelerated since: D Dorling, *All That is Solid*, Penguin, 2015, dannydorling.org/books/allthatissolid

35 S Hickey, 'Would a rent cap work for tenants facing £1000 a month rises?' *The Observer*, 1 May 2016. A copy can be found at the bottom of the page here: nin.tl/rentcap

36 P Collinson, 'Boom in office-to-home conversions drives rise in housing stock', *The Guardian*, 15 Nov 2016, nin.tl/officetohome

6

Where equality can be found

It is fair to say that heaven on earth has not been achieved yet, anywhere on earth, nor will it be soon. But it is perfectly possible to identify countries that are already benefiting from higher levels of equality and to try to learn from their examples. Just as important is to identify what goes wrong in the most inequitable countries so as to avoid taking their routes. This chapter looks at a variety of topics, from happiness to handguns and from holidays to murder, but it begins with the notion that we may already be nearer our goal than we realize, especially at the weekend. The search for a better life is a continuous search, but along the way you get to visit some very interesting places.

> 'A map of the world that does not include Utopia is not worth even glancing at, for it leaves out the one country at which Humanity is always landing. And when Humanity lands there, it looks out, and seeing a better country, sets sail. Progress is the realization of Utopias.'
>
> Oscar Wilde, 1891

For many, greater equality happens at the weekend, which may be partly why we look forward to it so much. It is during the weekend that you are freer to choose how to use your time and, with family and friends, everyone is treated much more equally.[1] During the week you are told where to sit in school, or which lectures to attend, or you have to obey your employer, or desperately search for work, or otherwise justify not being in paid employment – unless you are deemed too old or sick to work, neither of which are much fun in a society that values individualism and selfishness above solidarity and care.

Caring more includes giving time to your children, your partner, your neighbor, but there always seems so little time to do that if you live in the rat-run of a more unequal society. Equality matters because it is freedom, including freedom to do the things that really count. The story of the weekend is one of a million stories of more equality being better than less. For those of us who do not have to work during it, the weekend is an equality that we have won. Just as there were times in the past when equality was greater, so too there are places near where you live where things are more equal, and places further away that can show us that very different social arrangements are possible. None of these places are actually Utopias, but they are places from which it is at times easier to look in the direction of Utopia. In many other places terrible events occur, freedoms are impinged on and poverty continues to damage lives; and yet even from the worst of vantage-points there are still many contemporary signposts to a better future and away from an inequitable past.

It is usually in comparison to other nearby countries, or to areas of similar wealth (but not similar equality) that places of greater equity look good. Compared to Haiti, which is the most *inequitable* of Caribbean nations, Cuba (the most *equitable*) looks great. Probably for you, as a reader likely to be living in a wealthier country, Cuba remains far from ideal. Many people in affluent countries associate Cuba with holidays, although very few of them can actually afford to fly there. Now the American boycott of Cuba is slowly being lifted, even Americans can more easily go on holiday to Cuba again. Like weekends, holidays are a time when you are free to do what you wish and in which those who are on holiday with you really do expect you to treat them as equals. Holidays, originally 'holy days', are breaks from work, like the Sabbath; they were originally imposed by religions but slowly converted into rights. Those religions imposed them as they recognized the need for people to rest.

Your right to a paid holiday varies by where you live. In the most unequal rich countries, many workers have few rights to paid time off work. In the most equal there are more generous holiday allowances. Gaining more holidays is a part of the equality effect! Greater economic equality is won in far more ways than just securing a fairer distribution of income. And one way is by learning from the example of societies that have already benefited from the equality effect.

Cuba, Costa Rica and Kerala

Cuba has two secret weapons. First, the state tries to reduce the gap between rich and poor. Like any state, this does not include the favored bureaucrats, who still benefit from being bureaucrats, though not by as much as do bureaucrats in rich unequal countries. Second, there is community self-help and care at local levels, which has arisen as a response both to the more regressive aspects of the state and to the US trading boycott. This community self-help actually reinforces the state's redistributive elements. Cuba shows you need a state to provide the necessary conditions, and you need sufficiently strong communities to take these forward.

Cuba stands out in international comparisons as a result of meeting both the necessary and sufficient conditions for greater equality despite the breakup of the Soviet Union, its former sponsor. In 2015 life expectancy in Cuba was 79.1 and in wealthier but also equitable Costa Rica it was 79.6 years. This compares with 79.3 in the very wealthy United States. In all other Caribbean islands it was lower, including the much wealthier Bahamas (76.1). In wealthier Europe it is usually between 80 and 83, but is only 77.5 in Poland and 75.8 in Hungary. In very wealthy Saudi Arabia it is only 74.5.[2]

The Gross National Income per person in the Bahamas is over $21,000 per person. In Cuba it is about a third of that, at $7,300. In Europe the Gross National Income per person is higher still, while in the US and Saudi Arabia it is almost $53,000. Thus, despite their relative income poverty, Cubans each live (on average) over two years longer than residents of the Bahamas, over four years longer than in Saudi Arabia, and have the same life expectancy as

US citizens. If a country as poor as Cuba can achieve all this, then what more would be possible if greater equality were achieved in more affluent nations?

In Cuba adults on average have received 11.5 years of schooling. That is less than countries like Germany, Australia, the US and UK (around 13), the same as Japan, but more than France (11.1), Austria (10.8), Singapore (10.6), Italy (10.1) Spain (9.6), or Saudi Arabia (8.7).[3] In 1990 the average for the United Kingdom was only 7.9 years (in Cuba it was 8.5 at that point). This was because the UK was so very elitist in its recent past, when most children were consigned to inferior 'secondary modern' schools or, before that, to no secondary education at all. In contrast, Cuba has had a more egalitarian schooling system for longer than most European countries. In September 2016 Cuban universities opened up their classes to a record 200,000 students, representing one of the largest increases in enrolment in recent years, so 'years of schooling' (which generally include university years) statistics can be expected to rise significantly in Cuba in future.[4]

How can levels of health and education be so much better in Cuba than in other, much more affluent nations? The simple answer is that how healthy the population is, and how much they all know, is taken much more seriously in countries where all other human beings are considered as being more equal in value. Many complain that in Cuba civil liberties are curtailed and it is certainly possible to imagine it becoming a much better country than it is. But it is also even more easily possible to imagine all those richer countries that are inferior to Cuba in terms of their health and education records doing much better than they currently do, if only they would learn to become a little more equal. So let's turn to another, less politically charged, example of where greater equality can be found.

Costa Rica sits not too far from Cuba and is another nation-state often presented as a role model demonstrating the benefits of greater equality. Because it has not had to suffer under a US embargo or to recover from the collapse of the Soviet Union, Costa Rica is a richer country than Cuba. Income is a little less equally distributed in Costa Rica than in Cuba, but it is still a remarkably equitable country.

As a probable consequence of Costa Rica's slightly lower levels of equality, despite having twice the per-capita income, it has only a similar life expectancy to Cuba. Maternal mortality is lower in Costa Rica, and its average 8.4 years spent in education is lower than Cuba's 11.5. Although women hold 37 per cent of parliamentary seats in Costa Rica, in Cuba women are nearer to achieving parity, holding 43 per cent of all seats. Both these proportions are far greater than those almost all rich countries currently achieve.

Before quibbling about different models and levels of greater equality, compare the statistics for both Costa Rica and Cuba with the latest for nearby Haiti, which is both incredibly poor and incredibly unequal. In Haiti, life expectancy had fallen to 61.7 years even before the 2010 earthquake and by 2015 was only 63.5 years; mean average years in education were only 4.9 in 2015; maternal mortality was a staggering 22 times more frequent than in Costa Rica; and, perhaps unsurprisingly, women made up only five per cent of all parliamentarians.

More equitable countries deal far better with natural disasters than do more inequitable countries. In fact, most of the effect of a natural disaster is not *natural* but is influenced by the nature of the society that is hit. When earthquakes hit Haiti or hurricanes hit the US, as in the case of Hurricane Katrina in 2005, the effects are far worse than they are in more equitable countries that experience similar disasters. This is partly because so many more people are so much poorer in more unequal nations, and partly because those with power care less for others there.

Cuba and Costa Rica differ in many ways but they are similar in two key respects. First, they are more equitable countries compared with those next door to them: Nicaragua and Panama in Costa Rica's case, every other Caribbean island in Cuba's. Second, they have resisted colonial and US interference, unlike Haiti.

In Haiti, revolution followed slave rebellion in 1791, but former slave owners were replaced by new elites made up of the better-off ex-slaves. In contrast, the Cuban revolution came much later (1953-9). Costa Rica, located much further to the west, resisted enslavement by the original Spanish colonizers more effectively. The death penalty was abolished in Costa Rica as early as 1877, at a point when Cuba was still a Spanish colony and when the Haitians were still paying reparations to France for their freedom.[5]

Costa Rica severed diplomatic relations with Cuba in 1961 and only reinstated them in 2009. Not all places on the road to Utopia are well connected. The government in Costa Rica was also initially hostile to Nicaragua when revolution was taking place there in the early 1980s, but later the Costa Rican president helped negotiate the 1987 peace plan whereby the US promised to stop funding insurrection in Nicaragua.

All this was done without Costa Rica having any armed forces. Costa Rica is today the most celebrated of about two dozen of the world's countries that have chosen to have no army, navy or air force. In contrast, the US is still trying to work out how it can close its prison camp on Guantánamo Bay in Cuba despite having decided it must do so many years ago.

Finally, what of Kerala, the third place in the title of this section? You don't hear much about Kerala because it is not a country. It is a state of India, much larger in area and population than most countries, but not a nation-state.

If Kerala were a country it would be with this little group of three places signposting various routes to Utopia. Its life expectancy is 75 years for men, 78 years for women and its literacy rate is unsurpassed in all of India, at over 95 per cent.

In 2005, Kerala was acknowledged as having one of the highest rates of improvement in human development in the world and *'after 10 years of secondary schooling, students typically enrol in Higher Secondary Schooling in one of the three major streams – liberal arts, commerce or science.'*[6]

Kerala is not a rich Indian state, but it is a very equitable one. In the 1991 census there were 3.6 per cent more women than men there, rising to 5.8 per cent more in 2001 and 8.4 per cent more in 2011.[7] This figure is so high because of the number of men from the state who have traveled to the Middle East to work, but that emigration also happens from many other areas in the sub-continent. Across much of the rest of Asia, and almost all of India, there are still more men than women despite more male out-migration because female fetuses are more often selectively aborted, young girls are less well cared for and die in childhood, while more young women die in childbirth, and elderly women are also less well cared for. Kerala shows how different things can be.

Kerala is known outside of India for being one of the states where the communist party does well in elections. But its greater equality will be a product of other factors that matter as well: its outward-looking cultural traditions; its efficient use of international trade and remittances; its centuries-old religious tolerance, including a long-established Jewish population; the mountains and jungle that cut it off from much of the rest of India.

Norway, Sweden, Denmark and Finland

If Cuba, Costa Rica and Kerala show what is possible in some of the poorer countries and states worldwide, then these four Nordic countries show what can occur when greater equality is mixed with great affluence. In Norway, the amount of wealth generated through extracting oil has been huge, but rather than use it to enrich a few individuals, as occurs in most places in the world where oil is found, it has been shared out far more equitably through state intervention, ensuring, among much else, affordable childcare and long periods of paternity leave for men.

Within Norway it is recognized by many that the real secret of its success is not its oil wealth but the high proportion of working women who are paid very similar salaries and wages to men. Many of these women are thus not only paying high taxes but may possibly also be helping to deflate incomes at the very top by their presence. In many professions, when women are first allowed access, wages tend subsequently not to rise greatly. It may be possible that greater gender equality in Norway, extending right up to the top of its society, and within all other Nordic countries, has helped to prevent top salaries rising as much as elsewhere in the rich world. However, recent events in Norway also illustrate well that greater equalities have to be defended, as the graph showing the share of income taken by the top one per cent demonstrates (Figure 6.1). In 2017 we learnt that Norway is the happiest country in the world, while Denmark is the second-happiest.[8]

Denmark is one of the best models in the world for reducing income inequality. This does not mean that all is equal in Denmark. Denmark has, in the recent past, reported relatively high rates of wealth inequality, but if income inequalities continue to be kept low, if rents for private housing carry on being regulated, if public spending is kept high and universities there remain free to attend, then the long-term effect of what Denmark has managed to achieve will be remarkable. This is what a country with solidarity looks like and this book is peppered with examples of how people in Denmark enjoy not only a very high standard of living but also high levels of happiness, and of child well-being, as a result of controlling inequality so well.

Norway and Denmark were remarkably similar in their achievement and sustaining of greater and greater equality until the late 1990s. By then the richest one per cent in both countries was only taking about five per cent of all income – or about five times the arithmetic average income. These were some of the best equality statistics ever produced in the world. However, shortly after that, the Norwegian official statistics for the take of the top

**Figure 6.1: The take of the best-off 1%
in Denmark and Norway, 1900-2011**

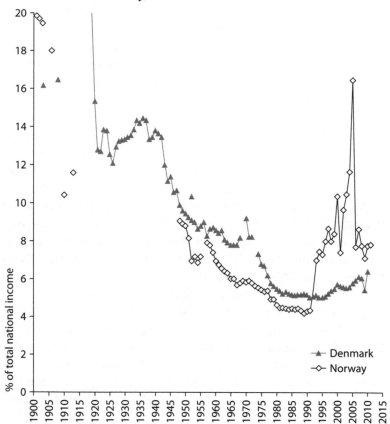

Years of consecutive data connected by a line. Where no data is shown it is missing for that year.

Source: World Wealth and Income database – accessed March 2017: http://wid.world/

one per cent skyrocketed and then were reported to have halved in just one year (2005-06). It is hard to believe such a turnaround is possible. But it did happen. And today Norway is fractionally more unequal than Denmark.

What happened was that the then Norwegian government announced, well before it was to be introduced, a new tax on *aksjeutbytter* (share income). In the following year there was a fire-sale and huge amounts of capital were taken offshore, with that slice of unearned income disappearing from the top one per cent's income-tax returns, to be brought back later in other, less heavily taxed, ways. There is tax dodging, it seems, even in the most equitable of countries.[9] Inequalities in Norway appeared to rise so quickly in the late 1990s because unearned income from having wealth began to be included more comprehensively in the statistics, and this income was then better taxed. A similar process may well have occurred in Finland, which has recently seen the income of its top one per cent come back down to similar levels to those in Denmark and Norway (just over six per cent of all

Figure 6.2: The take of the best-off 1% in Sweden and Finland, 1910-2012

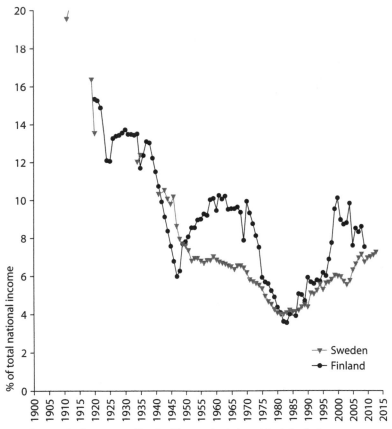

Years of consecutive data connected by a line. Where no data is shown it is missing for that year.

Source: World Wealth and Income database – accessed March 2017: http://wid.world/

income). Figure 6.2 shows the equivalent graph for Finland and Sweden. Note that these two were the fifth- and tenth-happiest countries in the world out of the 155 that were compared in 2017.

There have recently been increases in income *inequality* in both Sweden and Finland, and very recently perhaps increases in *equality* again in Finland (the most recent trend is downwards), but one of the things that has helped slow the effect of recent reversals has been the much greater sense of social cohesion that exists in all these countries. What follows is a very short story about Norway to try to explain this.

Greater cohesion is not the result of the shops in Norway being shut on Sundays, or the lack of a financial sector, but the consequence of many years of redistributive policies reaching deep down into the fabric of society or, as my colleague, geographer Simon Reid-Henry (a part-time resident of Norway), puts it, 'nourishing its bones'.[10]

Deep down, Norway and the other Nordic societies have the firm foundation of an intentionally redistributive economy, which itself provides the basis for a more caring society. Many of those who favor these models suggest that it is *care*, as a political philosophy, that provides the basic capital for mending broken societies. Partly because people in Nordic countries care more, they have recently accepted more than their fair share of refugees. The same has happened in Germany.

In recent years, newspapers began reporting that tensions were breaking out in Nordic countries as 'immigrant' populations grew and 'locals' began to resent wealth being distributed beyond the cohesive whole. If you look at the graph above, it suggests that in reality wealth was being redistributed towards a few well-established, affluent locals at that point in time. Whenever that happens in the world, there is a tendency for the rich to try to divert attention away from their appropriations towards some scapegoat – and immigrants all too easily fit the bill.

Immigrants are often incorrectly blamed for part of the damage done by allowing inequalities to rise. This is done through perniciously claiming that it is immigrants who are taking the jobs, houses or school places, which all actually become harder to fund when the rich take so much more in income, acquire more and more wealth, effectively reducing both the incomes of all other people, and the income of the state. The rise of rightwing extremism, even in Nordic countries, shows that they are not immune from such scapegoating when income inequalities rise.

In Denmark, in the summer of 2016, there was widespread condemnation of the use of a new law that allowed the police to seize jewelry from refugees, allowing them to keep no more than 10,000 kroner in cash and valuables. A similar ruling applied to Danish citizens before they could receive benefits, but of course that was rarely all they had left. Human Rights Watch described the action as *'despicable'* and *'vindictive'* and the UN said these actions would *'fuel fear and xenophobia'*.[11]

Sweden is the Scandinavian country most often cited as exemplifying success. In 2010 it had the highest secondary-education enrolment rate in the world, with 99 per cent fully completing high school. Compare that to just 91 per cent in the UK (but at least rising) and 82 per cent in the US, which was not showing much sign of rising, according to the latest UNDP figures at that time.

More recent UNDP statistics are probably not comparable because, strangely, they often report enrolment rates of over 100 per cent so we have to use figures from a few years ago here. Those 2010 figures showed that only 0.1 per cent of pupils drop out of school in Sweden compared with 1.5 per cent in the US and an unreported but possibly even higher proportion in the UK.[12] In Sweden there is one teacher for every 10.7 pupils; in the US one for every 14.3; and in the UK just one for every 20.1 (in most British state schools the ratio is nearer 1:30 for under 16-year-olds). By 2015 Denmark was spending 8.7 per cent of its GDP on public education, Finland and Sweden both 6.8 per cent, Norway 6.6 per cent, but the UK only 6.0 per cent and the US only 5.2 per cent.[13]

However, it is not Denmark but Finland that most often tops international comparisons of learning. Here, pupils do exceptionally well at school more often than anywhere else, and there is the highest level of enrolment in higher education. In addition, Finland's scientists publish more papers per citizen in international peer-reviewed journals than the academics of any other country. A few years ago Sweden topped that list.[14] This includes papers in journals covering physics, biology, chemistry, mathematics, clinical medicine, biomedical research, engineering, technology, and earth and space sciences.

It is perhaps not surprising that the Nordic people do so well in research given that they perform so well at school and at university and are all so well encouraged to learn and be imaginative compared with children in other countries. Research and learning is best done under more egalitarian conditions – the process of peer review is itself egalitarian, with your peers deciding whether the paper is good enough for publication.

It is not just greater ideas that are more often forged in conditions of greater equality. The more mundane creation of everyday knowledge and information is also sped up when more people's talents can be better employed. Today, innovation is most frequently found in the most equitable of countries that are also affluent enough to foster it. There are far more innovative companies produced per head of population in places like Finland (think Nokia), Denmark (think of Bang and Olufsen for adults, or Lego for children) and Sweden (think IKEA).

In Norway, which is the most efficient producer of petroleum in the world, it was announced in March 2010 that plans were afoot to build the world's largest wind turbine.[15] It is easier to think ahead in more equitable circumstances. Just as Denmark has quickly moved to ensure that most of its electricity will be generated by wind power, other Scandinavian countries are following suit. Meanwhile, the greatest numbers of patents are registered (per head) in even more equitable Japan.

Very unequal places like Britain and the US like to think of themselves as home to unusual numbers of inventors and especially to brilliantly imaginative *entrepreneurs* (a word of French origin), but no figures can be found to back up such claims. This is particularly evident in the recent most inequitable decades in the UK and US, an era which has been especially lacking in innovation other than in financial services, where many newly devised financial instruments, including derivatives, are often just repackaged debt, which recently turned very sour.

Ultimately it is innovation in thinking which is most free to evolve when greater equality is being realized. The stultifying atmosphere of feudal serfdom constrained the imagination of both serfs and rulers. In affluent inequitable countries, where education is highly stratified and where money buys very conventional teaching that is often (misleadingly) presented as being the best, those at both ends of the social scale end up being less creative. The young adult children of the rich talk of 'start ups' with little idea of what they might be starting up, other than getting someone else without capital to do most of the hard work for them.

Most children who attend the most expensive private schools in the most unequal affluent countries can usually be trained to get A* grades. This is not just due to the amounts of coaching they receive. Schools are ranked by exam results and university-entrance rates obtained, and private school fees usually reflect those rankings. The system is often presented as if parents should send their children to the most expensive school that they can just about afford, so that it is almost unthinkable for their children not to concentrate on getting A*s. However, good education cannot happen in an atmosphere of such intense pressure. Being trained to get an A* isn't the same as learning. Education, which should expand your imagination, should not restrict you to being able to produce standard answers. People from the top echelons of more *equitable* affluent countries, the Nordic people and the Japanese, tend to have a broader understanding and to be more aware, more creative and less arrogant.

Children who attend schools towards the lower end of the very wide spectrum of 'opportunity' offered in more unequal countries almost never attain an A*, particularly in the lower 'sets' in those schools. The OECD counts secondary-education spending as the total sum of both state and private spending. If you are reading this in a normal affluent country you may not be aware that in a few countries, such as Chile and the UK, at least 25 per cent of total secondary-education spending is spent privately on the schooling of just seven per cent of children.

If you are living in a normal affluent country you may also not be aware that in more unequal countries many children are routinely put into low-ability groups at school so that those seen to be below average do not put off the more 'gifted and talented'. Children really are given these labels in the UK, and in 2016 the

Prime Minister of the UK, Theresa May, suggested re-introducing the selective grammar schools of the 1950s. Under this system, at the age of 11 years, less than 20 per cent of children were deemed capable of benefiting from a superior education, leaving many of those children feeling smug but then suffering segregation, and many of the rest feeling defeated.

Where people are far freer to think and to reflect, where sham competition to identify talent is less encouraged, where there is no great corralling of children into separate classrooms for those of supposedly greater and lesser ability, a different atmosphere pervades. Youngsters are freer to play and associate with each other if they choose, rather than being forced to learn certain prescribed facts and to mix mainly with their own small group. Children can become interested in particular subjects and issues, and they can learn and think for the right reasons, rather than simply to try to secure future advantage over others: just to get an A.

It is easy to become good at mathematics if you find mathematics interesting – and if you are introduced to it as interesting and fun, rather than as a difficult subject in which you need to be coached to get the highest possible grade after several years of cramming (see Figures 4.13 and 4.14 in Chapter 4).

Later in life, as adults, if your views are listened to in the workplace, you can help make that place operate better. Within your organization, the more similar your pay is to others, the more you know that your views will be valued. If they say they value you, but you are paid only a fraction of what they receive, then you know that your opinion is likely to be ignored or valued as lowly as you yourself are valued.

You can be a saint or a sucker and work hard in trying to suggest changes to your bosses under inequitable circumstances, but the more equal you are, the more autonomy you have to say and do what you think is best.

It is when people are given the greatest autonomy that they become most creative, that their imagination flows, that they choose to make something good. Music, sculpture, painting, writing, running, dancing, entertaining: which of these things is best done under the cosh of inequality and which do we perform best when we are treated as equals?

Fit for what ?

Crime, gender equality and intervention

In Chapter 4 of this book a graph of crime rates by inequality was shown (Figure 4.12). The graph suggested that crime rates tend to go up as inequality rises but that there were some exceptions because different countries treat some types of antisocial behavior as more criminal than others. In Finland in 2013 a (male) motorist was fined the equivalent of $100,000 for speeding because in that country speeding is seen as a serious crime, whereas in the UK speeding in a car is usually not recorded in crime statistics.[16]

In Switzerland in 2010 a wealthy male motorist (who was a repeat offender) was fined $225,000 for driving his Ferrari through a village at 85 miles per hour. Owning a fast car is permitted almost everywhere, but driving it too quickly is not allowed in those places that know the value of life over wealth. But the highest recorded fine for a motoring offense to date was that given to a 25-year-old footballer in Germany in 2014, Marco Reus, who was fined $540,000 for driving without a license. The fine was based on his annual salary. He had, according to newspaper reports, never taken a driving test despite having previously been given numerous promptly paid speeding fines.[17]

More equal countries may record more crimes because they take them more seriously, but in general there is less antisocial behavior in such places. For instance, there is only one country in the world where, on average, just one person in every 200,000 is murdered each year, where only one person in every 30,000 is robbed each year, and where less than one in a hundred people have ever reported being a victim of assault of any kind (according to UNDP statistics used in Table 7 below). That country is Japan. This is the country that imprisons the fewest people, not because it is the most tolerant but simply because it has the lowest proportion of people committing any action for which they might face the threat of imprisonment.

In countries where both income and wealth distributions are very equitable, where almost everyone else has roughly what you have, why would you plan to steal from or rob others? Japan was only the 51st-happiest country in the world in 2017 – though the concept of 'happiness' may have lost something in translation to Japanese. But in general the countries that ranked highest in Table 7 – which orders them by their 2000-10 Gini coefficient of inequality – were also the best performers when the World Happiness Survey results were released in 2017.

By 2015 the association between inequality and several of the measures shown in the table below had in many ways strengthened. In terms of gender inequality, for example, the US fell from 37th to 55th place and the UK from 32nd to 39th, while the Czech Republic improved to 15th place and Slovenia jumped from 17th to first. Unhappiness rose in the UK and the US, according to the 2017 World Happiness report. None of these relationships are simple or deterministic but neither is there no correlation.

The 2015 UNDP report showed that life expectancy in Denmark had increased rapidly, from 78.7 in 2010 to 80.2. Older Danes had grown up in a far less equitable and less healthy country. In contrast, life expectancy in the US was recorded as falling from 79.6 in 2010 to 79.1 – a remarkable six-month fall in life

Table 7: The 26 most affluent large countries in the world – various indices of equality

	Gender inequality index 2010 (world ranking)	Life expect-ancy at birth (2010)	Gross national income (GNI) per capita (PPP US$ 2008)	Income Gini co-efficient (2000-2010)	Homicide rate per 100,000 people per year 2003-08	Popu-lation (millions 2010)
1 Denmark	2	78.7	36,404	24.7	1.4	5.5
2 Japan	12	83.2	34,692	24.9	0.5	127.0
3 Sweden	3	81.3	36,936	20.0	0.9	9.3
4 Norway	5	81.0	58,810	25.8	0.6	4.9
5 Czech Rep	27	76.9	22,678	25.8	2.0	10.4
6 Finland	8	80.1	33,872	26.9	2.5	5.3
7 Germany	7	80.2	35,308	28.3	0.8	82.1
8 Austria	19	80.4	37,056	29.1	0.5	8.4
9 Netherlands	1	80.3	40,658	30.9	1.0	16.7
10 Slovenia	17	78.8	25,857	31.2	0.5	2.0
11 Korea	20	79.8	29,518	31.6	2.3	48.5
12 Canada	16	81.0	38,668	32.6	1.7	33.9
13 France	11	81.6	34,341	32.7	1.4	62.6
14 Belgium	6	80.3	34,873	33.0	1.8	10.7
15 Switzerland	4	82.2	39,849	33.7	0.7	7.6
16 Ireland	29	80.3	33,078	34.3	2.0	4.6
17 Greece	23	79.7	27,580	34.3	1.1	11.2
18 Spain	14	81.3	29,661	34.7	0.9	45.3
19 Australia	18	81.9	38,698	35.2	1.2	21.5
20 Italy	9	81.4	29,619	36.0	1.2	60.1
21 UK	32	79.8	35,087	36.0	4.8	61.9
22 NZ	25	80.6	25,438	36.2	1.3	4.3
23 Portugal	21	79.1	22,105	38.5	1.2	10.7
24 Israel	28	81.2	27,831	39.2	2.4	7.3
25 US	37	79.6	47,094	40.8	5.2	317.6
26 Singapore	10	80.7	48,893	42.5	0.4	4.8

expectancy over a five-year period that needs examining in further research. The table above is ranked by the Gini index of income inequality as reported by the UN between the years 2000 and 2010. In the latest UNDP report, for 2015, no equivalent Gini index was reported for Singapore, New Zealand or Portugal. But the index rose further in the US, Israel and the UK – to 41.1, 42.8 and 38.0 respectively. Thus the most unequal countries of the 26 listed in Table 7 either became even more unequal, or failed to report their inequality statistics to the UN.

Inequalities as reported by the Gini index also rose a little in many other countries although they fell markedly in Slovenia from 31.2 to 24.9, which might partly account for why that country now ranks as having the least gender inequality – because high income inequalities tend to mean greater inequalities between men and women. And it might also help to partly explain why Slovenia had such a high increase in its country's average level of happiness in the 10 years to 2015, although it still has a long way to rise if it is to join the happiest and most equitable group of affluent countries.

South Korea and Japan are the only countries among the best-off 25 in the world where women are at least four per cent *more* likely to say that are treated with respect than men responding to the same question.[18] You might find this odd, since Japan ranks only 12th in the world on the gender inequality index, which reflects women's disadvantage in three dimensions – reproductive health, empowerment and the labor market. However, it may be that, where there is greater overall equality, where incomes are more similar, and where paid employment is not put on so high a pedestal, gender gaps diminish.[19]

In more equitable South Korea, and especially in Japan, people live much longer lives than in less equitable countries with similar average incomes. It is women who have gained the greatest advantage, with some cohorts living up to eight years longer on average than the already very long-lived men of these countries. Overall life expectancy is especially high in these countries largely because of how high it is for women.

Some measures of social well-being are only weakly correlated with inequality. Life expectancy is one such measure where, for example, heavy smoking increases death rates in otherwise equitable and healthy Denmark (though we also know that smoking levels there are now improving very rapidly). Similarly, the physical exclusion from Singapore and Israel of the poorest potential citizens when they stop working and are deported or leave before facing deportation means that the average life expectancy of all those permitted to remain within the official borders is artificially high.

Another of the weaker but still significant correlations concerns how homicide rates tend to rise with inequality, as Figure 6.3 illustrates. This is a graphic representation of three of the columns of data from Table 7. Each circle represents one of the 26 countries in the table, with the size of the circle proportional to the country's population. Each circle is then positioned horizontally according to how high income inequality in that country is – as measured by the Gini index – the further to the right each circle is, the more inequitable are incomes in that country. The vertical position of each circle is then determined by its annual homicide rate per 100,000 residents.

In this sample, the country with the highest homicide rate in 2010 was the US; and the UK then ranked second. The number of homicides in England and Wales fluctuated, but did not rise between 1898 (when there were 320 murders) and 1964 (when there were 300), despite the population increasing on average by just over two per cent a year. After 1964 the homicide rate steadily rose by about four per cent a year despite little growth in population until 2001.[20] However, in 2005 it was belatedly realized that a respectable general medical practitioner, Dr Harold Shipman, had murdered about 250 elderly women between 1971 and 1998. Deaths like these may have contributed to the very high homicide rate for the UK shown in Table 7 and Figure 6.3.

Handguns are prohibited in the UK and this reduces the number of murders there. The rate reported in 2015 was four times lower at 1.0 murders per 100,000 people whereas the rate in the US remained at 5.2. However, regardless of the validity of this one statistic for the UK, the overall relationship between inequality and the murder rate seems clear from the graph. It also needs to be noted that murder can go undetected in the UK, possibly more easily now than in the past. In 2015 it was reported that one UK NHS trust had failed to properly investigate over 1,000 unexpected deaths since 2011, mainly those of people with learning difficulties or of adults over 65 years of age with mental-health problems.[21] In great contrast, in 2015, the homicide rate for Japan had fallen

Figure 6.3: Inequality and homicide rates in affluent countries 2003-08

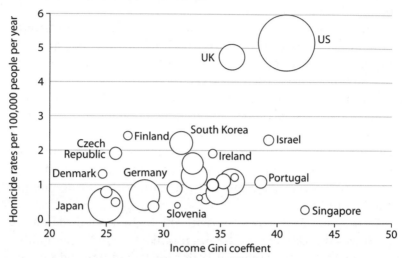

Note: The Y axis is rate per 100,000 people per year, X axis is Gini coefficient of income inequality. The size of each circle is in proportion to population. Data is for 2003 to 2008. See main text for notes on the UK rate.

Source: The World Top Incomes Database, and UNDP.

to 0.3 per 100,000 people, the lowest in any large country in the world and 17 times lower than in the US.

Japan, Germany, despair and hope

Japan's world-lowest murder rate of 0.3 per 100,000 people is only equaled by Iceland, which is also one of the most equitable countries of all, though its population is too small for it to be included in the graph above. Outside of rich countries, one of the lowest homicide rates is to be found in Bangladesh, one of the most equitable poor countries, which, most probably as a consequence of becoming more equal, has seen its infant mortality rate fall so that it now equals the world average. However, on the UN gender equality index, rather like Japan, Bangladesh ranks relatively low.

Comparing Japan, a country that has kept its border intact for centuries, with Bangladesh (formed only in 1971) may appear a little foolish. Bangladesh was in crisis in the 1970s, while in Japan the government was steering the economy to become the world leader in the per-capita production of high-tech goods. However, it may well be as a response to different national crises that greater equality has now been secured in both Japan and Bangladesh.

It was following its defeat in the Second World War that Japan became a far more equitable nation and subsequently saw such a great rise in living standards and freedoms. Between 1900 and 1940 the income share of the top one per cent in Japan had been around 18 per cent. After 1945 it fell to around eight per cent. It was the intervention of US troops, which disbanded the aristocracy of Japan and began land reform in the late 1940s, which set the country on the path to greater equality. The US did this not because it was a great advocate of equality worldwide, but rather because it feared Japan would otherwise turn to communism. In fact, the whole periphery of the communist bloc may have benefited from their geographical proximity in the sense that this made greater equality desirable to those who feared communism.[22]

There is no determinism in history, just associations, rhymes recognized in hindsight and trends that often cease once identified. It was also out of defeat in World War Two that Singapore became, after initial anarchy, both much more equitable, then a part of Malaysia, then separate and eventually incredibly inequitable. Despite this inequality, it boasts an even lower official homicide rate than Japan.

An affluent unequal population can be policed to be peaceful. Singapore has one of the largest per-capita military budgets in the Asia-Pacific region.[23] Japan has one of the lowest military budgets. Similarly affluent countries can be at opposite extremes for both income equality and military expenditure. But where greater equality is found there tends to be less violence, more harmony and greater well-being in many areas of life.

One thing that is remarkable about Germany and Japan is what happened after the First and Second World Wars. In the First World War Japan sided with the UK and its high level of inequality was unaffected. Germany lost and the take of the top one per cent fell from a pre-war level of 18 per cent to under 12 per cent, though it rose rapidly again in the 1930s.

Figure 6.4: The take of the best-off 1% in Germany and Japan, 1900-2010

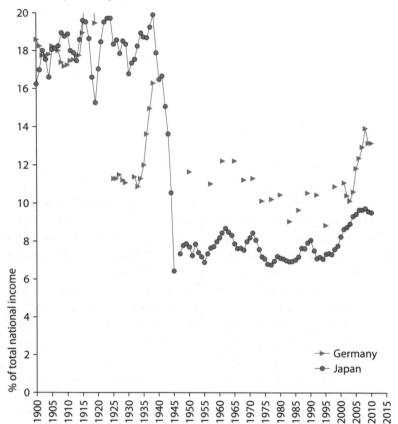

Years of consecutive data connected by a line. Where no data is shown it is missing for that year.

Source: World Wealth and Income database – accessed March 2017: http://wid.world/

In that Second World War Japan and Germany were both on the same side and lost. As a consequence, the take of the elite in Germany fell back to 12 per cent and in Japan it plummeted from 18 per cent to 8 per cent. In the past decade the take of the best-off one per cent rose in both Japan and Germany but in the last three years in both countries that rise in inequality appears to have halted, which again fits into a worldwide picture of a possible tipping point being reached with the global financial crisis of 2008 and its aftermath.

Most of the world is home to people who have experienced much more rapid social change than is usual in richer places, but even many wealthier countries have experienced occupation by hostile forces relatively recently. It is countries that have not suffered invasion, such as the US, Portugal, New Zealand/ Aotearoa, Australia and the UK, where old inequalities have often persisted and become worse.

Figure 6.4 shows the share of wealth held by the richest one per cent within Japan and Germany stabilizing in recent years and earlier in this chapter four Nordic countries were shown to be doing the same. At the start of the next chapter Portugal and Spain are shown to now have stable, if not falling income inequalities, along with New Zealand and Australia, as also do the last pair of countries compared in this book – the Netherlands and Switzerland.

All 12 of these countries show it is possible to hold the line. It is possible to curtail increases in inequality shortly after they begin, and even to reduce inequalities. But it is generally much easier to do these things if your parents or grandparents saw their world up-ended, their country surrounded by troops or invaded, dictators taking control, or as in the case of much of Scandinavia, your grandparents can remember poverty and did not live under the illusion that they were naturally superior because they had an empire.

Oases in apparent deserts of inequality

In June 2011, some remarkable research was reported.[24] The *Journal of the American Association for Psychological Science* announced that an upcoming issue would show that there was a psychological reason to narrow income disparity – economic inequality makes people unhappy (see text box below). Five years later, in 2016, the World Happiness Report revealed just how often this was the case and a few statistics from it have been used above and in earlier chapters. It is not that people are always happier in countries that are more equitable. There are often short-term reasons why they might not be. But it is the case that the happiest people of all in the world live in the most equitable of affluent nations today.

Reports of this kind have been published and publicized more and more widely since 2011. Very often they are produced from

Americans are becoming less happy

In its press release, the American Association for Psychological Science reported that, over the past 40 years, *'we've seen that people seem to be happier when there is more equality,'* according to University of Virginia psychologist Shigehiro Oishi, who (it was reported) conducted the study with Virginia colleague Selin Kesebir and Ed Diener of the University of Illinois. They found that *'Income disparity has grown a lot in the US, especially since the 1980s. With that, we've seen a marked drop in life satisfaction and happiness.'* The findings were claimed to hold true for about 60 per cent of Americans – people in the lower- and moderate-income brackets.

The researchers wanted to know why what they had observed had occurred. To find out, they looked at data gathered by the General Social Survey from 1972 to 2008. The survey was a poll of 1,500 to 2,000 people randomly selected from the US population every other year. The survey used to take place every year, but as a society becomes more unequal, less money tends to be spent on social-science research. The total study sample included more than 48,000 respondents and the answers they had given to that survey over the course of some 37 years.

The researchers concluded: *'That grim mood cannot be attributed to*

within some of the most unequal places on earth, in this case from within the US. It might well be because universities tend to be more collaborative places (you don't get much done in research if you don't collaborate) that these findings can often emanate from a country where so many people often appear to have no great political problems with living within, and sometimes even advocating, gross inequalities.

Two years earlier, in 2009, Richard Wilkinson and Kate Pickett published very similar results in *The Spirit Level*, but for mental health rather than overall happiness. A few people, mostly people who do not see inequality as a problem, immediately and viciously attacked their findings. Such attacks are now far less common as in the intervening seven years it has become widely accepted that economic inequality is a huge problem for us in so many areas of our lives – such can be the speed of social progress.

thinner pocketbooks during periods of greater inequality... the gap between people's own fortunes and those of people who are better off is correlated with feelings that other people are less fair and less trustworthy, and this results in a diminished sense of well-being in general. Interestingly, the psychologists found, the inequality blues did not afflict Americans at the top.'

The academic report concluded by suggesting that, for the richest 20 per cent, income disparity or its absence did not appear to affect their reported feelings about fairness and trust – or their own happiness – one way or the other. However, other research has found that, when it comes to harm to psychological health, 'all Americans, rich and poor, are suffering the consequences' of living with high inequality.[26]

The positive psychological impacts of living with greater equality can be added to all the other benefits. Where there is more trust of others and less destructive competition with others, people have more respect for each other and so, individually and on average, will be held in more respect and are less likely to feel so nervous, anxious and concerned. Writers such as Michael Marmot, a recent president of the British Medical Association, have linked such feelings to concerns over status in unequal settings, and the adverse effects of the hormones the human body releases into the blood stream under such stressful conditions.[27]

The oasis of greater equality amid huge deserts of inequality in some of the largest countries of the world shows us what is possible. Whether we live in the US, India, China, Brazil, South Africa or Russia, we need to understand that underlying so many of our problems is that we are living more economically unequal lives than is necessary. In particular, through studying the problems of the US we can see what goes wrong even when a country has phenomenal wealth and power but allows economic inequalities to rise and rise. As yet there is no sign of any slowdown in the growth of inequalities in the US. As the *Financial Times* made clear in 2017 when analyzing President Trump's proposed tax cuts: 'Simple arithmetic ensures the gains would go disproportionately to the top one per cent.'[25]

In the US, a tenth of all adults in the labor force are currently out of work or do not have enough well-paid work to gain them an income they can reasonably survive on. About one in five young people are similarly out of work, and in some areas two out of five (but most are not formally registered as unemployed). One out of six Americans who wishes to work full-time cannot find a full-time job. There is massive hidden underemployment. One in seven Americans survives only because they are given food stamps. A similar proportion suffers from what is officially termed 'food insecurity', and is on the breadline, being very near to needing food stamps. If you live in a normal affluent country you won't know what food stamps are – look them up on the Web.[28]

The economist Joseph Stiglitz listed all the above statistics in 2011 before he wrote in *Vanity Fair*, a magazine aimed at the rich, that:

> '...given all this, there is ample evidence that something has blocked the vaunted "trickling down" from the top one per cent to everyone else. All of this is having the predictable effect of creating alienation – voter turnout among those in their twenties in the last election stood at 21 per cent, comparable to the unemployment rate.'[29]

Again, it is possible to see signs that even the very affluent are beginning to realize that greater equality is in their interests.

Americans spend more on healthcare than any other people in the world in both absolute terms and as a proportion of their incomes. Given this, it is remarkable that only 76 per cent of them say they are satisfied with that healthcare. Table 8 below shows which countries have the greatest and least popular satisfaction with the healthcare provided.

The Comoros islands, at the foot of the list, are among the more inequitable of the poorest countries of the world, along with Haiti and Liberia. In contrast, Austria, Switzerland and Belgium are amongst the 15 most equitable rich countries. The Netherlands and Iceland are in the top 10. But both Singapore and the UK show that it is possible to have a good public health system in an otherwise economically unequal country. It just takes a past history of greater equality and an enormous amount of defending.

But why are people not happier with their healthcare in

Table 8: Adults who are satisfied with the quality of healthcare – most and least in the world, 2006-09

Proportion most satisfied			Proportion least satisfied		
Rank	Country	%	Rank	Country	%
1	Austria	93	10	Nigeria	24
2	Switzerland	92	9	Haiti	22
3	Belgium	91	8	Côte d'Ivoire	21
4	Luxembourg	90	7	Liberia	20
5	Singapore	89	6	Togo	20
6	Malaysia	89	5	Sierra Leone	19
7	Netherlands	89	4	Ethiopia	17
8	Iceland	88	3	Ukraine	17
9	United Kingdom	88	2	Senegal	16
10	Thailand	87	1	Comoros	13

Source: UN World Development Report 2010 Table 10 (based on Gallup world surveys)

Sweden, Norway, Finland or Japan? Perhaps people in more egalitarian countries question more what might be possible. The British people might express satisfaction in their health services, but they know they need to defend them to keep them from being privatized. Britain spends one of the lowest proportions of GDP on health in Western Europe. If it fought fewer wars and did not try to maintain its nuclear weapons, it could spend more on health at home, but it would need to spend that money wisely rather than in the way the US does. The world's biggest spender on war by some distance is the United States. It has almost 5,000 military facilities, some 662 of which are in foreign countries. It spends roughly $900 billion a year on its military and related 'security' facilities. It is, in effect, running an empire, but late in 2016 it became obvious that '...America's declining economic pre-eminence guarantees the ultimate failure of this imperial vision.'[30]

The US now faces a choice. It can continue to spend so highly on war abroad and so inefficiently on health at home, continue to allow inequality to stay so very high or even increase further, and at some point face potential mass bankruptcy, civil unrest and international humiliation. Or it can look towards the oases where greater equality can now be found and pull out its military from abroad, reform its health service at home and slowly but surely become a more equitable, less harmful country.

It is hard to see how the most unequal affluent countries in the world today can become even more unequal. Do the leaders of the UK and US really want their countries to become more like Brazil, Russia and South Africa? Do people in those three countries not also want to begin to change their current status as international pariahs of inequality? But perhaps Donald Trump admires Russian inequality and Theresa May admires South African inequality? Those who replace them in future should look elsewhere. The world is full of oases of greater equality. Greater equality can be found within the family, at the weekend, on holiday, in many countries in the world and in any organization where people have more respect for each other. You just have to look for it to find it.

1 JC Myers, *The Politics of Equality*, Zed, London, 2010.
2 World Health Organization, *Global Health Observatory, Life expectancy data by country*, updated 6 June 2016, nin.tl/WHOlife Other figures come from the UN Human Development Report 2015, nin.tl/HDI2015
3 This schooling is defined by UNDP as 'the mean average number of years of education received by people ages 25 and older in their lifetime based on education attainment levels of the population converted into years of schooling based on theoretical durations of each level of education attended'. For historical data since 1980 see 'Mean years of schooling (years)', UNDP, *Human Development Report* Indicators, nin.tl/UNDPindicators
4 YS Correa, 'Cuban universities open their doors', *Granma Blog*, 27 Feb 2017, nin.tl/GranmaHE
5 World Guide, 11th edition, *New Internationalist*, 2007.
6 Indian government, *Education in Kerala*, 2005, referenced in en.wikipedia. org/wiki/Kerala and nin.tl/Keralaedu
7 Kerala government, *Kerala at a glance*, August 2015, expert-eyes.org/kerala. html (more male migration of laborers to the Gulf States may be part of the reason).
8 See Figure 2.2 of: J Helliwell, R Layard and J Sachs, *World Happiness Report 2016*, Vol 1, The Earth Institute, Columbia University, nin.tl/HWorldHappiness
9 L Gunnesdal & ME Marsdal, *Det Nye Norge*, Manifest, Senter for Samfunnsanaluse, 2011, nin.tl/ManifestOslo
10 Personal Communication with Simon Reid-Henry, 2011. See also 'What we can learn from Scandinavia', *New Statesman*, Feb 2010, nin.tl/w4T1Mj
11 H Agerholm, 'Denmark uses controversial "jewellery law" to seize assets from refugees for first time, *The Independent*, June 2016, nin.tl/jewellaw
12 UNDP, *Human Development Report 2010*. The UK has an even less comprehensive system of education than the US.
13 These are all UNDP figures from the latest 2015 *Human Development Report* that was published in 2016.

14 SASI group and Mark Newman, Science Research, *Worldmapper poster 205*, 2006, worldmapper.org/posters/worldmapper_map205_ver5.pdf

15 Alternative Energy, *Norwegian company develops world's largest wind turbine*, 1 March 2010, nin.tl/tSM9H1

16 'Motorist gets £80,000 fine for speeding in Finland,' *Daily Mail*, 14 Oct 2013, nin.tl/Finnfine

17 A Flanagan, 'Marco Reus' $540,000 fine for driving without a licence is "fair enough", says Jurgen Klopp', *Daily Mirror*, 19 Dec 2014, nin.tl/Reusfine

18 UNDP, *Human Development Report 2010*.

19 C Fine, *Delusions of Gender*, Icon, London, 2010.

20 P Stubley, Homicide in England and Wales 1898 to 2012, *Murder Map*, 21 July 2012, nin.tl/murdermap

21 M Buchanan, 'NHS trust "failed to investigate hundreds of deaths",' *BBC News*, 10 Dec 2015, bbc.co.uk/news/health-35051845 Full report B Green et al, nin.tl/NHSfullreport

22 Britain, the US and Canada were then free to become most unequal, as none of them was next door to a communist state except over great distances of sea or ice.

23 For details of this and of the worrying new training center for practicing fighting in urban areas see: en.wikipedia.org/wiki/Singapore_Armed_Forces [as last accessed 27 Feb 2017].

24 Science Daily, *Income disparity makes people unhappy*, 13 June 2011, Association for Psychological Science, nin.tl/vGzpwL

25 E Luce, 'Donald Trump is creating a field day for the one per cent', *Financial Times*, 26 Feb 2017, nin.tl/Trumpfieldday

26 K Weir, 'Closing the health-wealth gap', *Monitor on Psychology*, American Psychological Association, Oct 2013, Vol 44, No 9, p 36, nin.tl/APAoct2013

27 M Marmot, *Status Syndrome*, Bloomsbury, London, 2004.

28 The Food Stamp Program was renamed as the Supplemental Nutrition Assistance Program in 2008, nin.tl/SNAPprog [as last accessed 27 Feb 2017].

29 JE Stiglitz, 'Of the 1%, by the 1%, for the 1%', *Vanity Fair*, May 2011, nin.tl/StiglitzVF

30 JD Sachs, 'The fatal expense of American imperialism', *Boston Globe*, 30 Oct 2016, nin.tl/SachsFatal

7
Firing up the equality effect

The equality effect is fired up by understanding, outrage and necessity. If you understand the benefits of greater equality for everyone in society then you are much less likely to oppose measures that will increase it even if they will not directly benefit you. And if you realize that poverty can never be seriously tackled without also reducing inequality, then you will work towards that goal. We can all now play a part in this sea change.

'The fight against poverty will not be won until the inequality crisis is tackled.'

Oxfam, 18 January 2016

Sometimes countries find it necessary to reduce inequalities because the incomes of the poor cannot be cut anymore and money simply has to be taken from the rich.

This is what happens when a country loses a war. When understanding and outrage combine with necessity, the effect is much greater than when a few simply wish and argue that we should be more equal.

The consequences of becoming more equal are often not immediately obvious, especially when it has been the result of necessity, when the rich get less but the poor (at first) get no more. However, in the succeeding years after such a change there is a sustained improvement in many social indicators – and that is a result of the cumulative equality effect. We originally taxed people to finance wars – and taxes in some countries still include a great deal of military spending – but we now tax mostly to promote the common good.

It is now being said loud and clear: The very richest people in the world are hiding much of their wealth. They do this in $7,600 billion worth of tax havens. By 2015 the richest one per cent, a far larger group of people than those who use tax havens, owned over half of all the wealth in the world, having taken half of all the extra wealth in the world generated since the year 2000. In 2016 we learned that the very richest 62 people in the world owned as much as the poorest half of humanity, having increased their wealth by 44 per cent in the five years since 2010. In contrast, the poorest tenth of people in the world have, on average, seen their annual income grow by just $3 a year for the past 25 years. Then by 2017 we learned that, by another way of counting, the eight richest people in the world now owned the same as the poorest half of humanity! You could despair, or you could recognize that it is only by repeatedly highlighting these injustices that change begins, because outrage grows. And you could recognize that it is the extraordinary levels of economic inequality in just a few countries that mainly sustain and increase inequalities worldwide.

Oxfam explains how the rich in the richest countries connive with the rich in the poorest countries to keep global inequality so high:

> 'Almost a third (30%) of rich Africans' wealth – a total of $500 billion – is held offshore in tax havens. It is estimated that this costs African countries $14 billion a year in lost tax revenues. This is enough money to pay for healthcare that could save the lives of four million children and employ enough teachers to get every African child into school.'[1]

The rich in the richest countries set up the tax havens in the first place and hold most of the wealth hidden within them. They collude with despots elsewhere to benefit from the exploitation of the poorest people on the planet. They are not just exploiting their fellow citizens at home. To make money on

What Oxfam is calling for[1]

- Oxfam is calling on leaders to take action to show they are on the side of the majority, and to bring a halt to the inequality crisis. From living wages to better regulation of the activities of the financial sector, there is plenty that policymakers can do to end the economy for the one per cent and start building a human economy that benefits everyone: Pay workers a living wage and close the gap with executive rewards: by increasing minimum wages towards living wages; with transparency on pay ratios; and protecting workers' rights to unionize and strike.

- Promote women's economic equality and women's rights: by providing compensation for unpaid care; ending the gender pay gap; promoting equal inheritance and land rights for women; and improving data collection to assess how women and girls are affected by economic policy.

- Keep the influence of powerful elites in check: by building mandatory public lobby registries and stronger rules on conflict of interest; ensuring that good-quality information on administrative and budget processes is made public and is free and easily accessible; reforming the regulatory environment, particularly around transparency in government; separating business from campaign financing; and introducing measures to close revolving doors between big business and government.

their investments abroad they are fueling worldwide exploitation and poverty.

It is not just Oxfam that is now complaining so loudly. Even the International Monetary Fund has discovered that those countries which tolerate greater income inequality also have greater health inequalities, as well as greater inequalities between men and women. Only 9 of the 62 richest people on earth are women, and in almost all cases they inherited their riches from men.[2] To raise outrage further, it is easy to explain that the lives of billions of people could be improved with just a fraction of the holdings of these 53 men and 9 women. But instead of calling for charity

- Change the global system for R&D [Research and Development] and the pricing of medicines so that everyone has access to appropriate and affordable medicines: by negotiating a new global R&D treaty; increasing investment in medicines, including in affordable generics; and excluding intellectual property rules from trade agreements. Financing R&D must be delinked from the pricing of medicines in order to break companies' monopolies, ensuring proper financing of R&D for needed therapy and affordability of resulting products.
- Share the tax burden fairly to level the playing field: by shifting the tax burden away from labor and consumption and towards wealth, capital and income from these assets; increasing transparency on tax incentives; and introducing national wealth taxes.
- Use progressive public spending to tackle inequality: by prioritizing policies, practice and spending that increase financing for free public health and education to fight poverty and inequality at a national level. Refrain from implementing unproven and unworkable market reforms to public health and education systems, and expand public-sector rather than private-sector delivery of essential services.

As a priority, Oxfam is calling on all world leaders to agree a global approach to end the era of tax havens.

from these multi-billionaires, instead of just asking for donations, organizations like Oxfam are now calling for the democratically elected leaders of those billions of people affected to take action (see box above).

The one per cent have the most to lose

Even as income inequalities are stabilizing or just beginning to fall in many places, wealth inequalities have still been growing across most of the world. Beneath the richest 8 and then the richest 62, however, they are now growing more slowly. Billionaires saw their collective wealth fall by $300 billion in the year from 2015 to 2016 and much of what is left will soon be passed on to their children: *'the younger generation stands to inherit a huge windfall from the one-third of billionaires that are over 70'.*[3] These children might not have quite the same greed as their fathers. They may still be greedy, but are unlikely to be quite as greedy as those who amassed the fortunes in the first place.

When we look just beneath the level of the billionaires at the next wealthiest group, the multi-millionaires, the rate of top-end wealth growth has slowed from an annual 7.5 per cent in 2014, to a 5.2 per cent rise in 2015. Each of these families has access to many millions of dollars of wealth in liquid assets.[4] In the same year, the average annual remuneration of the highest-paid people in the US – the 1,000 highest-paid Chief Executive Officers – fell from $13.5 million to $12.4 million; over a million dollars less being taken by each in just one year. Again, this may be an early sign that the tide is turning.

High wealth and high income statistics are closely linked because the highest-paid US executives compare themselves to the wealthiest of families in the world and, to justify their greed, falsely argue that they 'deserve' an annual income commensurate with the annual interest very rich families usually simply receive on their 'investments'. Thomas Piketty has dubbed this 'meritocratic extremism'; it is a fallacious argument that falls flat on its face when the net wealth of so many of the richest is starting to fall.[5] It also presumes that the very wealthy have somehow deserved to become that wealthy. No-one on earth deserves such enormous wealth. There is *nothing* they could have done that justifies possessing it.

As we have seen, to try to protect their wealth from shrinking further, more and more of the very rich hide their money in tax havens. They know we know they should not have so much. 'Haven' is an unfortunate word to use for a form of theft. The most famous tax havens are small islands, often in warmer parts of the globe. But one of the world's most unequal countries is now often said to also operate as a tax haven because of a raft of tax measures. These include different tax arrangements for people it deems as 'non-domiciled', low property taxes, and peculiar inheritance taxes that can be avoided by the rich by putting monies into 'family trusts'. This particular tax haven is the

United Kingdom, in which the 1,000 richest families are wealthier than the poorest 40 per cent of all UK households combined – wealthier than over 26 million people. In the year to April 2016, despite the reduction in the wealth of billionaires globally, the wealth of the richest 1,000 families in the UK rose by £28.5 billion (currently around $36 billion), enough to fund 1.8 million jobs at the living wage or one million jobs on an average UK salary for a year. Alternatively, this increase in the wealth of the richest 1,000 could have paid 20 years' worth of grocery bills for all the families who have to use food banks in the UK, or 10 months' energy bills for the entire UK population, or the entire annual council tax bill of all households in England. The UK does not have an effective wealth tax because it is a tax haven.[6]

Since the UK voted to leave the European Union in June 2016, much of the wealth of the 1,000 richest families will have declined in nominal terms, especially when they try to spend it abroad, because the value of the pound fell by about a fifth. That vote to leave was partly driven by the realization that it was becoming harder and harder to fund a decent health service, to start a family or to find realistically affordable housing in the UK.[7] The very rich owned the newspapers that informed the public that these problems were supposedly caused by migrants and EU regulation, while even most of those supporting 'Remain' largely preferred not to discuss the inequality that was a more obvious cause.

The very rich thought they stood to benefit from leaving the EU because their wealth would then not be scrutinized at the European level. They thought the financial sector would then not have to operate under European laws such as that which forced bankers to declare their extremely high salaries. Outside of the EU they could continue to demand that the UK had some of the lowest rates of tax in Europe, including very low taxes on the corporations they owned and no tax on transactions involving shares, bonds and derivatives. Ironically the very rich then realized some of the largest falls in wealth in the UK when, immediately after the Brexit vote, the UK saw:

'$1.5tn [$1,500 billion] wiped off its wealth during 2016 after the Brexit vote sent the pound tumbling and the stock market into reverse, according to a survey by Credit Suisse. A fall in values at the top end of the property market also contributed to about 400,000 Britons losing their status as dollar millionaires and one of the biggest drops in wealth among the major economies. But the UK remained third for the number of ultra-high-net-worth individuals, who own more than £50m in assets, behind the US and China.'[8]

Not all is well in Spain

Greater equality is, in general, better for everyone but there are always exceptions, real and apparent. Before lambasting the most unequal affluent countries for promoting and tolerating inequality and for harboring so many of the greediest people in the world, it is important to look within some of the more equitable affluent countries and ask why all is not always better there. This is because advocates of greater inequality constantly point to exceptions to the rule and then claim that, because of these few exceptions, it is not possible to sustain the argument that living in a country with

Figure 7.1: Median housing cost as a percentage of income among poorest quintile of renter households

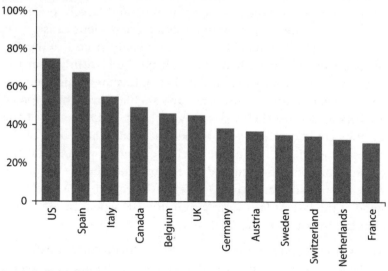

Source: nin.tl/internatrental

greater overall economic equality benefits everyone.

Figure 7.1 shows how much the poorest fifth of renting households have to pay each month for their home as a proportion of their total income. In general, the most equitable European countries have well-regulated rents and try to ensure that their poorest citizens are not destitute. In Germany, Austria, Sweden, Switzerland, the Netherlands and France, the poorest households have to pay between 31 per cent and 39 per cent of their monthly income on rent.

Figure 7.2: The take of the best-off 1% in Portugal and Spain, 1976-2012

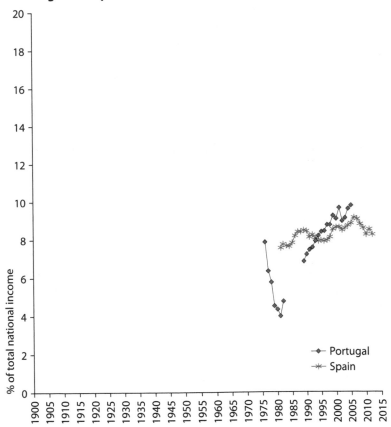

Years of consecutive data connected by a line. Where no data is shown it is missing for that year.

Source: World Wealth and Income database – accessed March 2017: http://wid.world/

In the more unequal affluent countries, such as the US, Canada and the UK, renters pay far more than is normal: between 45 per cent and 74 per cent each month of all the income they receive. This has a huge effect on what the poorest fifth of renters have left to pay for food or transport, or to buy their child a birthday present. There are, however, three exceptions in the graph, as there are always exceptions to all the generalization made in this book. In Spain, Italy and Belgium, all relatively equitable European countries, the poorest fifth of renting households are having to pay far too much in rent.

One reason why the situation in Spain appears so bad is that far fewer households rent privately there compared with the countries next to it in the graph above. So this worst-off fifth of renters comprises a far smaller group than the same group in the US. In both Spain and Italy many more families own their homes. In Belgium, meanwhile, the size of rental units tends to be larger and therefore more expensive for that reason.[9] Spain and Italy were especially badly hit by the 2008 global financial crisis, and the austerity that their governments then imposed cut the benefits of those at the bottom very severely.

If we step back and look at a longer time series of data (in Figure 7.2) we can see that Spain appears to have managed to hold its top one per cent in check, especially if Spain is compared to neighboring Portugal. Data for both Portugal and Spain only date back to the 1970s and the early 1980s respectively. The data for Spain begin three years after 1978, the year when Spain became a democracy again (following decades of fascist rule). For Portugal the dataset starts in 1976, two years after democracy was re-introduced in 1974 in the Carnation (peaceful) revolution. Democracy increases openness, release of information and more available statistics.

In Portugal a huge amount of land was seized from the very wealthy following the Carnation revolution and the wealth and income of the aristocracy collapsed. However, many of the land occupations were ended in 1978 and the land returned to its previous owners, so the take of the best-off one per cent quickly returned to what it had been at the time of the revolution and then slightly surpassed that, with the latest estimate for the annual take of the best-off in Portugal being 9.8 per cent in 2005 (a dozen years of data are still missing) We do not have any statistics after 2005, but we do know that Portugal was, after the UK, one of the most unequal countries in the rich world in 2010 and that this was no longer the case by 2015.

In Spain the restoration of democracy was less dramatic. A coup designed to halt that restoration failed in 1981 and a leftwing government came to power in 1982. Inequality has been falling in Spain since 2006, at which point the best-off hundredth took 9.2 per cent of all income. By 2012 they were taking 8.2 per cent, the latest figure we have. That 1.0-per-cent difference may not look like very much but it is a huge amount of money. Something similar may well have happened recently in Portugal. We live at a time when levels of inequality are in flux, both within countries and between countries. The changes are no longer slow and steady. What was thought to be impossible just a few years ago now often happens.

Most people are unaware of how different their country is compared to similarly rich or poor countries. When politicians do not want to change things, they often falsely suggest that 'this is just how it is everywhere nowadays'. The various ways in which inequality can be measured often cause confusion, even after people do become aware of the importance of inequality. The most commonly used measure, the Gini coefficient, is bewildering.[10] But it was used to rank countries at the end of Chapter 6 in this book (in Table 8) to show that much the same countries rank highly by that measure as by any other inequality measure.

The income take of the top one per cent is a particularly effective measure of inequality because it is both easy to understand and currently appears to represent the part of the income distribution that most affects overall attitudes in a country. Even a very small decrease in the take of the top one per cent represents a huge potential realignment within a national economy – the money can be used so much more effectively by the other 99 per cent, who always have far greater need of it.

That fall in the take of Spain's top one per cent between 2006 and 2012 is particularly significant because the country's total income also fell during those years – so a shrinking cake was more fairly shared out. It also entails falls in the incomes of the groups just below the top one per cent. The wild fluctuations in Portugal shown by Figure 7.2, meanwhile, demonstrate just how much the greedy can grab back. When inequalities rose again in Portugal, many poorer people migrated to live elsewhere in Europe. They had also left in large numbers under the dictatorship. Great inequality does not just attract in more migrants to do the low-paid jobs, it also creates more emigrants who want a better life elsewhere.

Of course, initially no-one feels better off if the take of the top one per cent falls substantially but everyone else also becomes poorer. That is what happens when inequalities fall out of necessity. However, in those countries where such a fall has occurred, it is normally followed by further rises in equality when the economy recovers. This is what happened across Europe from the late 1940s through to the late 1970s, and also in much of the rest of the world at that time. As wages rose again they rose most at the bottom, aided by trade-union pressure. In both Spain[11] and Portugal[12] there have been many general strikes in very recent years, but today many people have no work, and so no union, although the unemployed often join demonstrations associated with general strikes.

Today strikes are far less effective than they were in the past not just because a lower proportion of workers now belong to trade unions, but also because the international elites more often organize their businesses across many different countries. Doing this means they can increase production where there are tax advantages or labor is cheaper but also can simply reduce or cease production where the trade unions are strong. There are also far more retired people than there were in the past and young adults tend to start work later in life and often study for longer – these groups are not helped by trade unions increasing their members' wages. Neither are the millions of unemployed people in Europe who now only just get by. New tactics are required for new times. One new tactic is to call for a basic income – to be funded partly from the excessive take of the top 'earners'.

Basic income and living wages

I had a shock a few years ago. I was reading the work of a well-known leftwing writer. I had read through all the pages in which he poured scorn on the stupidity of those who favor greater inequality, and the weakness of those who would just keep the status quo or want to change it ever so slightly. I was expecting to reach the usual long list of everything that needed changing, culminating in calls for revolution of some kind, but the list never came. Instead he just suggested one thing – the provision of a subsistence-level basic income.

He then suggested that *'If such a proposal were seriously canvassed by a major party with a serious prospect of holding office anywhere in the advanced world, the reaction of the privileged would be extravagantly ferocious'*.[13] How quickly things can change. Major political parties have now advocated the introduction of a basic income, most promisingly in Scandinavian countries, but it is also creeping into the rhetoric in one way or another almost everywhere. If you really want to reduce inequality, then one of the best ways to ensure that no-one has too little to live on is to fund this by taking from those who have more than they need – providing a basic income directly reduces inequality. Its introduction is the equivalent of other preventive measures like vaccination, clean water supply and safety belts in cars – it is about stopping problems before they start, or at least making their repercussions far better than would otherwise be the case.

In Britain, where (as you know too well by now) I live, there is already a basic income for pensioners. There is also one for most people bringing up children, though not enough for many of those families to avoid poverty. People who are seriously disabled also qualify for one (although that eligibility has recently been attacked). Britons have accepted that it is the responsibility of government to ensure that all these groups have enough to live on, although there are now many attempts to backtrack on that acceptance. Nevertheless in Scotland pilot basic income schemes have been proposed in both Fife and Glasgow.[14]

The privileged in Britain are furious at the current size of the welfare budget despite the fact that it enables them to pay inadequate wages and to charge unreasonably high rents for housing. They and their representatives in the Conservative government are trying to dismantle much of what the country already has in terms of a welfare state. The Scottish government and many groups south of their border are fighting that. The benefit system is very complex, many do not get all that they are entitled to, bureaucratic inefficiency and increasing heartlessness have left huge numbers of people in a desperate state, and there has been a dramatic rise in the need for food banks in the space of just a decade.[15] Notwithstanding all this, even the UK – now the most inequitable country in Western Europe – provides a basic income for many of its citizens. How much more would be possible if the equality effect were fired up, not least in other European countries with far better welfare systems?

In a later book, the same writer (Alex Callinicos) who suggested that no major political party would advocate a basic income continued to make this single key suggestion. In 2010 he suggested that, to gain greater equality:

> 'In my view the best way to do this would be to introduce universal direct income. In other words, every resident of the country would receive, as of right, an income that met their basic needs at a relatively low but nevertheless decent level. This would serve two goals. First, it would ensure a basic level of welfare for everyone much more efficiently than existing systems of social provision... Second, having a guaranteed basic income would greatly reduce the pressure on individuals to accept whatever job was on offer in the labor market.'[16]

The concept of basic income was at this point becoming closely linked with the concept of freedom.

A year later, another writer, John Welshman, explained to the UK government that the single most important thing government could do to end poverty would be to play down the emphasis on work. This was because so many currently in paid work still remain poor.[17] In contrast, so-called social democrats pretended that what they called 'Welfare Reform' would give people a choice – but this kind of reform usually means no alternative to the particular paid work on offer. As former British and German leaders Tony Blair and Gerhard Schröder wrote early on in their premierships, *'New policies to offer unemployed people jobs and training are a social democratic priority – but we also expect everyone to take up the opportunity offered.'*[18]

So what is unreasonable about that? Surely, you may be saying, everyone who is able to do so should take up paid work? Well, first,

Blair and Schröder imply that, by comparison, all the unpaid work people do is not worthwhile. That would include much of the work currently done by women. Second, if everything that people in paid work did was beneficial, the Blair-Schröder argument might make some sense, but many jobs are not obviously beneficial – especially in more affluent countries where so few now work the land or make goods – or, if beneficial, they usually come with barely reasonable remuneration.

Many jobs today involve trying to encourage people to buy things they do not think they want – all the way from advertising executives spending a lifetime creating false desires, through to shop assistants asking 'would you like any help?' when you walk through a store. There are many jobs that simply serve to increase unnecessary consumption and actively detract from efforts to create a sustainable world. Other jobs involve making arms that are used to kill, working in security because crime is high where inequality is high, or in the surveillance of people just surviving on benefits because so many benefits are means tested. This idea,

that we should be forcing people to take such jobs and organizing our societies so that *as many people as possible* always have to take paid work, is one that relies on seeing money as the best measure of everything.

Almost 120 years ago Thorstein Veblen explained that most economic activity appeared to be addressed to trying to sell objects rather than to make them – let alone to teach, help or cure people.[19] He was writing long before the advent of television advertising, long before the Web itself could become populated by advertising (both overt and covert), but his message is as apposite today as it was then, because he was writing at a time of great inequality when, as now, the assumption was that the market knows best. His writings and the ideas that they spawned were a small part of what was later required to usher in greater equality around the world after the 1913 inequality peak.

Many jobs people currently do are needed less in more equitable societies: prison guards, people guarding doors to offices and to the sanctuaries of the wealthy, all that paraphernalia called 'security'. Similarly, if no-one is too lowly paid then it will no longer be economic to employ many people to do such menial tasks as serving coffee or cleaning somebody else's home. Much can be done by machine, or by the beneficiary themselves, or by not owning a property that is so much bigger than you need. The list of jobs that we could do without and the better things we could be doing with our time (other than being paid to work) is very long indeed.

Basic income is also often called a citizen's income, though that term carries with it the danger that only some people will receive it and others deemed not to be citizens will not. Like the idea of a tax on land value, along with many other progressive proposals, it can attract enormous scorn, especially when it comes to the technicalities. It is important not to underestimate the degree of intimidation that can keep good ideas for greater equality in an apologetic shade.

Greater equality can scare people, especially when you are suggesting paying people to do 'nothing at all for their handout'. But these same fears were raised when maternity pay was first introduced ('people will have to do nothing but get pregnant'),

Figure 7.3: Increase in disposable income (%) from implementing UK scheme B basic income

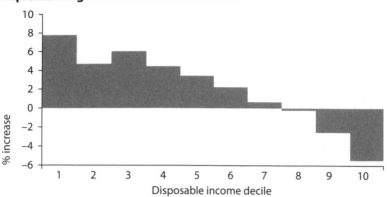

Source: M Torry, *Two feasible ways to implement a revenue neutral Citizen's Income scheme*, Euromod Working Paper Series, 6/15, Apr 2015, nin.tl/euromod

child benefit, pensions, and so on and on, through to every benefit that we now consider vital and humane. They were all once opposed by someone – usually and most effectively by someone wealthy.

The cost of implementing a basic income would not be huge. In a country as unequal as the UK only the best-off 20 per cent of society would lose anything, as Figure 7.3 shows, and even then only a tiny fraction of their disposable income. Everyone else would gain.[20] The biggest losers would be the top one per cent. It is hardly surprising that the political parties they fund and the newspapers they own pour scorn on the idea of ensuring that everyone has enough to live on and prefer complicated means-tested benefit systems. However, there will always be those whose complex needs mean that they will need more than a basic income to live decently. And introducing a basic income would initially be done gradually, so means testing and assessment would not be either immediately or ever entirely replaced, but it could be greatly reduced.

At first glance it looks as if the graph in Figure 7.3 does not balance, but that is only because we have used percentages to show the gains and losses. The better-off love percentages when it comes to discussing their pay rises so it is only fair to show what little they would lose in the same way. A one-per-cent rise for the poorest is a dramatically smaller amount than a one-per-cent rise for the richest. Remember this graph when people say that a basic income would be unaffordable.

It might be easier to introduce a basic income in a more unequal country. This is because inequitable countries already spend an enormous amount on welfare systems that are very complex and expensive to administer. Thus the cost saving of introducing a basic income in an unequal country is higher. And fewer would lose out, as there are fewer people who earn enough to have to pay the higher taxes. More unequal countries also tend to have a far more complex state apparatus, wider surveillance, a more complex sanctions regime, a larger social service to take care of poor, abused and abandoned children, as well as a far larger prison and criminal-justice system. But the existence of charities for the poor, which are more prevalent where there is more poverty, would not in itself make it easier to introduce a basic income, as those charities would have to contemplate their own demise.

Criticism of egalitarian ideas, such as basic income, often comes from the traditional Left as well as from the Right. A member of The Socialist Party of Great Britain sees it like this:

> 'For socialists, as for Marx, the concepts of justice and fairness are not so much wrong or false as not relevant for our purposes. They misrepresent the exploitative social relations of capitalism and are inappropriate to the struggle for socialism. Socialists operate within a different frame of reference, using different principles which transcend present-day society. Socialism will undoubtedly be a more materially equal society, but that is not the objective. Common ownership of the means of life will be a social relationship of equality between all people. This establishes a classless society. That is the socialist objective and not a "fairer" capitalism...'[21]

Thus, when it is suggested that people might be able to live more equitable lives, for example following the introduction of better basic income, leftwing detractors often suggest that this isn't real utopia, or 'socialism' as the version of utopia being described in the quotation above would have it. But one person's utopia can be another's nightmare. What is included and excluded in the *'Common ownership of the means of life'* and how? A basic income would ultimately show how much everyone in a society was valued at the most fundamental level. And the higher it could be set, the more successful such a society would be seen to be.

The political labels of old

Great inequalities have often been perpetuated under regimes which have described themselves as socialist, just as so-called 'free market' states often contain some of the least free markets, and so-called anarchists (meant to oppose over-arching forms of regulation) are often found protesting against firms that fail to pay their taxes and so are in effect calling for more regulation. The political labels of old are often not especially useful.

Socialism means so many different things to so many different people that I am not going to venture yet another definition here; all I will say is that the word is often used to describe a world of great equality but also of Spartan living and state surveillance. In similar ways, monasteries, kibbutzim or barracks, all unusual places of high levels of internal equality, are often put forward as dystopian versions of Thomas More's fabled Utopia, particularly because all are constantly surveyed with little individual freedom being permitted. However, we can already see what more equal societies are like, not from the above, but simply by going to visit them.

There is no such thing as full equality, no perfect model. You just need to see how living just a little more equally next year, as compared with last year, could be beneficial. It is already so hard to win greater equality that worrying about exactly what level of equality is ideal is largely a waste of time, especially if you already live in a country that is more unequal than most. Greater equality allows you much more easily to love whom you wish and to trust whom you want to trust; it means you need have less fear of strangers or of being at the mercy of landlords, banks and other moneylenders.

A more equal society is a society with more liberty and fraternity, one in which people are freer to be different, rather than being so similar to each other within their very stratified

245

groups. Under inequality, you are encouraged to blame others all the time for whatever predicament you find yourself in – especially immigrants and other 'strangers': *'The Germans blame the Poles, the Poles blame the Ukrainians, the Ukrainians blame the Kyrgyz and Uzbeks.'*[22] And most recently the British have blamed the Poles, Bulgarians and Romanians for their plight and wish to stop them coming freely to the countries of the UK (although a majority of people in Scotland and Northern Ireland did not agree). The UK is not well co-ordinated.

To gain greater equality requires co-ordination. There are groups and networks campaigning for the introduction of basic incomes and for wider social changes that often include such universal provision. In the past, change has occurred when it has been well organized: *'The way forward toward social equality cannot come about simply through the generation and discussion of ideas... organizations are responsible for bringing about political change...[but] organizations must be brought together around [ideas] and animated by ideas.'*[23] Ideas can also occasionally profoundly change the structure of entire societies. It took only a few feminists and, perhaps the birth-control pill, to lead *'...to women-friendly changes in... America after 1970'*.[24] Ask any woman old enough to have been working in the 1960s about how different life was then for women and you will quickly appreciate just how fast change can occur. And, if you are such a woman yourself, please do tell others just how much can change in a lifetime.

Basic income is a form of affirmative action and one that is not obviously leftwing or rightwing. As Lyndon B Johnson said in his inaugural address as US president in 1965:

> 'You do not take a person who for years has been hobbled by chains and liberate him, bring him up to the starting line of a race and then say, "you're free to compete with all the others", and still justly believe that you have been completely fair. Thus it is not enough just to open the gates of opportunity. All our citizens must have the ability to walk through those gates.'[25]

To be able to walk through most gates today you must first have the ability to feed and house yourself without fear, and the time to pursue your dreams.

Basic income should be seen as a way to give people freedom of choice. It opens up many more gates than just undertaking paid work, as well as giving everyone the ability to walk through those gates. It allows you to care for others that need your care without having to argue for a 'carers' allowance'. It allows you to study without having to apply for a grant or take out a loan. It sounds as ridiculous as the idea of regarding women as entitled to equal pay sounded to many men half a century ago, or treating as equals people who were not white sounded to most white people half a century before that, or how allowing working people to vote sounded a half century further back in time.

So how does a society go about introducing a basic income, where every adult resident receives a single equitable amount, simply for being a resident? You begin by introducing it at a low level, or at first for particular cohorts of the young, and by recognizing that, in many cases, for many groups, such a situation already exists where you live. The example of Britain has already been mentioned, but it is also a salutary warning that some will try to take basic incomes away. Until recently the parents of almost every child in Britain received child benefit. Now that is means tested. Under basic income, child benefit would not only be restored for all children but it would also provide enough for their parents to bring them up without any child having to live in poverty (defined in the EU as less than 60 per cent of median household income). Poverty greatly affects children's behavior and academic achievements. It dramatically reduces their chances of a university education.

Many affluent countries now have a basic income for pensioners that no old person need live below. Similarly, basic allowances are usually awarded to all parents of children, to people when out of work, to everyone who lives in the state of Alaska or in the north of some Scandinavian countries (as incentives to live there). The result of giving all citizens in Alaska an equal share of royalties from state oil exploration licenses is that it has risen to be among the most equitable US states – with the poorest tenth of citizens seeing their income rise by 28 per cent since the fund began, compared with a 7-per-cent rise for the richest.[26]

Once a principle is accepted for one group, it is easier to extend it more widely. Once a principle is accepted at all, starting with a very low basic income, it is then possible to increase the amount without needing to argue the point of principle again. This is exactly what happened in the reverse direction when tuition fees of £1,000 a year were introduced for UK students and then increased to £3,000, £9,000, and today to even more. The battle for basic income has already been fought for many years and many minor and major skirmishes have been won. There have been setbacks, too, but the long-term arc of change is progressive. We are slowly winning the argument that in affluent countries there is no need for poverty and that poverty is maintained by economic inequality. If you want many positive changes then you cannot allow the rich to continue to be so rich. Basic incomes will be introduced, just as welfare states were introduced, first in one country and then by copying that country's achievements. And all the implementations will differ, but a minimum requirement for all will certainly be that taxes are paid.

How to ensure that taxes are paid

A basic income would reduce the number of people defrauding the benefit system because many benefits can largely be done away with when you already have a basic income. Means testing invites fraud. There will still be a need for some assessment, as a basic income would not be enough for someone with much greater needs than most to survive on. If you are very disabled you may need help to buy and run an adapted car or you may need a specially adapted bed. A basic income should eventually be enough for the vast majority of people to be able to live on decently and then to be able to choose what paid work, if any, they wish to do. The availability of high-quality paid work rises when people are not forced to undertake it. But to make all this possible income and wealth have to be properly taxed.

Figure 7.4 shows how, in Australia, cases of benefit fraud had been rising from the 1990s through to when the graph was first drawn in 2003. This is not just because more fraud was taking place, but also because more surveillance was taking place. The other line on the graph shows that between 1989 and 2003 there was no increase in surveillance and prosecution of those who did not pay all the tax they should, which often constitutes a fraud several orders of magnitude greater than even the most imaginative of fraudulent benefit claimants can achieve.

After the graph below was first drawn, and then people like this author repeatedly drew attention to it, the Australian authorities were shamed into treating tax fraud far more seriously. A record amount of fines were issued in 2013/14, with 1,773 prosecutions resulting in 13 million Australian dollars being confiscated. By 2015/16 the number of prosecutions for tax crimes in Australia had increased to over 2,000 in a single year, a huge jump from the pathetic total in 2003 shown below.[27] Without widespread agitation and complaint it is unlikely that the authorities in Australia would have altered their policies on tax fraud, especially fraud by the rich. Amazingly, they now routinely issue press releases of the kind reproduced in the text box below.

Figure 7.4: Social security and taxation prosecutions, Australia

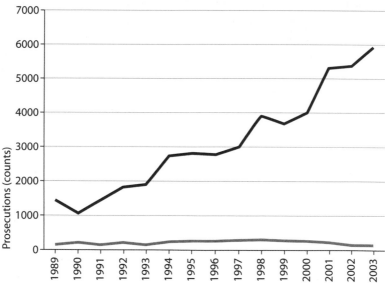

Graph first drawn by Greg Martin, the top line is the annual number of prosecutions for welfare fraud, the bottom line is prosecutions for tax fraud.

Source: Figure 19, page 251, Dorling, D. 2010. Injustice, Bristol : Policy Press.

Tax cheats brought to justice

Two men have been convicted of serious tax offenses following successful investigations under the Serious Financial Crime Taskforce (SFCT).

A 61-year-old former financial advisor was on Friday convicted in the Sydney District Court for tax fraud offenses totaling over $700,000. Jeffrey Conklin was sentenced to five years and nine months' imprisonment with a non-parole period of two and a half years.

Mr Conklin used a scheme involving various offshore entities and trusts to hide his income and then attempted to conceal the return of this income to Australia. He subsequently left Australia and was arrested at the border when attempting to re-enter the country in June 2014.

ATO Deputy Commissioner Michael Cranston said the conviction demonstrates the value of cross-agency investigations in detecting and dealing with offenders.

'We use every resource available by working closely with partner agencies to identify and prosecute these criminals. Those who commit tax fraud are stealing from the entire community and will be brought to account for their actions,' Mr Cranston said.

This verdict follows a second successful tax crime prosecution on 29 April 2016, when Timothy Charles Pratten was convicted and sentenced in the NSW Supreme Court to five years' imprisonment, with a non-parole period of two years, for failing to declare income

---

Compare the UK to Australia and New Zealand/Aotearoa. Child poverty in Australia is rising. More than one in six children in Australia live in poverty. When it comes to reducing poverty a commentator in Australia told the BBC in late 2016 that: *'One hundred years ago, Australia showed the way'*.[29] Child poverty is also very high in the UK but income inequality, educational inequality and child-health inequality are all not as bad as in the UK and in general children's satisfaction with life is higher in Australia than in the UK.[30] New Zealand's results show a similar story and an even better record a century ago. Now, in all three countries, *'children's economic security has declined in the past 30 years'*[31],

in his income tax returns for the financial years ending 30 June 2003 to 2009.

The 55-year-old former insurance company director used a web of offshore entities in Vanuatu, including trusts and companies, to conceal approximately $4.552 million in income from the ATO, resulting in a tax shortfall of approximately $2.055 million. Mr Pratten used these funds to support a lavish lifestyle, buying multiple properties, a helicopter and luxury boat.

The Commonwealth Director of Public Prosecutions (CDPP) last week lodged an appeal with the NSW Court of Criminal Appeal in the matter of Mr Pratten as it is of the view that the sentence imposed was manifestly inadequate for the crimes he committed.

CDPP Deputy Director Shane Kirne said abuse of the tax system through intentional and dishonest behavior is a very serious offense that warrants the imposition of strong penalties.

'These offenders both used calculated and deliberate tactics to attempt to evade their tax obligations,' Mr Kirne said.

The two guilty convictions are successful results under the SFCT, established 1 July 2015, which focuses on serious international tax evasion as well as other criminal activities related to phoenix businesses and abusive use of trusts.

'By sharing intelligence under the Taskforce we can build a detailed understanding of the criminal activity and ensure offenders face the full force of the law,' Mr Cranston said.[28]

14 June 2016

reflecting the rises in economic inequality in those three countries in the past three decades, which have been higher than in most other affluent nations.

Figure 7.5 tracks the rises in inequality from the 1980s through to the 2000s in Australia and New Zealand/Aotearoa and the leveling off in recent years (although the very latest two years have seen inequality rise again). The graph also highlights key events. It shows how New Zealand became much more equal earlier on than Australia, but that Australia also saw its top one per cent generally take less and less in the 1920s and 1930s. New Zealand famously had the world's first welfare state in the 1930s – it was in

Figure 7.5: The take of the best-off 1% in Australia and New Zealand/Aotearoa, 1921-2012

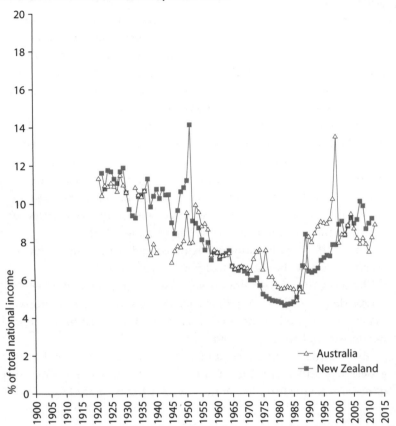

Years of consecutive data connected by a line. Where no data is shown it is missing for that year.

Source: World Wealth and Income database – accessed March 2017: http://wid.world/

part copied by the UK in 1945. The graph shows that inequalities in Australia rose abruptly in the years up to 1951, then in both countries fell through to the late 1980s before climbing again – with a particular spike apparent in New Zealand in 1999 following a period of political support for inequality. At that point a Labour government was elected committed to reducing inequality and it quickly achieved this goal.

So inequalities have fallen in New Zealand from their 1999 high and remain lower than their 2007 high in Australia. What would have to happen now in both countries to begin to reduce them further? In 2016 the New Zealand Labour Party announced that it was considering the idea of introducing a basic income for all.[32] The idea was also being widely debated in Australia that year.[33] Suddenly a basic income is becoming a mainstream idea in more affluent countries all around the globe. Circumstances change, often remarkably quickly; but we then get used to the change very quickly and forget that rapid change is so possible. We are currently approaching a time when rapid change could again become possible because the nasty minority who try to claim that poverty is not poverty, or that 'it will always be with us' are falling into disrepute.[34]

The most common question asked in response to the idea of introducing a basic income or of extending existing basic incomes to more groups is *'Where will the money come from?'* Answering this is far easier than you might think. Usually the money is saved from existing inefficient schemes by reducing the need for means-testing and other bureaucracy. For example, to ensure that each child receives a basic income you simply pay all parents a child allowance and you tax income and/or wealth to pay for it. Much of this will amount to a transfer of money from richer childless couples to poorer parents with children. There is plenty of money in Australia, New Zealand, the UK and the US. It is just that too much of it is currently held by (and flows to) those who need it the least.

Imagine how much money would be saved if a basic-income scheme one day replaced all the numerous different benefit and taxation systems existing across the whole of the European Union, or the states of the US, or in both Australia and New Zealand? How else could there ever be a unified system of social security to go with the free movement of labor that already exists across mainland Europe, the US and Australasia? There has been free movement of labor between New Zealand and Australia since 1973. As people move more often across national borders, existing national social security and pension systems begin to fail.

The money needed to fund a basic-income scheme could not only be raised by ensuring proper levels of taxation but also by ensuring people are prosecuted for not paying the taxes they owe, as Australia has recently begun to do. Take one step further and you could fine accountants and accountancy firms for aiding and abetting tax avoidance. Why not add a clause to your tax laws saying that tax exemptions can only be used for their obviously intended purpose and bring in a jury to determine cases who will be happy to say 'rubbish' to a defense that this is 'technically legal'? Not paying tax is theft.

Among many other advocates, a basic income has been argued for by the Green Party in most countries for at least a decade, and for just as long by Vivant in Belgium, the Socialist Party of South Korea, the New Zealand Democratic Party, the Liberal Party of Norway, the Workers' Party of Brazil, and the New Party Nippon in Japan.[35] To be sustainable, ultimately a universal basic income would involve continuous redistribution of wealth – and perhaps eventually reparations between countries. If this sounds fanciful, remember that the alternative is the continuation of poverty, even in the world's richest countries.[36]

Redistribution and reparation

There are more dramatic ways to reduce economic inequalities, including introducing a maximum income. Table 9 below shows what the effect of this would be in the US. The table does not include the total income of the US – to work that out, you need to multiply each group's average salary by the number of people in the group and sum the totals. When the financial crash hit, in the year 2008, the total income of all US citizens was $8,250 billion a year. If pay differentials returned to their 1970 levels, working from the bottom up, total US income would be reduced to $6,400 billion a year. If a limit were imposed of 20:1 on what the richest could receive each year (compared to the mean average), you would see that annual US income bill drop to $5,430 billion a year – less than two-thirds of the total bill in 2008, yet with 90 per cent of people receiving a pay rise. None of these figures are hard to calculate, so why are they so rarely discussed? It is because we have come to accept very high levels of inequality as inevitable. The years 2007/8 were recent high points in US inequality. In contrast, inequality in 2014 – the most recent year for which the take of the one per cent is known – has been somewhat reduced. The US may be moving towards greater equality (at least pre-Trump), but only ever so slightly, and with no firm commitment.

Now imagine that this commitment began to grow, as it has in other countries. Some of the money saved by this move towards greater equality could be used to fund a US basic income scheme. Just as most of us now accept that there should be minimum incomes, living wages, for those in work, so we could come to accept that there should also be maximum incomes, with taxation above that sum at 100 per cent. Other parts of the savings could be used to establish a better (more universal) health service, to pay off some of the deficit and perhaps also to mitigate some of the inequities the US has helped to build up worldwide. However, it might well take a great shock before any such scheme were ever introduced in the US, such as the election of a president from the extreme right who then fails to deliver on his promises to the people.

All the figures required to calculate total US incomes are shown in Table 9. In short, the richest 0.1 per cent of Americans in 2008 had an average annual income of $5.6 million each. This would

Table 9: Income inequality in the US, change since 1970 and the level to which a 20:1 limit would further reduce incomes

Income level	Number of people	Current average income	Overall change 1970-2008 % and graph of annual change	Annual salary in 1970 (in 2008 $'s)	Salary with 20:1 limit (in 2008 $'s)
Top 0.1%	152,000	$5.6 million	385%	$1.15 million	$631,000
Top 0.1-0.5%	610,000	$878,139	141%	$364,000	$199,000
Top 0.5-1%	762,000	$443,102	90%	$233,000	$127,000
Top 1-5%	6.0 million	$211,476	59%	$133,000	$72,000
Top 5-10%	7.6 million	$127,184	38%	$92,000	$50,000
Bottom 90%	137.2 million	$31,244	–1%	$31,560	$31,560

Note: Final two columns calculated for this book given the information in the first three columns.

Sources: P Whoriskey, 'With executive pay, rich pull away from the rest of America', *Washington Post*, Washington, 19 Jun 2011, nin.tl/Postinequality which in turn used The Top Incomes Database and reports by Jon Bakija, Williams College; Adam Cole, US Department of Treasury; Bradley T Heim, Indiana University; Carola Frydman, MIT Sloan School of Management and NBER; Raven E Molloy, Federal Reserve Board of Governors; Thomas Piketty, Ehess, Paris; Emmanuel Saez, UC Berkeley and NBER.

be reduced to $1.15 million each if income differentials were to return to 1970s levels. If American society were to become even more equitable than it was in 1970 – perhaps out of necessity following a massive and prolonged stock-market and housing-price crash resulting from inept political leadership – and this top group were paid 'only' 20 times the average, they would each have 'just' $631,000 a year to live on.

In the US, the UK and a few other very unequal countries, it is still almost taboo to suggest redistribution of income and wealth. A better word than 'redistribution' would be 'a fairer distribution'. When a journalist asked Tony Blair during his 1997 campaign to become UK prime minister *'if there might be some small role for wealth distribution in the politics of the center left'*, the response made him feel *'It would have been safer to venture he regularly beat his wife'*.[37] Just two decades earlier a leader of the same political party, Labour, far from responding arrogantly and rudely as Blair did, would have given a very different answer. And just two decades later, in 2017 the current leader of the same party (Jeremy Corbyn) cannot give a speech without mentioning inequality as the greatest evil of our times. But his speeches are rarely reported in the press because making a priority of actually reducing economic inequality is still a political taboo in the UK. For the British mainstream press it is still currently only acceptable to talk about reducing inequality in public if you do not actually mean what you say but are just paying polite lip service. This might help to explain why the UK still has the highest rates of income inequality in Europe – though this could change soon and there are already many quiet, unreported changes under way.

What was once possible becomes impossible and then strangely possible again. Maximum incomes have already been, in effect, introduced into much of public life in the UK as pay ratios are now published annually for civil servants by government department and, to date, they have fallen as the pay of the person at the top of each UK ministry has in effect been frozen while the median pay continues to rise ever so slightly.[38] This is a start, but the greatest inequalities are in wealth holdings as decade after decade of rising income inequalities automatically results in enormous inequalities in wealth.

It was in 1974 – at the height of income equality in Britain – that the only Labour Party manifesto ever to include a wealth tax was written. The party won the election – but the promise was not implemented.[39] Instead, growing price inflation led to instability. It was as if the golden age of the greatest equality that the UK had ever seen contained the seeds of its own destruction. However, that was not the case in other more equitable affluent countries that usually now tend to tax wealth, though not at a very high level. Wealth taxes are normal in more economically equitable affluent countries: they help to keep those places equitable.

Partly because no wealth tax was implemented in the UK in the 1970s, inflation was not curtailed and housing prices rose sharply, even though unemployment was then allowed to grow. By the 1980s, people in their thirties whose parents had been poor were four times more likely than average to be poor themselves compared with only twice as likely in the 1970s.[40] If you don't keep moving forward it is very easy to slip backwards, to see social mobility reduce and poverty and inequality become entrenched.

Moving forwards in the 1970s required an idea of where you were trying to get to and determining the means to get to that destination. Many countries moved backwards at the time. In places like Chile, Guatemala and Brazil, elected governments were overthrown, orchestrated by US intervention. In places like Britain and the US, often the dreams presented as more equitable alternatives were simply seen as too implausible. In both countries the media were largely controlled by an elite very similar to that before the Second World War – often they were their children. In more equitable countries the pre-war elite often held far less sway in the 1970s, often because those countries had been invaded in the 1940s. But in the UK and US there had been less social change. People agreed that measures to increase or maintain equality were 'all well and good' but were convinced, often by the media, that they were 'totally impractical, hideously expensive, and showed economic incompetence'. It so often appeared safer to stick to the status quo. However, the status quo was not static, but moving in the opposite direction.

What we dream of

Many still think you have to choose between socialism, capitalism and anarchy. But there is no need to have to make any of these choices to begin to benefit from the equality effect. None of the most equitable countries of the world operate as pure socialist states, discourage capitalism, or have embraced libertarian ideals. We all live in societies that are a mixture of these three extreme models, none of which ever operate purely in any setting. Here are the three extremes explained using a simple story about tractors.

First, the socialist extreme. Local food production requires tractors. Regional manufacturing plants that assemble the parts provided by national or international factories make tractors. Local ploughing requirements are calculated, orders sent to the regional manufacturers, which show in turn what requests for tractor parts they need to make to the national factories. These parts are then delivered in the knowledge that food will flow back in return. Lots of committees monitor everything – committees instead of money. A world without money is what some dream of. If this sounds like a nightmare, imagine another dream.

The second extreme: money and the free operation of the market rule everything. A tractor is then made only if it can be sold at a profit. To make a profit, the person who has the most marginal land, but can still just afford to buy a tractor, must exhaust that land until he or she goes bust. Other people must mine for the metal needed to make the tractor in the cheapest possible conditions, often the most dangerous. More tractors will be built than are needed but also more people will go hungry.

Or imagine a third extreme: anarchy, no state control at all. Should some groups get together and wish to build tractors they might choose to. However, if some of the groups wish to make their tractor work with petrol and others with clean electricity then there will be conflict, or pollution and unfair competition. No state control means no committees, but also no police and no regulation, no control of pollution and exploitation, and no creation of things that are too complex for more than a small group of people to create – which would almost certainly include a factory to build tractors.

These three are all old arguments for what we dream of – and all three could produce examples of extreme equality or extreme inequality. Actually, the argument that you can choose between having anarchy, or socialism, or capitalism in its purest form is silly. Nowhere do these pure, theoretical forms of society exist. You always end up with some form of balance between state control and regulation, individual liberty and market forces, and quite how that balance is achieved can determine how equitable or inequitable your society becomes.

Figure 7.6: The take of the best-off 1% in Switzerland and The Netherlands, 1914-2012

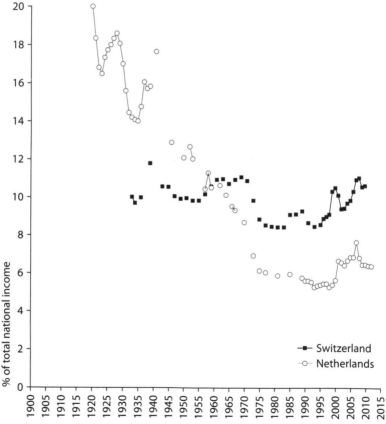

Years of consecutive data connected by a line. Where no data is shown it is missing for that year.

Source: World Wealth and Income database – accessed March 2017: http://wid.world/

As an aside, and to encourage a little optimism and realism at this point, if you do not think it is possible to see equality grow and grow, and to see the share of income held by the rich continuously fall, then consider the Netherlands and Switzerland. These countries are hardly Utopias although Switzerland in 2016 was reported in the World Happiness Report to be the second happiest country in the world and the Netherlands to be the seventh happiest.[41] The Netherlands is the average country in the rich world by its quintile income inequality range, but it does an especially good job of controlling its top one per cent. The Swiss are famous for their secretive banks, but also ensure that their best-off one per cent do not take excessively. To see this in detail look at Figure 7.6, at what people in both countries have achieved and continue to achieve when it comes to curtailing the greed of the rich.

Both the Netherlands and Switzerland have suffered small rises in inequality in recent years, peaking around the end of the 'dot.com bubble' in the year 2000 and the great financial crash year 2008 in Switzerland; and around 2002 and 2007 in the Netherlands, which is not quite as closely tied to the world's financial markets. Despite being home to so many bankers, Switzerland is far more equitable than the UK and the US. In the Netherlands the best-off hundredth took 6.3 per cent of all income at the latest count. In both these countries the share of the one per cent has been reduced from very high levels in the recent past and, when it appeared to be rising again in the 1990s and 2000s, steps were taken to curtail those rises, because most people in these two countries do not want to see their societies become dysfunctional.

Switzerland and the Netherlands are also countries in which people tend to be more innovative (on average) and hence their economies do well, with concentration on pharmaceutics among much else in Switzerland and computing in the Netherlands (which was where wi-fi was invented). The US is dominant in certain industrial sectors such as aircraft manufacture and mass-market computing not just because it is so large and rich but also because it was more equitable in the past, when these sectors were first beginning to grow. Today, however, it is frequently within smaller, more equal nations that new ideas spring up most frequently and successfully.[42]

More equitable countries produce innovators because they give more people a chance and they tend to have an educational ethos that is less about competition and more about collaboration and imagination. This was most recently recognized in the UK by an inquiry into the English school system that succinctly described all that is wrong in England's schools and universities today:

'The big problem is this – how small our education system has become. By small we mean narrow, restrictive and lacking in ambition and imagination. For both learners and teachers the space in the system is claustrophobic and does not allow people to stretch and expand, to push and be pulled, to know a life without limits. Schools have become factories of limited learning to fit with one dominant view of what it means to be human – the worker-consumer in the competitive global economic race at a time when for so many work no longer pays enough to live by – let alone provide work that allows us to flourish. It is small in the sense that too much of it is selfish and self-serving at [a] time when success increasingly comes from collaboration and co-operation. It forces us to look down at short horizons, not up at the vast landscapes of what a good society could be like.'

Final Report of the Compass Inquiry into a
New System of Education, March 2016[43]

The authors of that statement are giving us just another of many thousands of examples of people trying to fire up the equality effect: 'Don't be so selfish, don't be so self-serving,' they say. Don't believe that what will serve our children best is equipping them to compete alone in a race that only a few can win. If you want children to do better then don't restrict their ambition and imagination by making them simply compete with each other in test after test. There will always be people who score high in tests and others who score very low: tests are designed to produce those results. You can easily have a high score but end up knowing very little of much value; equally, some people with low scores in tests at certain times in their lives have gone on to make some of the most positive changes in their societies. But they are often too embarrassed to admit that they did not always 'come top'.

Other writers, researchers and analysts try to fire up the equality effect in far more opaque ways, but fortunately there are hundreds of thousands of such writers and thinkers. One large study of schools in a small part of England, concentrating on measures more than ideas, recently concluded, succinctly but somewhat opaquely: 'Eliminating social-class inequalities in educational achievement thus requires the elimination of social-class differences in school effectiveness.'[44] In other words, as long as you have schools that are essentially for children in different social classes, separated between richer and poorer neighborhoods, you will find that poor children appear to do even worse and richer children appear to do superficially better. In the long run of their lives this disadvantages them all.

Who would choose to live in a segregated country in which most people were poor or living near poverty, in which the better-off lived in different neighborhoods and went to separate schools, and in which the best-off children rarely saw their parents and were looked after by people with no long-term commitment to them?

Four years after the great financial crash, one of the most successful writers on that crash tried to explain to a group of mostly successful Americans why most of his own and his audience's success would be down to luck, with the odds just tipped a little in their favor if they were born with a silver spoon in their mouth:

> 'People really don't like to hear success explained away as luck – especially successful people. As they age, and succeed, people feel their success was somehow inevitable. They don't want to acknowledge the role played by accident in their lives. There is a reason for this: the world does not want to acknowledge it either.'
>
> Michael Lewis, Princeton University's
> 2012 Baccalaureate speech[45]

The world Michael Lewis was talking about was not the whole world, but the world as seen by the elites in unequal counties. By 'world' he really meant 'America', and in particular he was talking about the 'American Dream' – the idea that anyone can make it if they try hard enough and are talented enough, no matter how economically unequal is the society they are competing in.

That dream is a myth. Those who make money are often not very talented at all. They were just lucky at the right points in their lives. They might have worked hard, but thousands of others will have worked as hard as them and never struck it lucky. Most often those who make money had money given to them in the first place, through inheritance. Don't believe the myth of the nice, kind, gifted, self-made entrepreneur.

What finally fires up the equality effect is realizing that we live in a world in which those who have got to the top have not got there out of great merit or desert, but because they often had a few unfair advantages to start with, such as being born male, white and rich, had many lucky breaks on the way up, and often because they were willing to stamp on others' chances as they rose. The human world does not consist of just a few superior beings able enough to do the key things that need doing, and a lumpen mass of inferior beings who could never do these things and so should be penalized appropriately.

All over the world today people are firing up the equality effect in one way or another. Between the lines of what they write, from inquiry panels and academic researchers to innovative journalists, from concerned actors and enlightened politicians to dogged authors, it is more and more common to read that inequality is the problem, that it narrows our collective outlook, harms our societies and fools us into believing that just a few of us are special – especially if we ourselves are one of the 'chosen ones'.

No-one is especially deserving of riches and no-one deserves poverty. There is no need for either to exist in abundance but one never exists without the other. These extremes return as commonplace when we forget the benefits of greater equality, when we become complacent or confused, when we are distracted by other events and when we do not think carefully or for long enough. They recede when events and our own collective efforts result in our becoming more equal, then less stupid, more caring, more able, and less fearful of one other.

Harmony

So far I have used the word equality throughout this book because it relates to things that you can measure. But there is one word that encompasses all those things and much more, and that is harmony: living in harmony within our community and in our country, living in harmony with other countries and with nature. Harmony is not something you can easily measure, but it is something you can aim for.

It is sometimes tempting to look back nostalgically to a happier past in which you feel there was greater harmony. In reality there was probably, in many aspects of life, also great inequality back then, much that you would not be able to stomach now, but for the last few generations people are likely to have had a sense that things were getting better, that inequalities were being reduced, and that everything was moving in the right direction. All that creates a greater sense of harmony.

Studying the past is valuable, but look more for the ideas that were never taken up, that were *before their time*, rather than harking back to solutions that *have had their day*. The necessity to keep looking back diminishes once you can see your way forward and things are again moving in the right direction. Moving in the right direction requires becoming more equal and when increasing equality is viewed as almost impossible then very few good new ideas are generated. Decent healthcare, good housing, education for all, work for all, pensions for all, clean water, healthy food: all of these were ideas whose time could only come after the equality effect had already been fired up.

We would never have been able to measure the equality effect today were it not for the example of a few extremely unequal countries that have, in recent decades, allowed inequalities to rise sharply away from the crowd, and that have become examples of great disharmony. And we would not know that greater equality was so beneficial were it not for those few extremely equitable affluent countries that demonstrate the effect so well.

In particular, it would not have been possible to tease out the specific benefits of increasing equality from the general benefits of affluence without the recent errors of countries such as the UK and the US. We would not have realized so clearly the close interrelationships between the many different aspects of equality – financial, gender, health, housing security, safety, employment, happiness and respect. And we would also not know of it but for those researchers who first looked for it when the data were hardest to uncover and the trends had only just become clear to see.

A decade has passed since Kate Pickett and Richard Wilkinson first produced two obscure academic papers that demonstrated a remarkable correlation between the level of economic inequality in a country and so much of the consequential social harm suffered there by its population.[46] By adding many more examples they turned these initial findings into the best-selling book *The Spirit Level* in 2009. In the ensuing decade recognition of the various harms caused by economic inequality has grown exponentially.

Hundreds of books on inequality have now been published in the US and the UK, and that is no spatial or temporal coincidence. Furthermore, the increase in inequality that was occurring in the decades up to 2009 in these and many other countries has since (in many cases) stalled or even been reversed. This was not just as a result of the financial crash of 2008, itself very much a product of rising inequality. It was also as a result of many of those in power coming to realize that they are part of a generation who have recently inherited rising inequality from their forebears, and all the problems, hurt, harm and disharmony that then flow from that.

Imagine again what was first described at the start of this book: a happy band of people going up a gentle slope, all helping each other. Yes, one is at the front and one is at the back (but definitely not left far behind), also some are short and some are tall, some fat, some thin, some disabled – we all have disabilities. If you have ever climbed hills, you will know what happens. You see the top and when you get there the view is much better but you also see another top. You might need a rest, but you don't give up because you want to see the view from even higher up. Stay too long at one spot and squabbles can happen, discord grows. Equality is not so much a goal, but a direction. There will always be another summit to reach, but we are spared from seeing them all at once. Together we can seek greater equality, achieving greater harmony by so doing – by firing up the equality effect. The alternative is not a gentle slope, but an impossibly steep ladder to climb.

Politicians around the world condemn inequality, but as yet hardly any recognize the full reach of its various effects because

Two ladders

they are only now being discovered. Humans have not evolved to be greatly different from one another in ability, temperament or aptitude. Within small groups we humans easily recognize that inequality can be damaging – for example, by reacting angrily to being demeaned, ignored or not respected. But human beings have only very recently lived in societies and cities as large as we live in today, within which it is possible to be so segregated from others and lead parallel lives to those beneath and above us, so rarely mixing and never properly talking to one another.

We have only very recently reached a point when theoretically we are sufficiently affluent for everyone to have a reasonable standard of living, where we have solved the technical problems associated with achieving that. New times present new priorities and we need to develop new arguments for increasing equality, and new ways of again firing up the desire, the demand and the necessity for more equality. The alternative is a Blade Runner dystopian future[47] in which all are fearful, even those who have the most.

As I was making the final changes to this book I was asked by my local student newspaper to make a comment about rising homelessness. I replied that when I was growing up in Oxford in the 1970s there was almost no homelessness, just a few very old men sitting in the town square. Today you walk past young adults on the street, some with all their belongings piled up by their sides. If I were an Oxford undergraduate today I would look at my friends and wonder which of us, in 10, 20, or 30 years' time, will find ourselves homeless. I told the students: 'You may think it will never happen to you, to your friends, or to someone in your family; but the rate at which the situation is worsening should worry you. Even if you currently have all of life's advantages, things still go wrong. So the next time you walk past someone on the street, think how you would feel if you recognized them – how you will feel in future as housing becomes more and more expensive and life in the UK becomes more precarious.' I told them that of course there are alternatives but that the generation which allowed the situation to become this bad is unlikely to implement them.

We have always made our own history, always from circumstances not of our own choosing, and we have always eventually succeeded in becoming more equal. The clamor has never been louder than it is today. There is collective outrage, a great wrong has to be put right and the fuse has been lit – but don't stand back, take part. Greater equality is realized through believing it is not only desirable, but also possible, and by refusing to accept anything that takes us further away from that goal.

1 Oxfam International, *An economy for the 1%*, Briefing Paper, 2016, nin.tl/oxfamrich

2 C Gonzales, S Jain-Chandra, K Kochhar, M Newiak & T Zeinullayev, *Catalyst for Change: Empowering Women and Tackling Income Inequality*, IMF, 2015, nin.tl/IMFonrich

3 B Blackstone, 'Billionaires fall on harder times', *The Wall Street Journal*, 13 Oct 2016, nin.tl/billhardtimes

4 A Monaghan, 'World's wealthiest people just got 5.2% wealthier', *The Guardian*, 7 Jun 2016, nin.tl/worldrichest

5 M Naim, 'Thomas Piketty and the end of our peaceful coexistence with inequality, *The Atlantic*, 19 May 2014, nin.tl/Pikettypeaceful

6 *Wealth Tracker 2016*, Apr 2016, The Equality Trust, equalitytrust.org.uk/wealth-tracker-2016

7 D Dorling, B Stuart, & J Stubbs, 'Don't mention this around the Christmas table: Brexit, inequality and the demographic divide', *LSE European Politics and Policy Blog*, 21 Dec 2016, nin.tl/BrexitXmas

8 P Inman, 'Brexit vote wiped $1.5tn off UK household wealth in 2016, says report', *The Guardian*, 22 Nov 2016, nin.tl/Brexitwiped

9 See pp 32 & 36 of: M Carliner & E Marya, *Rental Housing: An international comparison*, Working Paper, Harvard Joint Centre for Housing Studies, Sep 2016, nin.tl/Harvardrental

10 Just look at the Wikipedia entry for the *Gini Coefficient*! en.wikipedia.org/wiki/Gini_coefficient

11 Progressives Spain, 'Podemos readies for "general strike" against Rajoy', *Progressive Spain Website*, 17 Oct 2016, nin.tl/Podemosstrike

12 'Civil service general strike set for 18 November', *Portugal News Online*, 31 Oct 2016, nin.tl/Portugalstrike

13 A Callinicos, *Equality*, Polity, Cambridge, 2007.

14 'Scottish government "interested" in universal basic income', *BBC News*, 26 Jan 2017, nin.tl/Scotbasicincome

15 Wikipedia, *Hunger in the United Kingdom*, page accessed 28 Feb 2017, nin.tl/WikiUKhunger

16 A Callinicos, *Bonfire of Illusions*, Polity, Cambridge, 2010.

17 B Knight, *A minority view: What Beatrice Webb would say now*, Alliance Publishing Trust, London, 2011.

18 A Callinicos, *Equality*, Polity, Cambridge, 2007.

19 PA Baran and PM Sweezy, *Monopoly Capital*, Monthly Review Press, 1966.

20 M Torry, 'Two feasible ways to implement a revenue neutral Citizen's Income scheme', *Euromod Working Paper Series*, 6/15, Apr 2015, nin.tl/citizenincome

21 Lew Higgins, Socialist Party of Great Britain, comment in book reviews Jun 2011, nin.tl/rXQ4wD

22 Z Bauman, *Collateral Damage*, Polity, Cambridge, 2011.

23 JC Myers, *The Politics of Equality*, Zed, London, 2010.

24 J Wright, 'More equal than others', *Geographical Magazine*, July 2010.

25 Cited in R Bell, *'Race and poverty: is affirmative action the answer?'* in B Knight, op cit.

26 S Goldsmith, *'The Alaska Permanent Fund Dividend: An experiment in wealth distribution'*, paper presented at 9th International Congress of the Basic Income European Network, 12-14 Sep 2002.

27 Australian government, 'Tax crime prosecution results', 13 Feb 2017, nin.tl/Oztaxcrime

28 Australian government, 'Tax cheats brought to justice', 14 Jun 2016, nin.tl/Oztaxcheats

29 P Mercer, 'Australia's child poverty "national shame"', *BBC News*, 17 Nov 2016, nin.tl/Ozshame

30 'New league table shows wealthy nations are failing children', UNICEF Australia, 14 Apr 2016, nin.tl/UNICEFOz

31 *New figures on growing inequality among children*, UNICEF New Zealand, 14 Apr 2016, nin.tl/UNICEFNZ

32 C Mortimer, 'New Zealanders want to give everyone a "citizen's wage" and scrap benefits', *The Independent*, Feb 2016, nin.tl/NZcitizenwage

33 M Liddiard, 'Could the idea of a universal basic income work in Australia?' *The Conversation*, 1 Jun 2016, nin.tl/Ozbasicincome

34 D Dorling, 'Housing is fundamentally a debate about social goods and social evils', *Taxpayers against poverty* Blog 6, 11 Nov 2016, dannydorling. org/?page_id=5730

35 Wikipedia, *Basic Income*, accessed 1 Mar 2017, en.wikipedia.org/wiki/ Basic_income_guarantee

36 P van Parijs and Y Vanderborght, *Basic Income: A Radical Proposal for a Free Society and a Sane Economy*, Harvard University Press, 2017.

37 P Stephens, *Financial Times*, 9 Apr 1997, cited in Callinicos, 2007, op cit.

38 See Table 3 on page 95 of D Dorling, *A Better Politics: How Government Can Make Us Happier*, London Publishing Partnership, dannydorling.org/ books/betterpolitics/

39 B Knight, op cit.

40 Ibid.

41 See Figure 2.2 of J Helliwell, R Layard and J Sachs, *World Happiness Report 2016*, Vol 1, The Earth Institute, Columbia University, nin.tl/ Worldhappiness2016

42 J Hopkin, V Lapuente L and Moller, 'Lower levels of inequality are linked with greater innovation in economies', *LSE American Politics and Policy*, 23 Jan 2014, eprints.lse.ac.uk/58473/

43 Compass, *Final Report of the Compass inquiry into a new system of education*, 20 Mar 2015, nin.tl/Compasseducreport and compassonline.org. uk/education-inquiry/

44 Conclusion of G Hobbs, 'Explaining social class inequalities in educational achievement in the UK', *Oxford Review of Education*, 8 Feb 2016, vol 42, 1, pp 16-35, nin.tl/Hobbseduc

45 M Lewis, Princeton University's 2012 Baccalaureate Remarks: 'Don't Eat Fortune's Cookie', 23 Jun 2012, *Princeton University News*, nin.tl/ Princetonaddress

46 RG Wilkinson & KE Pickett, 'Income Inequality and Population Health', *Social Science & Medicine*, 62, 1768–84, 2006; and RG Wilkinson & KE Pickett, 'The problems of relative deprivation', *Social Science and Medicine*, 65, 9, 1965-1978, 2007, nin.tl/relativedeprivation

47 The dystopian 1982 film *Blade Runner* was based on the 1968 novel *Do Androids Dream of Electric Sheep?*, a fictional account of life in San Francisco following nuclear war. There has been no nuclear war, but socio-economic trends in the US since 1968 have rendered the film an iconic warning of what might result from increasing inequality.

List of Figures

List of Tables

List of Illustrations

INDEX

Page numbers in **bold** refer to 'take of the best-off 1%' graphs.